# PICTURING POWER IN THE PEOPLE'S REPUBLIC OF CHINA

# PICTURING POWER IN THE PEOPLE'S REPUBLIC OF CHINA

*Posters of the Cultural Revolution*

Edited by Harriet Evans and Stephanie Donald

ROWMAN & LITTLEFIELD PUBLISHERS, INC.

*Lanham • Boulder • New York • Oxford*

ROWMAN & LITTLEFIELD PUBLISHERS, INC.

Published in the United States of America
by Rowman & Littlefield Publishers, Inc.
4720 Boston Way, Lanham, Maryland 20706
http://www.rowmanlittlefield.com

12 Hid's Copse Road
Cumnor Hill, Oxford OX2 9JJ, England

British Library Cataloguing in Publication Information Available

**Library of Congress Cataloging-in-Publication Data**

Picturing power in the People's Republic of China : posters of the
    cultural revolution / edited by Harriet Evans and Stephanie Donald.
        p.   cm.
    Includes bibliographical references and index.
    ISBN 0-8476-9510-7 (cloth : alk. paper)
    ISBN 0-8476-9511-5 (paper : alk. paper)
    1. China—History—Cultural revolution, 1966–1976—Posters
Exhibitions.   2. Political posters, Chinese Exhibitions.
3. Political posters—England—London Exhibitions.   4. University of
Westminster Exhibitions.   I. Evans, Harriet.   II. Donald, Stephanie.
III. Title: Posters of the cultural revolution.
DS778.7.E93   1999
951.05'6—DC21

99–24279
CIP
rev.

Printed in the United States of America

# Contents

# Acknowledgments

A first exhibition of the University of Westminster collection of Chinese posters was held in Regent Street, London, in 1979 under the title "Political Art and Popular Culture in China." Since then, apart from sporadic loans to documentary-film makers and publishers and occasional viewing by students as documentary material to accompany courses on modern Chinese politics, the contents of the collection have not been widely seen. This book is part of a project to bring these posters back to public attention (albeit in a public sphere different from the one they first inhabited). We have received generous sponsorship from Indiana University's East Asian Studies Center to prepare this book and its accompanying exhibition. The Center's enthusiasm is indicative of the excitement the posters have generated as materials for pedagogical and scholarly reflection. We are particularly grateful to the Center for its subvention for the color plates reproduced in this volume. We have also received support and funding from the Centre for the Study of Democracy at the University of Westminster and the School of Media, Communication and Culture at Murdoch University. Research and presentation support has been given by the John Curtin Gallery in Western Australia, Teresa Hwang at the Taiwanese National Film Archive, and Murdoch University's small-grants scheme. For their inspirational and pioneering work in producing the poster catalogue—now two decades ago—we would like to thank John Gittings and Anna Merton. Without the catalogue, and the time and commitment that went into producing it, editing this volume would have been an impossible task. For her more recent work on the catalogue and the posters, we wish to thank Anna Johnston. We would also like to acknowledge Paul Crook's loans to the collection, as well as his contribution to the ideas explored in this book. Others have also offered us invaluable help. Our first thanks are due to Jeffrey Wasserstrom, for all his insights, comments, and sustaining good humor. Michael Schoenhals has given us detailed advice about the production, display, and reading of posters during the Cultural Revolution. We also thank Barbara Abrash, the late Anne Benewick, John Cayley, Sudipto Chatterjee, Timothy Cheek, Susan Daruvala, Vera Fennell, Faye Ginsburg, Gail Hershatter, Carma Hinton, Emily Honig, Michael Palmer, Paola Voci, Rae Yang, and Marilyn Young for their input and wisdom and for the opportunities they have given us to explore many of the ideas developed in this book. Thanks also go to Peter Stuart of Murdoch and Ted Welch of the University of Westminster for their computer literacy, and to Isabel Hilton, whose 1974 photograph is in the frontispiece of this book. We would like to acknowledge as well the very useful and rewarding comments made by our two anonymous readers. Finally, but not least, we wish to thank our editor, Susan McEachern, for her indispensable help and encouragement in bringing this project to completion.

This book, then, can be thought of as the outcome of our collective realization of the vibrancy that this particular visual form brings to the study of China's recent history. It suggests ways in which visual forms may be used in both teaching and research, not simply as supplementary materials to the main texts of conventional political studies, but as main texts in themselves, which tell identifiable narratives through a diversity of forms, images, and symbols.

# A Note to the Reader

This volume contains many references to posters in the University of Westminster's collection. The letter in each alphanumeric designation (e.g., N43) indicates the category to which the poster has been assigned in the Westminster collection. The categories represented in this book are:

A   Agriculture

B   Four Modernizations

C   Industry and Commerce

D   International Relations

E   Politics

F   Revolutionary History

H   Health, Education, and Society

J   Military and Sport

K   National Festivals and Patriotism

L   Art

M   Children

N   Leaders

Q   Women

Z   *Nianhua* (New Year Prints)

Posters referred to but not pictured are listed in the poster references beginning on page 145. Those pictured are, of course, contained in the list of illustrations, which begins on page xi.

# Illustrations

**Figures**

# 1

# Introducing Posters of China's Cultural Revolution

*Harriet Evans and Stephanie Donald*

What color was the Cultural Revolution? What did it look like? What did people see around them as they went to work, to a political meeting, or to play? What pictures hung on the walls at home, in the factory, or in the train stations crowded with young people on their tumultuous way around the territory of the People's Republic of China (PRC)? One way to find out: look at the posters. You won't find out what people looked like, nor even what they did, but you'll know something of what they *saw*. You will begin to think about what graced the walls of the streets and homes and hospitals and meeting rooms, all those places where people gathered to live through both the everyday and the extraordinary days of the "Ten Years of Chaos."[1]

Posters, as well as other visual images such as portraits of Mao Zedong and paintings, were distributed in vast quantities during the Cultural Revolution.[2] With the exception of the 1966–1968 period of Red Guard violence, when the images that appeared in public were mainly those that "smashed the class enemy" or "upheld the great red banner of Mao Zedong Thought," posters were ubiquitous in public and private space.[3] They were displayed on billboards and classroom walls and in clinics, workplaces, and domestic spaces. Whether applauding the inspirational authority of the Great Helmsman or exhorting students to "learn from the peasants," they were inescapable.

A great deal has been written about the Cultural Revolution, both in Western languages and in Chinese. It inspired an enormous amount of instant commentary when it was taking place; some writers sought to praise it, others to condemn it, and still others to explain what remains a complex, even incomprehensible, series of events. Since the late 1970s, sociologists and political scientists have made creative use of official publications and interviews with Hong Kong refugees. Thanks to them, we have a good sense of various issues, such as the class backgrounds from which Red Guards tended to come and the ways in which top-level factional struggles influenced the course of the Cultural Revolution. These studies have given us a fuller understanding of the patterns of violence that were a key feature of the conflicts between 1966 and 1969. The *cultural* dynamics of these struggles have, however, received scant attention. In particular, we still know far too little about the visual texts, such as posters, that were used as a major vehicle for the transmission of political messages at the time. Until very recently, for a variety of reasons that are explored briefly in the following pages, trajectories in Cultural Revolution studies in both China and the West have ensured that issues associated with cultural discourse and symbolism did not attract much serious attention.[4]

This book about posters of China's Cultural Revolution is an introduction to new ways of looking at a particular visual form that was central to the political culture of the time. It approaches its subject from a variety of disciplinary perspectives, moving outside the parameters of analysis normally associated with art history and political science and philosophy. It also provides an opportunity to think about how, as spectators acquainted in very different ways with China's recent history, we think about a specific visual form in the production of a particular past. In the chapters that follow, we do not provide a history of Cultural Revolution posters, any more than we attempt to offer a definitive analysis of their aesthetic qualities and techniques or their political function within the broader ideological frame of the time. All those necessary aspects of analysis are addressed to some degree, but our priority is to examine posters as a dominant visual discourse—complementary to, but distinct from, other official discourses in structuring and establishing ideological positions—through which the power relations of the Cultural Revolution were played out at the time and through which the history of that time is evoked three decades later. This book seeks to bring posters to the center of our understanding of the Cultural Revolution, not as an aside or a colorful visual accompaniment to the dominant texts of written documents, but as a major visual text central to the processes of constructing meaning and practice.

### Posters and the "Great Proletarian Cultural Revolution"

Officially launched in 1966, the Cultural Revolution was initially described as "a revolution to touch people's souls."[5] It was to overturn established structures of bureaucratic power and challenge conventional social and political hierarchies. Under the attack on the Four Olds (old ideas, old culture, old customs, and old habits), it sought to introduce new educational, social, and cultural practices to undercut the privileged position of professionals and intellectuals. Its proponents wanted to expose and destroy power-holders within the Communist Party, whose political prominence gave them access to wealth and influence. In its overall vision, the Cultural Revolution was inspired by Mao Zedong's concerns that the gains of revolution not fall to the exploitative uses of the "capitalist road."

> At present, our objective is to struggle against and crush those persons in authority who are taking the capitalist road, to criticize and repudiate the reactionary bourgeois academic authorities and the ideology of the bourgeoisie and all other exploiting classes and to transform education, literature and art and all other parts of the superstructure that do not correspond to the socialist economic base, so as to facilitate the consolidation and development of the socialist system.[6]

This characterization of the Cultural Revolution belongs to a recent period of China's history that has been all but obliterated from official memory by another, dominant narrative. According to this history, disseminated by the post-Mao governments in China and by many Western analysts, the Cultural Revolution centered on a factional power struggle. The players were, on the one hand, Mao Zedong, his "closest comrade-in arms" and army chief of staff, Lin Biao, and the radical Gang of Four, and, on the other, the more moderate and pragmatic Liu Shaoqi, China's head of state, and his major ally, Deng Xiaoping. In this version, many of the key events and images associated with the terror of the Cultural Revolution, such as the violence of the Red Guards, the enforced dispatch of millions of students to the countryside under the "rustification" campaign, or the suppression of open intellectual and artistic endeavor, were the result of Mao Zedong's misconceptions about revisionism and class struggle. He exaggerated the dangers of the former and devastated the lives of many innocent individuals by his erroneous application of the latter. Mao's central role in this factional struggle explains the expansion of his personality cult, deliberately cultivated by Lin Biao and his followers to reestablish Mao's waning authority over his opponents. It also explains Mao's support of a vast movement of revolutionary youth, the Red Guards, to attack the practices and symbols associated with the "feudal" past and to preach the thoughts of their "great leader."

The posters produced during the Cultural Revolution contain images that cut across these different approaches. Some themes correspond to general messages of proletarian solidarity and collective unity. Some are iconic adulations of Chairman Mao. Others address the interests of specific campaigns at particular moments of the period. The night scene of small boats full of people approaching a large junk for a "criticize Lin Biao–criticize Confucius" political meeting (see figure 1.1 [A40]) refers to the campaign to attack Lin Biao that was launched in 1973. This followed revelations about Lin's alleged assassination attempt on Mao Zedong in 1971 and his own death in an air crash in Mongolia while fleeing China. The image of the young woman striding through the fields, bedding roll on her back and eyes gazing toward a bright future (see figure 3.1 [H15], 1975), corresponds with a particular stage of the movement to send young urban students to the countryside, which continued throughout the early and mid-1970s. Deng Xiaoping's view that economic development could be divorced from class struggle and from political interests is attacked in *Oppose economism* (E9, 1967). Collective agriculture is promoted in posters encouraging peasants to "learn from Dazhai," the model commune. Gender and ethnic equality also emerge as major themes. These emphases changed as the ascendancy of the Cultural Revolution waned. Mao Zedong died in 1976, and the influence of his intimates and of those who used him as an iconic patron quickly deteriorated. Not all these changes were immediate or absolute; questions of continuity in style and form remained. It is even possible, as Paul Clark has suggested in relation to film, to date the end of the Cultural Revolution at 1978, thus extending the ten years to twelve.[7] Whichever endpoint is chosen, the problem of description remains and takes much of our attention here.

As the discussion in the following chapters shows, the stylistic forms of the posters of this period were neither as uniform nor as limited as received wisdom about socialist propaganda art suggests.[8] The posters varied in technique, in composition, and in color and in many instances evoked visual links with traditional Chinese painting *(guohua)*. Despite these differences, they all conformed to the same basic principles of artistic creation initially set out in Mao Zedong's famous "Talks at the Yan'an Forum on Literature and Art" delivered as part of the Party's 1942 rectification campaign, carried out in the revolutionary base area of Yan'an. These talks set out the major principles for the production of socialist art and literature that were followed for the next three and a half decades. Mao Zedong rejected the theory of art for art's sake and stipulated that the political criteria of art were primary, while the aesthetic ones

Fig. 1.1 [A40]. *Angry waves in fishing waters (Yu hai nu tao).* N.p., n.d.

were secondary. Later reworked into the dual conceptualization of "revolutionary realism" and "revolutionary romanticism," the Yan'an Talks became a byword for rigid political control of all aspects of artistic production. During the Cultural Revolution, under Jiang Qing's supervision, this particular rendering of Stalin's socialist realism was reshaped as the *san tuchu* ("three prominences," according to which the good are more prominent than the bad, the very good are more prominent than the good, and the one outstanding figure is more prominent than the very good).

Writing about these posters is no easy matter. They belong to a period that, whatever the interpretation or experience of it, defies simple characterization and recollection through any text, including the poster. They date from a historical and cultural moment when artistic endeavor, whatever its form, was subjected to perilously exacting standards of political and cultural purity. Painting the image of Mao Zedong in ways that departed from the approved version, for example, could earn the artist condemnation as a counterrevolutionary, as was the case with a Mao-badge designer from Inner Mongolia who altered the profile of Mao to face right and not left.[9] Poster art was a politicization of aesthetic practices and the development of aesthetic genres through political motivation. On the one hand, it was produced and disseminated to educate the mass public in ideological values defined by the authoritarian party-state. It was one arm of the project of political power. The production of posters was itself marked by other practices of political control, through the modification of laws, rules, and regulations and the generation of funds through tax breaks to factories producing revolutionary art.[10] On the other hand, effective posters had to have an immediate, direct appeal to their audience. Their aesthetic construction grew from a sophisticated notion of political spectatorship. They had to compress information, and provide contextual hints on that information, in visual forms to which their audience could respond. A successful poster had to retain an internal aesthetic cohesion in order both to attract the eye of the beholder and to lend visual coherence to the political message expressed through the image.

Writing about these different attributes of Cultural Revolution posters is also complicated by the passage of time. Looking at the posters now, three decades or so after their production, evokes a range of contradictory responses. For many people who lived through the experiences graphically represented in the posters, these images are harrowing reminders of a painful past. Although revolutionary representations often seem to be forgiven the specificities of history—in the case of the Cultural Revolution, scholarly analyses have largely ignored such representations as components of a discourse of utopian lies and impossible promises—such images can have horrific resonances. They are graphic reminders of mass insecurity, arbitrary violence, and personal trauma. Paradoxically, however, looking at these posters can also give pleasure. This may be simply the pleasure of generic recognition. Posters usually deliver a clear and confident message. For those, including some of the contributors to this book, who were distant from the abusive politicosocial culture in which they were produced, that confidence is untainted by personal scars that furiously contradict its clarity. It may also be the pleasure of nostalgia, bitter as well as sweet. Most of the contributors to this volume first became acquainted with China as a living and lived experience in the early and mid-1970s, in the days of Europeans' privileged access to China, before it "opened up" to the United States and the global economy.[11] The posters of the period are, for us, strongly associated with affective memories of youthful commitment to the ideals of Marxism-Leninism, to exploring the visions represented by the rhetoric of the Cultural Revolution, as well as with our often cynical dismissal of stories of revolutionary success. Hours spent simply looking at and talking about the posters with colleagues and friends, Chinese and otherwise, have enabled us to share familiar images that belong to our subjective pasts. These pleasures are associated with the aesthetic and political mix of the posters and with beholding a spectacle long obscured from public view and barely referred to by the collective subject. The revelation of objects and their circumstances is a primary motivation for historians and cultural analysts, and that is one of the principal appeals of this collection.

In analyzing the poster from a range of different perspectives and disciplines, this book seeks to acknowledge its prominence in the processes through which the Cultural Revolution was produced and played out. It is a collective project that draws together analyses from modern social and cultural history and criticism, film and media studies, art history, and political science. Our decision to produce such a book has been inspired by three main impulses. First, we hope to make an intervention in the current reassessment of the Cultural Revolution by examining a specific and so far underestimated aspect of its processes, effects, and legacy. Second, we want to acknowledge subjectivity as a valuable concept in social and political analysis. In Craig Clunas's chapter, for example, the subjective emerges as a critical issue in notions of authorial authority; it informs self-reflexive questioning about how we approach analysis of these posters. In John Gittings's chapter, subjectivity is a clear issue in understanding the raison d'être of the poster collection on which our analysis is based. The contributors were drawn together by a common experience of China in the 1970s; the notion of the subjective that emerges here is primarily, though not entirely, that of the outside spectator. Academic attention cannot manufacture an account of the subjective experiences of Chinese citizens in the 1960s and 1970s. What we can do is offer careful observations in the context of our own experiences and areas of expertise. It will be for others to revisit the collection and discuss what it was like to be a Chinese citizen at the moments at which these posters were produced and consumed. What were the conditions of embodiment? How did people understand themselves in relation to others and in relation to their own circumstances? Was it possible that the ideal of a collective subject was realized as people glanced at, read, admired, or ignored the posters on the walls that surrounded them?

These questions are difficult for us to answer, but we share with a number of other scholars a concern with the construction of "the ideal Chinese political subject," as well as with the subjects who were excluded from this position. Alongside other visual and written texts, posters' picturing of women, children, and other subgroups at particular moments was indicative of their subjective textual subordination as well as their subordinate place within the political and social order. Some of the essays that follow match empirical data with visual evidence or confirmation—or contradiction. Others examine the importance of visual meanings without reference to other discourses and disciplines. We therefore move away from the habit of using visual material as a secondary source and instead analyze it through an approach that involves a serious consideration of the symbolic worlds of the visual text. Where visuality *is* taken seriously, notably in the fields of film and media theory and art history, it is often accompanied either by a denial of the political or by a correspondence of visual grammar with ideological manipulation. We hope to avoid these reductions here.

Finally, we would like to offer a contextualized reappraisal of the value and scope of the process of collection. Collecting is a process of preservation of a synchronic chunk of a material past as well as a necessary disavowal of that past as a series of events and experiences that can be retrieved in the present "as it really was." The collection thus offers the opportunity to construct a history at the same time that that history constructs the present. This book celebrates the analytical complexity that these possibilities of "the collection" offer in producing, not a perfectly packaged and rounded analysis, but different "takes" on the posters, all of which re-create history and the present in specific ways.

## The University of Westminster's Poster Collection

The posters we analyze in this book come from a collection held by the University of Westminster in London. This collection contains some five hundred catalogued items, plus many more uncatalogued posters and papercuts as well as Cultural Revolution memorabilia, including children's toys, handkerchiefs, and badges. It was initially put together by John Gittings when he first went to China in the early 1970s as a lecturer teaching Chinese politics in what was then the Polytechnic of Central London. The collection expanded with donations and loans from friends and colleagues who lived in, or traveled to, China. Paul Crook, who spent his adolescence and early adulthood in China during the 1960s and the 1970s, made important contributions, as did Anna Merton, who in 1974 was one of the first British students to study in China under the auspices of the British Council and the Chinese government. She later worked with

John Gittings to catalogue the collection. As it is now, the bulk of the posters spans the period from the early years of Cultural Revolution through to the early 1980s, when, in its political form, the poster effectively disappeared from production and public life.

The collection is organized into categories that, taken together, reveal the range of subject matter, imagery, and politicosocial concerns that are represented in this book. Categories include women, children, national minorities, sports, leaders, personalities (from Charles Darwin to Lei Feng), political leaders, agriculture, industry, science and modernization, fine art, folk traditions, health, education, and, of course, politics. Within the categories there is great variety. Some posters categorized as "art" deal with overtly cultural material while others are themselves self-consciously artistic. In *Art comes from a life of struggle; the working people are the masters* (plate 1 [L17]), peasant painters are at work on a mural. In *Spring colors fill the gardens* (L40, 1980) a rush of color, peacocks, and peonies produces the typically optimistic dazzle of revolutionary romanticism. Posters about women's status include vibrant scenes that range from a local sports competition (plate 2 [Q7]); to a two-woman-operated television station, *Good news travels ten thousand miles and warms ten thousand families* (figure 2.2 [B9]); to girls doing embroidery, *Embroidering goldfish which make the waves red* (Q22, 1979). Still others are concerned with the political status of the main figure. In *Let new socialist culture occupy every stage* (N28, 1967), Jiang Qing stands in army uniform, holding Mao's *Quotations* against a background of revolutionary "cultural" scenes, including a man playing a cello. The hierarchy of address invokes first the army and the Maoist faithful and then a narrative of revolutionary culture appropriated to vindicate Jiang Qing's own claim for political center stage. The address is to differently prioritized groups and political standpoints. Each level supports the other(s) and ensures the poster against criticism. The appeal to the artist, perhaps in the figure of the cellist, is less than convincing. His position as an artist necessarily trained in the ideologically dubious years before the Cultural Revolution is, after all, under continual review, given his choice of instrument and his need to participate only in appropriate cultural scenarios. The same point is made, although this time stripped—at least overtly—of Jiang's personal ambitions, in *Our literature and art must become a component part of the whole revolutionary machine* (L16, 1967). Young female soldiers dance with castanets and copies of Mao's "little red book" above a quotation from Mao's Yan'an Talks (1942). Here it is the legitimation of the Yan'an narrative and Mao's place in that story that is central to the message. The poster inscribes Mao's place in history at the same time that it asserts his overarching patronage—or control—of the army and the arts. The connection between the two is further emphasized by the feminization of the army's image in this instance. In the same category of "leaders," a more specific target is tackled in *Oppose economism* (E9, 1967), a slogan specifically associated with Deng Xiaoping's "revisionist" policy of economic development. The poster shows a worker writing a slogan on a wall while a rebel troop member tears up papers marked "economism" *(jingjizhuyi)*. Here, the opposition is set up between the masculine activity of revolutionary practice and the fragile paperwork of bureaucrats. Neither Mao Zedong nor Deng Xiaoping is mentioned by name or image, but their presence is clearly felt. That the poster—itself paper—can deride the use of paper in favor of writing directly on the wall also gives it a breathtaking confidence.

The collection also covers most of the artistic techniques developed in poster art between the 1960s and the early 1980s. Many techniques borrow from the earlier-twentieth-century interest in woodcuts and the New Year picture (*nianhua*, simple colored woodblock prints made to celebrate the new year) tradition that figured prominently in commercial Shanghai art of the 1920s and 1930s.[12] The work of a number of well-known artists who shifted their aesthetic attention from traditional landscapes to scenes of industrialization and collectivization was also used in posters. Indeed, the continuum between academic art and propaganda art that John Gittings refers to in his chapter was a key element of Cultural Revolution art, as Julia Andrews has so clearly argued.[13] The main omission of the collection is the category of cartoon art, generally associated more with the "big character" wall poster than with the posters produced for mass distribution. Cartoon posters were often drawn by hand and in limited numbers or as one-offs. Though photographs taken at the time tell us quite a bit about the contents of these posters and the contexts in which they were displayed, none, according to the historian Michael Schoenhals, has survived in the original.[14] Many cartoon posters dealt with a number of dubious issues, such as the "debauchery and repulsive features" of criticized leaders. Others, which appeared on the streets of Beijing in 1967, depicted the violent atrocities being perpetrated by Red Guards in different parts of the country. Perhaps the most famous of this almost satirical genre was *A Crowd of Clowns,* featuring a ridiculous parade of disgraced Party leaders. Arguably, the poster's effect was to disgrace the Party as a whole rather than a selection of its leadership.[15]

A *Crowd of Clowns* clearly showed the potential of an image to undermine, not just competing authorities, but authority itself. Directives distributed by the Party authorities sought to produce political affiliations and actions by associating "political correctness" with power and prestige, so the particular visual form of the posters clearly constructed positions of power and authority as well as exclusion and marginalization. Many of the political issues fought out through the Cultural Revolution can be "read" from the poster text as much as from the more familiar written texts. This returns us to the known, but seldom noted, fact of the centrality of posters in public discourse of the 1960s and 1970s. Indeed, given the physical presence of these posters in the spaces of daily life, it is extraordinary that so little has been written about them.[16]

The configuration of circumstance and intent—of working in an institution housing a unique collection and our own interests as teachers and researchers—has produced a space in which posters, by virtue of concentrated spectatorship, are seen again and anew. The movement of images into the present, still bearing the traces and inscriptions of the past to which they contributed so greatly, retrieves their visibility. We are now one of their publics, and this book is just one more public space in which they may be seen.[17]

## Writing about Posters

Writing about posters is a strangely ambiguous project. Posters are ephemeral inasmuch as they are produced for immediate and short-term appeal. Those produced in the Cultural Revolution also had to meet exacting standards of political precision. A few posters, notably those that reproduced pictures from another medium, remained in circulation for a long time. Posters are a relatively cheap way of addressing a mass audience. They are inexpensive to produce and require no technological investment on the part of the spectator. A successful poster must have an immediate and direct appeal to its audience. It must also compress information in forms and contexts that are familiar to its audience. A poster extolling the qualities of Chairman Mao, for instance, needed to represent him physically in a positive light and in an appropriate symbolic context. An appropriate text gave added meaning to the image of the leader without detracting from this image as the central focus of the complete composition. Such a poster had to appeal to people's existing knowledge of the man and of the particular context in which his image appeared, but it also had to contain an element of surprise to attract their attention. During the Cultural Revolution period, poster artists were required to produce representations of the leader in his many pastoral and international guises: the young scholar turned into national saviour, the Great Helmsman, the inspiration to the new, young, revolutionary generation, and so on. The Mao painting-cum-poster operated within a political marketplace in which his image occupied the top position in the iconography of power. Hitting the right political note of the moment through visual means therefore granted the poster the precious status of privileged public attention, as the print runs for some of the most famous images of Mao indicated. However, given that one of the main political motivations in the Cultural Revolution, particularly in its early stages, was to substantiate Mao's personality cult, artists not only had to affirm his authority, they also had to keep his image fresh and responsive to shifts in the public and political mood. A Mao poster worked for the cult of Mao Zedong in a two-way complementary fashion. Furthermore, to succeed in pleasing the eye of the beholder, a poster had to have an internal aesthetic cohesion sufficient to lend visual coherence to the political tenor expressed through the image.

The posters we analyze in this book have an additional quality that has no uniform authority but derives from their status in a permanent collection. These are posters that transcend the ephemeral, although they still share the characteristics outlined above. Their appeal has outdistanced the original intention of the artists and their political masters and has entered the international time and space of collection, categorization, and display. Placing these posters in a permanent collection is an indication of their aesthetic merit, their historical importance, and their enduring appeal to the memory, and possibly the nostalgia, of the collector and spectator. Removed from the moment of their production and intended public dissemination, they now contribute to the historicization of their political subjects in different ways. They are now seen by spectators inserted into systems of visual and political discourse that reject the poster as an appropriate public form, as John Gittings discusses in his chapter. Yet it is the particular success of these compositions that they endure as visual mementos of their own creation.

We have referred to the variety of images and themes within the categories listed in the University of Westminster poster catalogue. However, the multiple possibilities and qualities of the poster make even their simple categorization problematic. Should they be described through their politics, their aesthetic organization, or their formal pictorial qualities? How, indeed, should one begin to categorize their politics in any case—by overt subject matter? by period of production? by political innuendo? In any event, can the political content ever be truly separated from the aesthetic form in Marxist-Leninist-Maoist–inspired cultural production? The relationship between form and content is possibly the most fundamental sticking point in most debates on art and politics. The complexities involved in identifying the boundaries—if there are any—within that relationship may explain scholars' reticence about poster art in

China. Refusal to acknowledge such complexities also explains the simple "condemnation" of China's poster art as "merely a form of politics," the product of Mao's insistence on "the unity of politics and art."[18] As in Golomstock's *Totalitarian Art*, it can make the analyst blind to the range of stylistic and aesthetic qualities used in political posters and to the different ways in which they constituted their spectators as political subjects. The collapsing of these different categories and features removes the political poster from specific political practices and historical contexts and transforms it into a monolithic tool of the undifferentiated totalitarian state. Such an analysis overlooks the means and discourses of control in different socialist and fascist states. In so doing, it fails to advance our understanding of the ways in which these states maintained their position vis-à-vis their subjects.

Our present methodological solution is to use a shifting model of analysis that acknowledges both political and aesthetic qualities. These posters are profoundly political, as Stefan Landsberger points out in suggesting that they were a particular instance of the relationship between party, state, and masses.[19] Their form was also partly determined by political necessity. They are, however, also at least aesthetically competent, and sometimes inspirational, in their mix of compacted imagery and vibrant color. Successful images achieve extraordinary narrative and emotional effect.

A further aspect of their status as collectors' items is that these posters may be read in diverse ways, depending on the space, place, and time of their exhibition as well as the position of the spectator. They may be politically harrowing or uplifting; they may suggest the artistry of the peasant muralist or the amateur animator; they may seem historically seductive or simply naive in their promise of a future socialist modernity. The spectator is the key to their categorization, whether this is in the private world of the academic collector or in the public realms of display and discussion.

In her collection of Russian avant-garde film posters of the 1920s, Susan Pack wonders at the craftsmanship and artistry of a medium that is so fleeting. After all, posters are usually made from paper, stuck up on walls with rough glue, then torn down or covered over, or—as she rather movingly describes—seen by "workers at the end of the day, running to catch their streetcars . . . for a few brief moments escap[ing] their everyday routine."[20] People and ideas move fast. This phenomenon is a thrilling dimension of creative endeavor, whether it be the work of the poster artist or the cultural events and products that advertising posters are designed to promote. When, however, the posters' primary function is disseminating political information, the rate of change becomes alarming. During the Cultural Revolution the demands on the spectator did not represent an equal address between artist and spectator. The patronage of a particular incarnation of the party-state intervened. The posters made specific demands on those who looked at them; they did not offer an "escape from everyday routine." Rather, they endowed that routine with an additional burden of political meaning, constraint, and even terror.

In many posters, in particular those of the early stages of the Cultural Revolution when the "enemy" was still given visual form, the political meaning of a poster was immediately evident to its spectators. For example, a poster from 1967 (N30) called "Long live Chairman Mao, we wish him a long life without end" has four scenes: Mao applauding (the people for applauding him?); Mao and Lin Biao in army uniform; revolutionary troops trampling on Deng Xiaoping and Liu Shaoqi; and Mao with a crowd of workers and peasants. The poster uses Mao's image to good effect. The spectator is reminded of his claim to authority, his military prowess, and his political standing (footage of Mao often shows him applauding the Party Congress after his own speeches). The poster sends a message to his constituencies, the workers, peasants, and soldiers, to remember their loyalty to his leadership. It also makes a clear political demand of them, that they physically and politically denigrate Mao's immediate enemies, Liu Shaoqi and Deng Xiaoping. These messages legitimate one another in a cycle of iconic effect.

In many of the posters examined in this book, additional meanings are not always obvious. As we have indicated, analysis and description of the poster must take into account a certain slippage between content, form, and politics. Such slippage is implicit in every piece of public information. The posters we discuss here introduce a further ambiguity. Posters printed in China between 1966 and the early 1980s are not all *political* in a narrow sense. Relatively few are directly concerned with matters of state, although almost all have a discernible political tenor underlying the obvious message. Many posters give general advice on how to live. There are posters on superior methods of agriculture, on the value of study and Chinese medicine, on the benefits of breast-feeding and birth control, and on the need to attend to matters of social order, morality, and "good manners." These messages are tied to an overarching political discourse that gives legitimation and force to their argument. Conversely, the concerns of the everyday give the weight of inevitability to the political discourse that frames their narration. A 1974 poster publicizing the "later, more spaced, and fewer" (*wan, xi, shao*) stage of the government's birth control policy, for example, pictures a smiling woman holding up a medical manual in place of the "little red book" in one hand and a bottle of pills in the other (see figure 1.2 [H8]). Under the slogan "Put birth control into practice for the revolution," the everyday concerns of reproductive health and fertility control are linked with a broader project of political authority, present in the title as well as the symbolic place of the manual. Another poster, produced soon after Mao's death, refers to the traditional parable of the old man who moved two mountains (A42, 1977). Entitled *Move mountains and make new land,* the poster pictures an irrigation project in a mountainous area, with peasants shifting earth with tractors, tying practical necessity to the mythic qualities both of the recently deceased Chairman and of the old man himself.[21] It is part of our project to look even more closely at those peasants, their tractors along with the accompanying exhortation, and the grid of political and cultural meanings implied. One question on this particular poster might be, for example, why was the connection between the parable and the laboring peasants not made even more explicit? What happened to the visual discourse around Mao's face and body in the years after his death, especially in the medium of poster art, which figured largely in the development of his personality cult in the 1960s and early 1970s?

Writing about posters is not, then, as straightforward as it might at first seem, especially given the present cultural and geographic distance from their moment of production. Doubtless, the intended audiences of the posters could interpret them immediately; after all, the posters we examine here were designed to be read for their immediate impact. Regardless of how they were, or were not, appreciated, their signs and images, their references, and their juxtapositions of subject and space were read at once aesthetically and politically. Describing the posters from the perspective of a collector or a scholar in a different time and space is, therefore, a challenging task. Strategies of analysis have to be chosen for their effectiveness as well as their cross-cultural fluidity. Different methodologies used in the course of a single analysis must be complementary and mutually supportive. Given the overriding political purpose of

Fig. 1.2 [H8]. *Put birth control into practice for the Revolution (Wei geming shixian jihua shengyu).* Shanghai 1974.

the posters, political analyses are essential. Semiotic and historical interpretations, linguistic competence, and a sense of the aesthetics of the period in its own particular context are all useful and valuable tools. This collection of papers offers perspectives that derive from all these methodologies and approaches. John Gittings discusses the production, distribution, and display of poster art within a historical and political analysis that draws on his own experience of looking at these posters in the early 1970s. Craig Clunas's revisiting of posters from a "known" and recent past becomes an argument for self-reflexivity as a priority of scholarship in art history. Harriet Evans shows how the politics of gender can be traced with careful attention to semiotic detail within a methodological context that acknowledges the barriers to retrieving the posters' "original" gendered meaning. Stephanie Donald looks at specific posters to give a distinctive account of the representation of children in poster art between 1965 and 1985. Using an analytic approach that borrows from film theory, literary theory, and psychoanalysis, she examines the continuities in representations of children as messengers for adult interests between the Cultural Revolution and post-Mao years. Xiaomei Chen seeks to retrieve a memory of the posters alongside other forms of visual culture that constituted the cultural "knowledge" of her childhood. Finally, Robert Benewick combines Mao's personal and political biography with, again, a semiotic approach to the iconography of power and the making of history through art.

The differing perspectives presented in this book converge on one notable point. Whatever their thematic content, these posters created and invoked the sense of a public—of a highly politicized publicness. Posters made direct reference to the nature of this public by including and excluding different political subjects. Indeed, given the persistent rhetoric of class struggle throughout the entire period of the Cultural Revolution, the absence of visual representation of political targets in the posters of the early to mid-1970s is striking, as Harriet Evans notes with reference to images of women.[22] These posters' textual detail and intertextual assumptions about power and exclusion produced a discursive insistence on linking the party-state with the politicized body, both individual and collective. In a sense the posters produced the politicized body through their persistent, often oblique, inscription in the individual woman or man of associations with, and loyalties to, the party-state. Such an association between body image and institutional belonging was made to seem a condition of being a social subject.[23] Our response to these posters is also telling in this context. For Craig Clunas, the posters demand of him reflection about his personal political positioning in the world of China that he experienced in 1974. For Harriet Evans, they urge reflection about the complexity of political, as well as gendered, meanings of the Cultural Revolution for women. Stephanie Donald, by contrast, sees the posters as a textual erasure of political agency. The construction of the image, of itself, works against the autonomous presence of groups in national and political structures. In particular, children's images tell us more about adults and the Party than about childhood on its own account.

### Texts and Memories: Recent Trends in Literature on the Cultural Revolution

The 1970s saw the publication of numerous works in English on the Cultural Revolution, many of them with clear ideological biases.[24] China-watching journalists and government personnel based in Hong Kong tended to emphasize high-level factional politics.[25] By contrast, writers who approached the Cultural Revolution from a Marxist perspective adopted a sympathetic approach to its innovative aspects, treating it as an unprecedented and profoundly important attempt to confront issues of Party bureaucratization and privilege.[26] As the 1970s progressed, scholars attempted to examine the movement's broader political and social issues, such as the widening gap between the elite and the masses, the dynamics of mass politics, and the ideological implications of the "two roads."[27] Some attempted to develop a comprehensive interpretive framework to analyze the Cultural Revolution as a whole, while others adopted a more focused approach, either on Mao Zedong and his political philosophy, on the role of particular individuals, or on particular case studies.[28] A few eyewitness accounts by foreigners in China at the time also appeared.[29] By and large, however, the focus on factional politics and the social bases of activism in the works of this period limited the methodological and conceptual tools available to analyze this extraordinary movement. A few works departed from these dominant approaches. The studies by Richard Solomon and Lucian Pye gave close attention to the problems associated with language and culture and to the psychological dimension of Mao Zedong's acquisition and use of power.[30] Chen Ruoxi and Lowell Dittmer's collaboration produced an important work on rhetoric.[31] By the early 1980s, the publication of village studies based on interviews with Hong Kong refugees, most notably Anita Chan, Richard Madsen, and Jonathan Unger's *Chen Village,* contributed important and innovative insights into the social and kin bases of political conflict during the period.[32]

As China launched into its "second revolution" in the 1980s, scholars' attention shifted to the radical changes of the reform era. Indeed, from the early 1980s until very recently, study of the Cultural Revolution was, to use Michael Schoenhals's words, "in limbo."[33] For a while, few serious scholars of politics in the PRC seemed to show much interest in events prior to the reformist era. When they did, their focus tended to be on high-level factional struggles and the meaning of mass violence or on revisiting the Cultural Revolution as a "variation on the Stalinist theme," a Chinese version of the great purges.[34] It was also assumed that there were no archives to facilitate new research. While during the 1980s and early 1990s a few notable scholars attempted to explain the limitations in contemporary analyses along lines that promised fruitful new avenues of inquiry, such as attention to local variations in how the Cultural Revolution was played out, the interpretive strategies used remained quite limited.[35]

The official Chinese evaluation of the Cultural Revolution has remained virtually unchanged ever since the Deng regime's characterization of it as a "tragedy for the entire state, nation and people of China" in June 1981.[36] The public memory of the "ten years of turmoil" has transformed the "revolution to touch people's souls" into a period of relentless political struggle synonymous with the "unlimited expansion and abuse of state power," the unbridled use of the "cult of the personality" to create an artificial backing for Mao's political fantasies, and the consolidation of a "feudal fascist dictatorship" dominated by a scheming ultraleftist clique whose rise to power depended on its personal links to Mao Zedong. The "*wenge*" now is a metaphor for cultural rigidity and intellectual repression, political brutality, and cunning manipulation of position and power by the demonized Jiang Qing and her cronies. That this view is widely held was apparent in 1989 when both protestors and the regime agreed that to be linked to the Cultural Revolution was the worst possible condemnation. Both sides of the struggle tried to smear the other with accusations of continuing and rekindling the years of chaos.[37]

Throughout the early and mid-1980s, the Dengist reformulation of the 1966–1976 decade was apparently welcomed throughout Chinese society. On the one hand, it acknowledged the devastating effects of an experiment to implement the aspirations of an ailing autocrat long out of touch with the "objective realities" of the society over which he ruled. On the other, it signified a clear commitment to a new strategy of political stability and unity. Condemnation of Mao's cult of the personality, for example, was paralleled by an explicit commitment to collective Party leadership. "Politics in command" was to be replaced by a "pragmatic" emphasis on economic development. "Class struggle" was discredited. The official reevaluation in many respects suggested the possibility of a new social and political space in which ordinary people—colleagues, former friends and fellow students, family members—could relearn how to acquire self-respect and tolerance in a society that had for too long been rent by vituperative hatreds, rivalries, and violence.[38]

Chinese scholarship on the events that engulfed China between 1966 and 1976 took advantage of these formulations but was also constrained by the political imperatives embedded in them.[39] The official histories, the biographies of Party leaders, and the various accounts of the inner workings of the Party that were published in the 1980s in varying degrees contributed interesting detail about particular aspects of the Chinese Communist Party's political practices. None of them, however, offered substantially different perspectives to add to, or modify, the official reassessment of the period. In different ways, they concurred with the prominence given to Mao's individual instrumentality in launching and overseeing the processes of the Cultural Revolution. Most notably, they did not seriously challenge the official rendering of the "masses" in the Cultural Revolution as passively "misled" by a manipulative bunch of power-hungry leaders. None included discussion about the cultural and symbolic fields of the Cultural Revolution. Instead, the official reworking of the Cultural Revolution found its way into a broad range of discourses—into literature, poetry, and film—and quickly defined the dominant terms of the new public memory of a devastating decade. This memory was such that to talk about its cultural dimensions seemed in some way to trivialize the central issues of political struggle and violence.

The total condemnation of the Cultural Revolution as the master plan of one misguided individual obsessed with his own vision of China's future is also prominent in English-language writings. It is common in many of the earlier works noted above. It is particularly noticeable in the autobiographical memoir, a genre of writing about the Cultural Revolution that has blossomed in the past decade or so. Ranging from the early accounts of former Red Guards to semifictionalized histories of entire families, these contributions to rewriting the history of the Cultural Revolution do not tend to challenge the major premises of the official version.[40] Many of them concur with its simple reversal of the polarized positions of the Cultural Revolution decade. They transform the former heroes of the revolution into its most hated and destructive enemies and turn its erstwhile capitalist-roading targets into exemplars of moral fortitude or hapless victims of an evil system. In depicting themselves, and all others who were targeted by the "ultraleftists," as prey to a pernicious system, the authors of these works tend to consolidate a view of the Cultural Revolution as a Manichean struggle between good and evil between the aggressors, who wielded and abused power, and their victims, who were condemned as the bourgeois representatives of the capitalist road. One exception to the genre is Rae Yang's recent *Spider Eaters*, which seeks to write the "victim's" agency and choice back into an analysis of the effects of the Cultural Revolution.[41]

The many ideological correspondences between official versions and autobiographical memoirs have reinscribed the Cultural Revolution in public memory—Chinese as well as Western—as anathema to all that is "good" in Chinese culture and society. One reason that the cultural dimension of the Cultural Revolution has been ignored, despite "culture's" prominence in the term, is that the political agenda molding cultural production at the time has come to be defined as a negation of culture. Mere mention of the Cultural Revolution is enough to bring to mind images of torture and deprivation. The common images are of millions of young students waving the "little red book" and chanting in a single voice in adoration of their godlike hero, and of humiliated teachers and professors forced to bow their heads low to withstand the attacks of their youthful assailants. These events are also used to explain the ruptures and conflicts that continue to characterize contemporary Chinese society and the limitations on the artistic, literary, and intellectual endeavors of the post–Cultural Revolution generations. For the protestors of 1989, one legacy of the Cultural Revolution was prominent in the devastating manifestation of force that the elderly leaders displayed on 4 June. For the exponents of Deng's regime, the youthful radicals of 1989 were reviving the "chaos" of the Red Guards.[42]

There is considerable evidence that many people, notably of the Red Guard generation, actually recall the Cultural Revolution as a time of exhilaration, experimentation, and freedom from parental constraints. Differentiated memories suggest that the effects of class, age, and gender on the experience of the period are an obvious area for further work. Some years ago Marilyn Young referred to women's affirmative identification with the opportunities for professional as well as social activity that the Cultural Revolution gender rhetoric of sexual equality offered.[43] In personal conversations, a number of women have talked with us about the excitement of being independent and empowered as political subjects during the early years of the Cultural Revolution. Recently, Wendy Larson has discussed the representation of the Cultural Revolution "not so much as a political ideal but as a decade of passion and devotion, symbolized by the Red Guards, whose unbridled forays around the countryside and violent attacks on all forms of authority become the most provocatively sensual liberation." She mentions Jiang Wen's 1995 film *Yangguang canlan de rizi* (Those brilliant days), which tells of a gang of young people in Beijing whose parents have been sent to the countryside. "Freed from the demands of school and work, the youths indulge themselves in food, sex, and violence, and create a sense of sensual immediacy that contrasts sharply with their later, middle-aged entrepreneurial selves."[44]

Scholarship on the "years of chaos" has acquired renewed vigor since the twentieth anniversary of Mao's death.[45] The third decennial of the Cultural Revolution in 1996 was marked not by commemorative celebrations but by conferences and special issues of journals.[46] A number of interesting and insightful works have been published; analysis is becoming more nuanced, with an exploration into new interpretive and theoretical strategies. Indeed, much recent research suggests an attempt at unraveling, even exploding, received assumptions about what the Cultural Revolution was, although it also demonstrates how much ground there is still to cover before any comprehensive assessment can be made of what for many people remains a very painful and still recent experience. There have been a number of exciting discussions about rhetoric and language, some focusing on written discourse and others on verbal representations and practices, such as political rhetoric and swear words.[47] Elizabeth Perry and Li Xun have published a meticulous reconstruction of the Cultural Revolution in Shanghai that contests the totalitarian version of the movement by examining the movement from below, in particular by explaining the political activism of ordinary factory workers.[48] Mobo Gao's articles offer striking critiques of the current assessment of the Cultural Revolution.[49] Rae Yang's *Spider Eaters* is a moving, sensitive, and deeply self-reflective attempt to understand—and articulate— the seemingly incomprehensible behavior of the Red Guards. A new research project on women in the PRC sponsored by the University of California, Santa Cruz, is devoting specific attention to women's participation, perceptions, and instrumentality in the Cultural Revolution.[50] Emily Honig has written a fascinating article on the gendered aspects of violence among the Red Guards.[51] Alessandro Russo analyzes a specific conceptualization—the "ultimate probable defeat"—of Mao Zedong's in a recent essay that seeks to relocate the Cultural Revolution as the political moment when the modern concept of the rational revolution came to an end.[52] Piece by piece, bit by bit, built on archival material hitherto assumed to be nonexistent, and using new theoretical approaches, these works are now helping to construct an understanding of the diversity of the social and political experience of the Cultural Revolution era, in terms that convey something of the multiple meanings it had for its participants and for those it affected. The obstacles, as Alessandro Russo puts it, to "discover[ing] any rational content in the Chinese Cultural Revolution" are only now beginning to be confronted.[53]

Though all commentators on the Cultural Revolution are certainly familiar with its visual characterizations, few studies to date have gone beyond brief passing references to their general educational and political role. Still missing from the literature is a significant set of works that look closely at the way visual discourses and grammars created in, and perpetuated through, various media, including posters, supplemented, reinforced, and provided alternatives to, written texts.[54] Geremie Barmé's recent exploration of the cultural *materia* associated with the posthumous cult of Mao contains many references to the popular art of the Cultural Revolution and its ironic reiteration in the writings of contemporary artists. A section of Wang Shuo's roaring parody of Maospeak, *Don't Treat Me as a Human Being* (*Qianwan bie ba wo dang ren*), is wonderfully conveyed:

> "Praise to you, Lord Clear Sky. . . . You have righted the wrong and crushed the bad in one fell swoop. Respected wise dear teacher leader helmsman pathfinder vanguard pioneer designer bright light torch devil-deflecting mirror dog-beating stick dad mum granddad grandma old ancestor primal ape Supreme Deity Jade Emperor Guanyin Boddhisattva commander-in-chief."[55]

Barmé's presentation of *visual* forms of pop culture unsurprisingly emphasizes Maoist iconography and memorabilia, but this does preclude a more comprehensive examination of the poster form. Stefan Landsberger's *Chinese Propaganda Posters*, the only significant study to date of Chinese communist posters, contains some wonderful reproductions of posters of the period.[56] Spanning revolutionary and reform eras (but with significant gaps), it offers a vivid visual essay on some of the themes developed in this poster art. However, Landsberger discusses the poster in basically the same terms as those that the Chinese Communist Party used to describe its function, as a "vehicle for the transmission of party ideology." It emerges once again as an unproblematic category, as a tool of political propaganda, which sought to present idealized "people's heroes" to the "masses" as models for the latter's ideological edification and emulation.[57]

## Looking at Posters of the Cultural Revolution: Theoretical and Analytical Approaches

In the chapters that follow, we borrow from notions of discourse developed by the French historian-philosopher Michel Foucault to identify the discursive patterns and impulses active in a particular visual form. Some visual discourses can be properly described as hegemonic. These are the layers or trajectories of meaning that are common throughout the visual imagination of a society or group and that operate on the level of assumption. A hegemonic discourse may be naturalized to the point of being synonymous with common sense; it is natural because it is there. This is not to say, of course, that a dominant visual discourse necessarily corresponds with the declared policies, acclaimed beliefs, legal positions, or moral stances that are articulated elsewhere in a society's system of communication. It may contradict them in important respects. Nor is it to suggest that the level of assumption at which a hegemonic discourse operates precludes subjective challenges to it; the public spectator neither condones nor rejects the meanings projected by a dominant visual discourse in any necessary way. During the Cultural Revolution, under the totalizing tendencies of the party-state structure, the different visual aspects of public discourses manifested a high degree of uniformity with official policies. Severe political constraints and pressures—among other factors—also ensured a high degree of subjective conformity to the official discourse.[58] Even this, though, was not enough to guarantee any particular response from the public, as the chaotic practices of the Red Guards indicated. The identification of such tensions both within a specific visual discursive mode and between one visual discourse and other media lends the analysis of visual culture great importance. Such analysis works as a discipline in its own right—a claim long made by art historians and film studies scholars—and contributes to an overall understanding of social organization and imagination.

How does this help us make a contribution to the study of the Cultural Revolution? First, posters are an exceptional visual form in that their function and design are geared to instant comprehension by a large proportion of the population. The poster artist relies on shortcuts to make a point and to create an immediate political or emotional impression. The poster emphasizes cultural and social literacy rather than literary knowledge or artistic sensibilities. Posters, in one form or another, were part of everyday life during the Cultural Revolution, as John Gittings shows in his chapter. Public spaces were almost definable by the presence of appropriate posters, just as advertising billboards are now inescapable in most urban spaces outside the home. Even domestic spaces were incomplete without some poster representation of the leader or the Party. Posters supplied a visual text that acknowledged "the people" as a unified public body accustomed to reading the visual image for political meanings. They addressed "the people" through a limited repertoire of mnemonics and clues, using "the people's" experience to build a grammar of signification in public space. Through discursive analysis and semiotic scrutiny, it becomes possible to find out how a certain kind of public was addressed. The next, maybe more interesting, step is to explore how such a method of address constituted the desired public.

Second, certain key words are associated with the study of the Cultural Revolution: chaos, class struggle, tragedy, humiliation.[59] How can we begin to think about these words through the posters, either in the original Chinese or in translation? Visual texts offer a different focus for thinking about concepts such as these. In posters of the Cultural Revolution, apart from the Red Guard years, there is, at first sight, very little chaos. Indeed, it is significant that images of the violence of revolutionaries "beating down" *(dadao)* their revisionist enemies disappeared from the public visual space by 1968. The foregrounding of chaotic violence in a 1967 poster of a man "smashing the old world" *(dasui jiu shijie)*—he is pictured breaking up statues, records, and books with a hammer—does not recur in later posters (E39). After 1970 the lines and shapes of the people and landscapes are bold, and the use of color is decisive. Transformations to eradicate chaos already seem to have taken place and are now being advertised for emulation. Tragedy is unthinkable for those within the picture, and humiliation is left to those outside the ideal world of poster people. In one poster a peasant militia leader exhorts a crowd of heavily armed young people to be vigilant in the struggle against Confucian ideas, here referred to under the slogan "restrain the self and return to the rites" *(ke ji fu li)*. It is telling that there is no reference to what, or who, might be the physical target of their armed zeal (J22, 1974?). The youth who has been relocated to the countryside, or "sent down," who strides joyfully through the fields seems to be in a kind of rural idyll (figure 3.1 [H15], 1975). Tension is, however, palpable in these images. It is located in the way the human bodies are contained by color-matching (that is, related by the way they are colored), by the direction of their gaze out of the poster's frame, and by the lack of plasticity in the drawing of limbs and flesh. These are images with little scope for excess or transgressions. Yet the sharp visual containment, which keeps them clear of the fuzziness of a less protective aesthetic, at the same time suggests the very levels of subjective chaos that these images are designed to deny.

Another aspect of the use and evocation of key words of the Cultural Revolution in the posters is the relationship between written word, as represented through a slogan, book title, wall poster, or the like, and the image. In many of the posters, word and image can be read as parallel texts, each discretely comprehensible and mutually reinforcing. In other instances, as Harriet Evans's chapter argues, the words sometimes have no apparent bearing on the image itself; rather, they invoke the broader political meaning, which gives legitimacy and status to the mundane image of the poster. Left to itself, without the words, the image in such cases could be read in a number of different, maybe contradictory, ways.[60] Word and image also appeal to different spectatorial modes; spectators take them in at different, though not necessarily hierarchically organized, levels. So the intertextual linkage of picture and text, of visual and written information, presents a complete amalgam to the spectator that is at one and the same time instructive, allusive, semiotic, iconic, symbolic, and inscriptive. It approaches the reader/spectator both through aesthetic forms and through historically, politically, and culturally embedded allusion. In so doing, it evokes a wide spectrum of responses, first through recognition of the image and then through recognition of a more specific kind that may exclude spectators who are not "in the know" or may bring spectators together in a trained response of respect, pleasure, or anguish. Stephanie Donald's chapter further suggests that pleasure is inscribed in the images of children's bodies, producing a visual rhetoric that announces the child as a continuing object of political and cultural spectatorship. She argues that pleasure is derived through the symbolic naturalization of childhood as a grammatical figure in adult visual discourse. Pleasure, too, is present in Xiaomei Chen's reflections on the visual images of her childhood. Having "grown up" with the posters of the 1960s, she explores the complex multiplicity of meanings posters could generate in their public. Both Craig Clunas's and Robert Benewick's chapters examine different aspects of spectatorial response. Clunas uses autobiography to trace the history of (his) perception of this particular cultural formation, the poster of the Cultural Revolution. He recognizes that the subjectivities of place (Scotland in the 1960s and Beijing in the 1970s), education, hindsight, youth, and age produce contingent psychical structures of reception that allow "natural" responses to fade and mutate with the passage of personal and global time. Benewick also refers to the contingencies of political expediency and the effects of power. The portraits of Mao and other leaders evoke a trained response of respect whereby significance is accorded through the signature of the icon. This is also true of the ironic revisits to Mao in Chinese pop art of the 1980s (and of Andy Warhol's technicolor Mao-as-Marilyn homage). In all these readings, satisfaction in spectatorship is central to understanding the power of the publicness of posters.

A third way in which we hope to contribute to the historical and social analyses of the Cultural Revolution is by foregrounding the notion of subjectivity in visual cultural production, a point that we have already mentioned briefly. The competence and artistry of revolutionary posters can be seductive. It is possible to describe—or dismiss—them as propaganda while at the same time accepting, provisionally, the often stereotyped messages they project. In documentary after documentary we see the same footage of frantic young Red Guards waving the "little red book," or of armies of students, banners in hand, marching in serried ranks to the beat of revolutionary drums. Many writings of the memoir genre, and particularly those that focus on the Cultural Revolution, tend to neglect the subject, collapsing subjective difference and agency into a political and social uniformity reminiscent of the features of propaganda art. The individual subject thus becomes part of an undifferentiated collective victim, ravaged by Maoist violence. The posters make concrete a version of the "average Chinese in the last years of Mao" in which the individual figure has no identity beyond her/his political expediency and social position; the complexity of individual and collective identities is lost in images of sameness. The model people of the posters were designed as much to project a socialism of the future as to provide exemplars for the present.[61] Despite—or very probably because of—this motivation, revolutionary poster art, children's cartoon books, scant film footage, and even personal memoirs seem to come together in extending the representations of propaganda into lived social experience. It goes without saying that this reduction of Chinese people to a few social models, politically sanctified at a moment in history, is ridiculous. Yet the question we face is how to break down the classic, rigid divisions of worker/peasant/soldier versus reactionary/revisionist/bureaucrat versus male/female,and so on, through a multidisciplinary and interdisciplinary account of the posters in the Westminster collection. In confronting these oppositional divisions, we argue that a close analysis of visual and other primary materials is required to explode the notion that all revolutionary art is the same—in other words, that it is a seamless version of authoritarian political rhetoric.[62]

We cannot fully realize our aims and objectives in this book without reference to other sources and cultural forms. Much of that information is contained in the endnotes and in the previous research of the contributors. John Gittings is not only a collector but also a writer and a journalist of modern China. Harriet Evans's gender analysis of posters and recent history is informed by her work on women's magazines and sex education manuals as well as by official documentation written by, and about, women. Xiaomei Chen's experience as a Western-trained academic struggling to find an appropriate way to represent China in the diaspora is central to the concerns of her essay. Craig Clunas draws on his knowledge of Chinese art and gardens and of the histories that produce, and are produced by, visual culture. Robert Benewick and Stephanie Donald have written on Mao through a consideration of badge collection in the 1960s and 1970s.[63] Perhaps the most obvious companion to our present study is film. The philosopher Walter Benjamin declared as early as 1939 that people could not survive without film to accompany them through modernity. Relatively few films were made in the Cultural Revolution years, but those that were stick in the minds of the spectators as beacons of memory and experience. The visual address of posters in a public place and that of film may surely be understood as relatively alike in the conditions of the Cultural Revolution:

> With the close-up, space expands; with slow motion movement is extended. The enlargement of a snapshot does not simply render more precise what in any case was visible, though unclear: it reveals entirely new structural formations of the subject.[64]

Cultural products, whether gardens, paintings, badges, magazines, film, or posters, offer sources for further reflection on the period of their production and consumption. The revolutionary operas *(geming yangbanxi)* and subsequent model films *(yangban dianying)* are available on compact video disk in urban China. These texts of a swiftly receding past are returning to the public sphere in the guise of film history. In the present book we hope to begin this work for the posters of the Cultural Revolution. We wish to make them visible, to reform their publicness, to picture their power, and to question "entirely new structural formations of the subject."

## Notes

1. The Great Proletarian Cultural Revolution is usually abbreviated as "wenge" (cultural revolution). Official texts tend to use quotation marks in referring to the *wenhua da geming* (Great Cultural Revolution) as a way of challenging its status as a revolutionary movement. The designation of the Cultural Revolution as "ten years of chaos" indicates both official periodization of the movement and official assessment of its effects.

2. In his lecture at the exhibition "Mao's Graphic Voice: Pictorial Posters from the Cultural Revolution," at the Elvehjem Museum in Madison, Wisconsin, Michael Schoenhals noted that a famous painting of Mao Zedong, *The Chairman Tours the Nation,* which depicted Mao on an inspection tour of rural China during the Great Leap Forward, had a print run of over 20 million copies. The source for his statement was a journal of national culture, *Zuojia wenzhai* 45, (5 November 1993). quoted in Michael Schoenhals, "Posters and Poster Art in China's Cultural Revolution: The Political and Social Contexts" (lecture given at the exhibit "Mao's Graphic Voice: Pictorial Posters from the Cultural Revolution," Elvehjem Museum of Art, University of Wisconsin, Madison, 1996), 7. Craig Clunas notes that an edition of 172,077 copies of one particular painting during the Cultural Revolution was not "unusually large." See Craig Clunas, *Art in China,* Oxford History of Art (Oxford: Oxford University Press, 1997), 214.

3. Thanks to Michael Schoenhals for this observation on the posters of the Red Guard period. In a discussion in March 1998, he described these years in China as a "visual desert."

4. A key exception in writings of the earlier period, in this case published soon after the official end of the Cultural Revolution, was Lowell Dittmer and Chen Ruoxi, *Ethics and Rhetoric of the Chinese Cultural Revolution* (Berkeley, Calif.: Center for Chinese Studies, University of California, Berkeley, 1981). There are notable works on art production that refer to posters, peasant painters, and paintings that became posters. For a comprehensive history, see Julia F. Andrews, *Painters and Politics in the People's Republic of China, 1949–1979* (Berkeley and Los Angeles: University of California Press, 1994). See also Maria Gallinowski, *Art and Politics in China, 1949–1984* (Hong Kong: Chinese University Press, 1998); Joan Lebold Cohen, *The New Chinese Painting 1949–1986* (New York: Harry N. Abrams, 1987), 21–23, 144–49; Ralph Croizier, "Chinese Art in the Chiang Ch'ing Era," *Journal of Asian Studies* 38 (February 1979): 303–11; Ellen Johnston Laing, *The Winking Owl: Art in the People's Republic of China* (Berkeley and Los Angeles: University of California Press, 1988), 58 ff; 71 ff.

5. See the Decision of the Chinese Communist Party Central Committee Concerning the Great Proletarian Cultural Revolution, often known as the "Sixteen Points," adopted on 8 August 1966 by the Chinese Communist Party Central Committee (CCPCC) Plenum to guide the progress of the Cultural Revolution.

6. "The Sixteen Points," in *CCP Documents of the Great Proletarian Cultural Revolution, 1966–1967* (Hong Kong: Union Research Institute, 1968), 46.

7. Clark also backdates the start of the Cultural Revolution to 1964, marking it by the advent of hostility toward certain films and film workers. Paul Clark, *Chinese Cinema: Culture and Politics since 1949* (Cambridge: Cambridge University Press, 1987), 126.

8. See, e.g., Igor Golomstock, *Totalitarian Art in the Soviet Union, the Third Reich, Fascist Italy, and the People's Republic of China* (London: Collins Harvell, 1990). This categorizes all socialist art produced in the Soviet Union and China and fascist art of Nazi Germany and Fascist Italy as monotonous, monolithic, and totalitarian.

9. Schoenhals, "Posters and Poster Art," 13.

10. Schoenhals, "Posters and Poster Art," 2.

11. Stephanie Donald is, by contrast, a relative latecomer to China "itself." She first saw the posters in 1979 in a "revolutionary" bookshop in a British university town and wondered at the gap between the Chinese she was studying and the Chinese experiences glimpsed in posters.

12. Two recent publications featuring women in Shanghai New Year posters and advertisements are Yi Bin, ed., *Lao Shanghai guanggao* (Advertisements of old Shanghai) (Shanghai: Shanghai huabao chubanshe, 1995); and Song Jiami, ed., *Lao Yuefen pai* (Old calendar pictures) (Shanghai: Shanghai huabao chubanshe, 1997). See also Stephanie Donald, "Children as Political Messengers: Art, Childhood, and Continuity," this volume, note 10.

13. Andrews, *Painters and Politics,* 315–16. Andrews points out that "most Cultural Revolution art was directly descended from the academic painting of the 1950s and early 1960s, and . . . the best of it was painted by academically trained artists," 315.

14. Schoenhals, "Posters and Poster Art," 16.

15. For a discussion about *A Crowd of Clowns,* see Andrews, *Painters and Politics,* 332–36.

16. An early publication on Chinese posters introduced one hundred items of the author's personal collection. See Stewart E. Fraser, ed., *One Hundred Great Chinese Posters* (New York: Images Graphiques, 1977). The only sizable monograph to date on poster art of the PRC is Stefan R. Landsberger, *Chinese Propaganda Posters* (Amsterdam: Pepin Press, 1995). A more recent work by Landsberger is *Paint It Red: Fifty Years of Propaganda Posters* (Gröningen: Gröninger Museum, 1998), published to accompany an exhibition of Chinese, Cuban, and Soviet posters held in the Gröninger Museum, 4 December 1998–28 February 1999. A website on the exhibition also contains Chinese posters from the entire period since 1949 and useful information on the artists. See <http://iisg.nl/exhibitions/chairman/index/html>. Other books about socialist art and posters have made passing, and often erroneous reference to China; see, e.g., Golomstock, *Totalitarian Art,* 121–30. One of Golomstock's most notable errors is misnaming Yan'an as Yangyang. Other recent publications on art and propaganda give barely a mention to the posters of the People's Republic of China. See, e.g., Toby Clark, *Art and Propaganda in the Twentieth Century* (New York: Harry N. Abrams, 1997).

17. John D. Thompson, *The Media and Modernity: A Social Theory of the Media* (Cambridge, England: Polity Press, 1995).

18. Golomstock, *Totalitarian Art,* 123.

19. Landsberger, *Chinese Propaganda Posters,* 172.

20. Susan Pack, *Film Posters of the Russian Avant-Garde* (Germany: Benedikt Taschen Verlag, 1995), 14–19.

21. Geremie Barmé quotes a Cultural Revolution joke that plays on both the excessive number of Mao texts given as presents on special occasions and the parable of the old man. The joke reminds us again of the multiple layers of spectatorship, both credulous and ironic, at play in the final ten years of Mao's life. Geremie Barmé, *Shades of Mao: The Posthumous Cult of the Great Leader* (Armonk, N.Y.: M. E.Sharpe, 1996), 5–6.

22. In "Posters and Poster Art," Schoenhals discusses the transition from posters that explicitly targeted named individuals for condemnation to the disappearance of class enemies from visual representation by the end of the 1960s. In his analysis, the transition could be explained with reference to the view of Mao Zedong, and presumably others, that explicit criticism through reference to individuals' "promiscuous and decadent lifestyles" did not serve "to politically educate the broad popular masses." *Wenge jianxun* (Cultural Revolution news in brief), no. 333 (6 July 1967), cited in Schoenhals, "Posters and Poster Art," 16–17.

23. Our use of the term the "politicized body" of course invokes Ann Anagnost's essay "The Politicized Body," in *Body, Subject, and Power in China,* ed. Angela Zito and Tani Barlow (Chicago: University of Chicago Press, 1994), 131–56. In this essay, Anagnost examines a peasant's desire for political legitimation by the local authorities as a means of reinscribing the Party as a benevolent, just, and fundamentally moral entity. Our analysis here, by contrast, focuses not on the authority bestowed on the Party by individual loyalties but on the ways in which the poster featured the politicized body as a visual form consolidating the individual sub-

ject's necessary ties with the state.

24. This brief review of secondary literature on the Cultural Revolution is necessarily a selection. For a useful bibliography, see "Further Readings" in Michael Schoenhals, ed., *China's Cultural Revolution, 1966–1969: Not a Dinner Party* (Armonk, N.Y.: M. E.Sharpe, 1996). A bibliographical essay on the subject is in Roderick MacFarquhar and John K. Fairbank, eds., *The Cambridge History of China,* vol. 15, *The People's Republic, Part 2: Revolutions within the Chinese Revolution, 1966–1982,* (Cambridge: Cambridge University Press, 1991), 880–911.

25. E.g., Edward E. Rice, *Mao's Way* (Berkeley and Los Angeles: University of California Press, 1972); Stanley Karnow, *Mao and China: Inside China's Cultural Revolution* (Harmondsworth, England: Penguin Books, 1972).

26. Jean Deaubier, *A History of China's Cultural Revolution* (New York:Vintage, 1974); Charles Bettleheim, *Cultural Revolution and Industrial Organization in China* (New York: Monthly Review Press, 1974).

27. Byung-joon Ahn, *Chinese Politics and the Cultural Revolution* (Seattle: University of Washington Press, 1976); Hong Yung Lee, *The Politics of the Chinese Cultural Revolution* (Berkeley and Los Angeles: University of California Press, 1978); Stuart R. Schram, ed., *Authority, Participation, and Cultural Change in China* (Cambridge: Cambridge University Press, 1973).

28. Maurice Meisner, *Mao's China and After: A History of the People's Republic* (New York: Free Press, 1977). Lowell Dittmer, *Liu Shao-ch'i and the Chinese Cultural Revolution: The Politics of Mass Criticism* (Berkeley and Los Angeles: University of California Press, 1974); Stanley Rosen, *Red Guard Factionalism and the Cultural Revolution in Guangzhou (Canton)* (Boulder, Colo.: Westview Press, 1982); William Hinton, *Hundred Day War: The Cultural Revolution at Tsinghua University* (New York: Monthly Review Press, 1972).

29. One of the first of these was Neale Hunter's *Shanghai Journal: An Eyewitness Account of the Cultural Revolution,* 2d ed. (Hong Kong: Oxford University Press, 1988) (originally published in 1969).

30. Richard H. Solomon, *Mao's Revolution and the Chinese Political Culture* (Berkeley and Los Angeles: University of California Press, 1971); Lucian W. Pye, *Mao Tse-tung: The Man in the Leader* (New York: Basic Books, 1976).

31. Dittmer and Chen, *Ethics and Rhetoric.*

32. Anita Chan, Richard Madsen, and Jonathan Unger, *Chen Village* (Berkeley and Los Angeles: University of California Press, 1984).

33. Schoenhals, *China's Cultural Revolution,* xvii.

34. Andrew Walder, "Cultural Revolution Radicalism: Variations on a Stalinist Theme," in *New Perspectives on the Cultural Revolution,* Harvard Contemporary China Series no. 8, ed. William Joseph, Christine Wong, and David Zweig (Cambridge: Harvard University Press, 1991), 41–61.

35. See, e.g., Joseph, Wong, and Zweig, *New Perspectives.*

36. This was in a document approved by the Twelfth Plenum of the Eleventh Central Committee of the CCP in June 1981, "Resolution on some questions concerning Party history." Publication of this document was accompanied by massive amount of explanatory texts detailing the specific points of this "new" narrative of the Cultural Revolution.

37. See Jeffrey N. Wasserstrom, afterword in *Popular Protest and Political Culture in Modern China: Learning from 1989,* ed. Jeffrey N. Wasserstrom and Elizabeth J. Perry (Boulder, Colo.: Westview Press, 1992). By contrast, a more recent article by Craig Calhoun and Jeffrey Wasserstrom looks at a series of parallels and continuities between the Cultural Revolution and 1989. See Craig Calhoun and Jeffrey N. Wasserstrom, "Wenhua da geming yu 1989 nian minzhu yundong zhijian de lishi guanxi" (Historical connection between the Cultural Revolution and the Democracy Movement of 1989), *Xianggang shehui kexue xuebao* (Hong Kong Journal of Social Sciences), no. 11 (Spring 1998): 129–49, also to be published as "Legacies of Radicalism: China's Cultural Revolution and the Democracy Movement of 1989," *Thesis 11* (forthcoming).

38. See Vivienne Shue, *The Reach of the State* (Stanford, Calif.: Stanford University Press,

1988), 23–24. The reformulations of the Cultural Revolution were also associated with the restoration of a moral and social order reminiscent of the "golden age" of the 1950s. The repeated references to the importance of the early 1950s for the new period of China's socialist development had different levels of meaning. On the one hand, the references were significant for symbolic reasons, since the 1950s represented, in public and official discourses, a period of political unity and stability, before the onset of Maoist "adventurism" with the Great Leap Forward in 1958. The 1950s were also significant in that the decade was commonly associated with the economic policies pursued by Liu Shaoqi, who, as Mao's number one enemy in the Cultural Revolution, was criminalized as a "renegade, scab, hidden traitor" and who was posthumously rehabilitated in 1980. For more on Liu Shaoqi's struggle with Mao Zedong during the Cultural Revolution, and for the continuities between Liu Shaoqi's "revisionist" economic program of the 1950s and early 1960s and the post-Mao period, see Lowell Dittmer, "The Chinese Cultural Revolution Revisited," *Journal of Contemporary China* 5, no. 13 (November 1996): 255–68.

39. For a useful review essay on Chinese literature on the Cultural Revolution, see Michael Schoenhals, "Unofficial and Official Histories of the Cultural Revolution: A Review Article," *Journal of Asian Studies* 48, no. 3 (August 1989): 563–72; a more recent though briefer review is in Mobo C. F. Gao, "Maoist Discourse and a Critique of the Present Assessment of the Cultural Revolution," *Bulletin of Concerned Asian Scholars* 26, no. 3 (July-September 1994): 13–31.

40. There are too many such titles to list here, but the following are some of the most important and popular: Gao Yuan, *Born Red: A Chronicle of the Cultural Revolution* (Stanford, Calif.: Stanford University Press, 1987); Cheng Nien, *Life and Death in Shanghai* (London: Grafton Books, 1986); Min Anchee, *Red Azalea* (New York: Pantheon, 1994); Yue Daiyun and Carolyn Wakeman, *To the Storm: The Odyssey of a Revolutionary Chinese Woman* (Berkeley and Los Angeles: University of California Press, 1985); Jung Chang, *Wild Swans* (London: Harper-Collins, 1991; New York: Doubleday, 1992); Rae Yang, *Spider Eaters: A Memoir* (Berkeley and Los Angeles: University of California Press, 1997).

41. For an interesting and welcome critique of the genre, see Mobo C. F. Gao, "Memoirs and Interpretations of the Cultural Revolution," *Bulletin of Concerned Asian Scholars* 27, no. 1 (January–March 1995): 49–57.

42. Examples of official use of the spectre of the Red Guards during 1989 as well as student responses to this charge are in Han Minzhu, ed., *Cries for Democracy* (Princeton, N.J.: Princeton University Press, 1990), 83–85, 131–36, 269–71, 305, 321. Other writers have also noted the ways in which the students of 1989, despite their efforts to distance themselves from association with Cultural Revolution practices, resurrected some techniques associated with the Red Guard years. See Anita Chan and Jonathan Unger, "Voices from the Protest Movement, Chongqing, Sichuan," *Australian Journal of Chinese Affairs* 24 (1990): 259–79.

43. Marilyn Young, "Chicken Little in China: Some Reflections on Women," in *Marxism and the Chinese Experience,* ed. Arif Dirlik and Maurice Meisner (Armonk, N.Y.: M. E. Sharpe, 1989), 253–68.

44. Wendy Larson, "Women and the Discourse of Desire in Post-revolutionary China: The Awkward Postmodernism of Chen Ran," *boundary 2* 24, no. 3 (Fall 1997): 204. See also Chen Xiaoming's account of Jiang Wen's film, "The Mysterious Other: Postpolitics in Chinese Film," in the same volume, 135–36.

45. For recent works, see Yan Jiaqi and Gao Gao, *Turbulent Decade: A History of the Cultural Revolution,* ed. and trans. D. W. Y. Kwok (Honolulu: University of Hawaii Press, 1996); Wang Nianyi, *Da dongluan de niandai* (Decade of great chaos) (Zhengzhou: Henan renmin chubanshe, 1988); Jin Chunming, *Wenhua da geming de shigao* (Outline history of the great Cultural Revolution) (Chengdu: Sichuan renmin chubanshe, 1995).

46. In 1996, in the PRC itself, there were at least half a dozen informal conferences on the Cultural Revolution, the most significant of which was convened by the Contemporary China Institute (Dangdai Zhongguo yanjiu suo). In January 1995, an international workshop on the Cultural Revolution was held at the Centre for Pacific East Asia Studies at Stockholm University, and a second follow-up conference was held in July 1996 at the Hong Kong University of

Science and Technology. A special issue of *China Information* (vol. 11, nos. 2–3 [Autumn/Winter 1996]) focuses exclusively on the Cultural Revolution, and the 1996 American Asian Studies conference held in Chicago had a panel discussion called "New Perspectives on the Cultural Revolution."

47.  One of the most important analyses of written discourses of the period to date is Michael Schoenhals, "Doing Things with Words," in *Chinese Politics: Five Studies*, China Research Monographs, no. 41 (Berkeley and Los Angeles: University of California Press, 1992). For studies of verbal practices, see Michael Schoenhals, "Talk about a Revolution: Red Guards, Government Cadres, and the Languages of Political Discourse," Indiana East Asian Working Paper Series on Language and Politics in Modern China, no.1 (Bloomington: Indiana University East Asian Studies Center, June 1993); Huang Shaorong, *To Rebel Is Justified* (Lanham, Md.: University Press of America, 1996); Vivian Wagner, "Die Lieder der Roten Garden" (Songs of the Red Guards), (M.A. thesis, University of Munich, 1995); Elizabeth J. Perry and Li Xun, "Revolutionary Rudeness: The Language of Red Guards and Rebel Workers in China's Cultural Revolution," Indiana East Asian Working Paper Series on Language and Politics in Modern China, no. 2 (Bloomington: Indiana University East Asian Studies Center, July 1993).

48.  Elizabeth J. Perry and Li Xun, *Organized Disorder: Shanghai Workers in the Cultural Revolution* (Boulder, Colo.: Westview Press, 1997).

49.  Gao, "Maoist Discourse" and "Memoirs and Interpretations of the Cultural Revolution."

50.  The main scholars associated with this are Gail Hershatter and Emily Honig, both of the University of California at Santa Cruz. My thanks to both of them for some fascinating discussions about this new project in May 1998.

51.  Emily Honig, "Maoist Mappings of Gender: Reassessing the Red Guards," in *Chinese Femininities/Chinese Masculinities,* ed. Jeffrey Wasserstrom and Susan Brownell (Berkeley and Los Angeles: University of California Press, forthcoming).

52.  Alessandro Russo, "The Probable Defeat: Preliminary Notes on the Chinese Cultural Revolution," *Positions* 6, no.1 (Spring 1998): 179–202.

53.  Russo, "Probable Defeat," 179.

54.  There have been accounts on the generic specificities of film form. Yau gives good accounts of the development of revolutionary narratives, which were taken to extremes in the model operas and model fictions of the 1970s. Esther C. M. Yau, "Filmic Discourses on Women in Chinese Cinema (1949–1965): Art, Ideology and Social Relations" (Ph.D. diss., University of California, 1990). Paul Clark has a lengthy section on the politics and aesthetics of film in "his" Cultural Revolution, in Clark, *Chinese Cinema,* 125–53. However, the volatility of political sentiment made filmmaking—a lengthy process—one of the main cultural sacrifices of the period.

55.  Barmé, *Shades of Mao,* 225.

56.  A much smaller volume, published as a guide to an exhibition based on a private collection in Shanghai, for the Elvehjem Museum of Art, University of Wisconsin, is Patricia Powell and Shitao Huo, eds., *Mao's Graphic Voice: Pictorial Posters from the Cultural Revolution* (Madison: University of Wisconsin Press, 1996).

57.  Landsberger, *Chinese Propaganda Posters,* 41.

58.  For a particular perspective on subjective conformity with the dominant discourse, see Gao, "Maoist Discourse."

59.  Incidentally, it is interesting to note in this context a change in the fortunes of the word *xuanchuan* (propaganda), a term that is closely associated with the kind of public information given out in the discourses of the Cultural Revolution. During a trip to Hong Kong not so long ago, John Gittings heard that the central authorities in Beijing had made a decision to change the English translation of the word *xuanchuan* from "propaganda" to "publicity."

60.  In a presentation "Presentations of Progress in PRC Primers and Pictorial Histories, or 'What Do Modern Cities and Citizens Look Like?'" at the March 1998 Association of Asian Studies conference in Washington, D.C., Jeffrey N. Wasserstrom pointed to some of the extraordinary contradictions between word and image in communist primers of the early 1950s.

61.  Victoria E. Bonnell makes this point very clearly in her analysis of Stalinist poster art. She writes that "the purpose of political art, beginning in the 1930s, was to provide a visual script, an

incantation designed to conjure up new modes of thinking and conduct, and to persuade people that the present and the future were indistinguishable. In important respects, the visual medium anticipated developments in Soviet society and provided a model for them, rather than simply reflecting processes already under way." Victoria E. Bonnell, *Iconography of Power: Soviet Political Posters under Lenin and Stalin* (Berkeley and Los Angeles: University of California Press, 1997), 14.

62.  In this context, it is worth quoting another comment made by Golomstock in his *Totalitarian Art*. For him, there appears to be a "seamless" sameness not only between Chinese and Soviet political art but also in the public's mode of response to it. Hence, "Inexperienced in dialectical subtleties, the Chinese mentality tended to take the statements of its revered leaders literally, and the principles of Mao, whenever and wherever they were stated, were immediately put into practice." Golomstock, *Totalitarian Art*, 122.

63.  John Gittings, *Real China: From Cannibalism to Karaoke* (London: Simon & Schuster, 1996); Harriet Evans, *Women and Sexuality in China: Dominant Discourses of Female Sexuality and Gender since 1949* (Cambridge, England: Polity Press, 1997); Craig Clunas, *Fruitful Sites: Garden Culture in Ming Dynasty China* (London: Reaktion Books, 1996); Robert Benewick and Stephanie Donald, eds., *Belief in China: Art and Politics, Deities and Mortality* (Brighton, England: Royal Pavilion/Green Foundation, 1996).

64.  Walter Benjamin, "The Work of Art in the Epoch of Its Technical Reproducibility" (1939), quoted in Howard Caygill, *Walter Benjamin: The Colour of Experience* (London: Routledge, 1998), 112. Full translation as "The Work of Art in the Age of Mechanical Reproduction," in *Illuminations*, by Walter Benjamin (reprint in translation, London: Fontana, 1992), 211–44.

# 2

# Excess and Enthusiasm

*John Gittings*

To travel in China during the Cultural Revolution was a bewildering business. The normal sense of disorientation in an unfamiliar land was heightened by the very special political culture of the time with its unwritten and usually unfathomable rules. In between set-piece visits to schools, factories, communes, and theaters the inquiring visitor would seize any opportunity to disengage from the guided tour, get down from the bus or out of the hotel, and try to see something that was not prefaced by an officially presented "brief introduction." This worried Chinese hosts considerably. At the lakeside resort of Hangzhou in 1971, an attempt to ride into town on an ordinary bus was frustrated when the bus was flagged down and the driver ordered not to move till the foreigners on board had been transferred to the safety of a hotel minibus. Later, in Beijing, a quiet stroll in the backstreet lanes, or *hutongs,* was abruptly terminated by a group of vigilant schoolgirls who arrested the two stray foreigners on suspicion of spying.

Deprived for most of the time of the normal contacts that help build up understanding in a foreign culture—the casual strolls, chance encounters, and random conversations—we searched for other reference points among the abundance of visual images on display. These ranged from stark slogans in black or red characters to colorful posters on billboards, or smaller printed versions on sale in bookshops. Designed to catch the eye and to convey propaganda—*xuanchuan*—the posters, literally "propaganda pictures" *(xuanchuanhua),* were emphatic and exuberant, often stating topics with greater emphasis and clarity than our own guides. Many of them delivered messages of harsh conflict and struggle, especially in the early phase of Red Guard violence and high-level political warfare (1966–1969). Yet others conveyed a sense of excitement and commitment to genuine social change that developed when the violence was reduced and attempts were made to "revolutionize" education, health, workplace relations, and local government. This aspect of popular involvement is now denied, and the years 1966–1976 have been officially designated as "Ten Years of Chaos" in which "nothing good took place." Poster art, too, has been written off by Chinese art historians as a worthless product of those years—a contention I shared neither at the time nor since.

The propaganda poster belonged to a much larger family of artistic endeavor of the time that will be described in detail later. From traditional painting to woodcuts and cartoons, all forms of art had been thoroughly "revolutionized" by the Cultural Revolution to convey a uniform range of aspirations and exhortations. For visitors to China the posters, on sale for a few cents per copy, provided the easiest access to this cultural continuum of revolutionary art. They could be purchased in the state-run New China Bookshop *(Xinhua shudian)* found in every town. In these usually cavernous premises, with their bored assistants, dusty windows, and half-empty shelves, they provided the one bright feature. Examples of posters in stock were pinned on the wall or ceiling and identified by numbers for easy purchase. Posters of Chairman Mao were naturally most prominent. The appearance of any other leader would be of political significance. Marx, Lenin, Engels, and Stalin would be on display. Figures from the revolutionary operas promoted by Mao's wife, Jiang Qing, were also frequent subjects, as were model heroes such as the soldier Lei Feng. Current campaigns in the Cultural Revolution generated posters illustrating the appropriate slogan. In the early years many were artistically very crude, but in the early 1970s the stark themes of "struggle" gave way to the advocacy of social goals, such as taking education to the countryside, promoting women's equality in the workplace, and working harder to help national construction. Posters of this period showed much more variety artistically, departing from the more hackneyed approach—familiar from the Soviet Union—to adopt images and techniques of traditional Chinese painting and folk art and making a conscious effort to look attractive.

Sold cheaply, they would be purchased for home use as acceptable decoration on bare walls, alongside the obligatory portrait or poster of Chairman Mao. They were displayed in school classrooms, on the walls of factory workshops, and in the corridors of government buildings. Larger-scale compositions appeared on billboards at road junctions and inside railway and bus stations. For the visitor, they offered a combination of realistic detail with imagistic allegory that richly illustrated the main political and social themes of the time. At both levels, such propaganda posters also provided opportunities for analysis and discussion at a level that was accessible to ordinary Chinese, for whom the images were part of everyday discourse. They sometimes offered clues to political trends or views that were otherwise concealed. Posters in a school showing Premier Zhou Enlai, who was regarded as a moderating influence in the Cultural Revolution, might indicate support for his efforts to restore social order and revive the importance of science and education. Posters in a factory that criticized bureaucracy or denounced "economism" might imply that militant workers were waging a campaign against the management. Billboards calling for fresh efforts to smash the class enemy could reveal a fierce political struggle; those exhorting people to support the Four Strike Hards would indicate problems with crime and theft in the area. Posters calling for good traffic discipline, better-quality goods, or care for the elderly indicated a return to "normality" in which less politicized social goals could again be expressed.

After the death of Mao Zedong in September 1976, his successor, Hua Guofeng, continued to assert the validity of the Cultural Revolution, while reviving the policy of the "Four Modernizations" (originally proclaimed by Zhou Enlai before the Cultural Revolution began and then dropped) as the emphasis began to shift from political struggle to economic reforms. Posters from this period provide an extremely sensitive indication of its changing values. I first visited China in 1971 and began a collection of Chinese popular art and ephemera at that time. In the late 1970s, I was teaching Chinese politics at the Polytechnic of Central London (PCL) to students who now had the opportunity to spend a year attached to a language institute or university language department in China. On pastoral visits to China, I found that the importance of posters as a guide to the rapid shifts in political culture under way was evident to both staff and students. The Chinese Visual Arts Project was established at the PCL, and a public exhibition of posters was held in April 1979. With generous help from a small number of colleagues and friends in the China field who had visited or lived on the mainland, the core of the present collection was quickly established, extending back into the 1960s.

The return to power of Deng Xiaoping, who stressed the need for economic modernization and the revival of education and science, gave poster art a new though short-lived lease on life. Images of thoughtful study and dedication were presented in softer colors with more subtle design. But posters suffered from being an art form so closely associated with the previous epoch of turmoil. The very word "propaganda" began to sound as old-fashioned as "comrade." Diplomats from the Chinese embassy in London invited to the PCL's exhibition found it hard to hide their incredulity at, and even distaste for, the organizers' interest. By the early 1980s, blank spaces were appearing on the walls of the New China Bookshops; very soon most poster themes became anodyne and their images purely decorative. A fresh source of visual appeal was to be found instead on the billboards where advertisements for consumer goods and films at first appeared side by side with, and then replaced, images of Chairman Mao. That is another area of enormous interest, in its blending of the traditional and the modern, the foreign and the domestic, but it lies outside the scope of this collection.

**History of the Poster**

Propaganda posters in the modern sense began to be produced for mass sale after the 1949 communist Liberation: specialized groups were set up to study Soviet experience of poster design and output, and modern techniques of reproduction became available for the first time. However, the use of art for propaganda was no novelty: it had been used extensively in both the nationalist and the communist revolutions, particularly in appealing to a largely illiterate population in the rural areas. Such propaganda struck a chord with the peasants, who were accustomed to "reading" messages conveyed visually through shop signs, New Year posters, pictures in the temples, flags and banners on the opera stage, and crudely printed fly sheets that began to circulate in the second half of the nineteenth century. (Antiforeign feeling that culminated in the Boxer Rebellion had been stimulated by illustrated tracts and leaflets depicting the atrocities committed by foreign missionaries.) The advertising poster, linked to commercial design work and influenced by the packaging of Western goods, established a distinctive style that reached its peak in 1930s Shanghai, but it developed in an entirely different world from rural society.

The theoretical basis for all cultural work under communist rule was Mao Zedong's "Yan'an Talks" (May 1942) in which he laid down the principle that literature and art must "serve the people." Mao was elaborating—and forcing into a more rigid mold— ideas which were already familiar. In 1976 an exhibition of "soldiers' art" in Beijing would give pride of place to an oil painting with the title *Chairman Mao teaches us to paint for the revolution*. This showed Mao smiling approvingly at propaganda sketches made by young soldiers in the period before 1927 of the joint Communist-Nationalist "united front."[1] In the Nationalist-led Northern Expedition (1926–1927) against the

Chinese warlords that followed, mobile propaganda teams would accompany the fighting troops to win over civilians. The Communist armies, who had to rely entirely on peasant support both to survive and to attract new recruits, made even greater efforts to appeal to the people. Pictures as well as slogans were painted upon walls, both inside and outside. The new woodcut movement of the 1930s, inspired by the writer Lu Xun, was enlisted in the service of the revolution by artists who moved to the Communist capital in Yan'an. They included Gu Yuan, Yan Han, Jiang Feng , Shi Lu, and others who became senior figures in the post-1949 art world. They adapted rural art forms common in New Year and other folk prints to serve the new political cause.Because access to printing presses was very limited, woodcuts usually offered the best way of making multiple copies. Political meetings were held and theater troupes performed on open-air stages, in front of banners painted with grotesque images of Japanese imperialists and Chinese puppets, as well as with appropriate slogans. Such ephemeral works were photographed by a number of foreign visitors to the communist areas.[2] More sophisticated work began to be produced during the civil war (1946–1949); some of this work survives in Chinese collections and has been republished or placed on exhibition.[3]

All of the art produced for propaganda purposes in this period was described as "propaganda pictures"—*xuanchuanhua*. A retrospective collection, published in Beijing in 1979, contained sketches, cartoons, woodcuts in the 1930s and peasant styles, New Year prints with revolutionary themes, all dating from the anti-Japanese war and described as xuanchuanhua.[4] Cartoons *(manhua),* illustrated strips *(lianhuanhua),* woodcuts *(banhua),* New Year prints *(nianhua)* and paintings in the traditional style *(guohua)* were the recognized forms of visual art production; all of these except the guohua were routinely used for propaganda work. The term *xuanchuanhua* was appropriated to describe the new mass-produced propaganda posters only after 1949. Many were specially composed to suit the new medium, but posters continued to reproduce compositions originally designed in one of the other forms, particularly modern-style New Year prints and the popular illustrated strips that are also available in smaller book-form versions. Propaganda posters are also known as "placard pictures" *(zhaotiehua),* meaning a picture that seeks attention and is attached to some object—an apt description for posters designed to be pinned or glued to walls.

An official history of Chinese art published in 1994 looks back on the 1950s as the golden age of propaganda posters; independent observers would be unlikely to agree. A huge quantity of very mediocre work was produced to support the war being waged by the Chinese People's Volunteers (the armed forces under a different name) in North Korea against the U.S.-led United Nations forces. Art workers rallied round, the story is told, to plaster the whole country with posters, many of which were sent to the front line to raise the troops' morale. Most fell into the category known as "we fervently love peace," showing wistful or smiling children, doves of peace, and other scenes of harmony. A poster with this title by Jue Wen showed two little children reproduced with photographic clarity and actually holding doves; it was regarded as a masterpiece.[5] In posters as with other art, the influence of Soviet socialist realism was only too clear—an influential exhibition of Soviet posters and cartoons was held in Beijing in 1951. Another obligatory theme of this period showed Mao Zedong meeting the people or displaying his wisdom in the manner of Joseph Stalin. The New Year pictures were at first less affected, showing rural reforms in the style developed by Gu Yuan and others with scenes such as *Ballot by beans* and *Acquiring new title-deeds to the land.* But the *nianhua,* too, was enlisted into the service of other themes that had little rural resonance; these included *Villagers welcome Soviet friends* and *Peasants sign the Stockholm Peace Appeal.*[6]

By the late 1950s, poster art was displaying more variety as the Soviet influence waned, though the most admired examples were still the most anodyne. The range included gouaches, oil paintings, woodcuts, and New Year paintings. Socialist realism was supplemented by a more imaginative style of revolutionary romanticism, combining elements of the traditional landscape with symbols of economic transformation. National-minority themes were encouraged and offered the opportunity for more diverse and colorful design. Foreign influences from Eastern Europe also were absorbed. A complex body of theory that linked political and social aims to artistic values and techniques of the propaganda poster was being built up. These were discussed at length at a 1960 conference, accompanied by an exhibition, summing up ten years of poster experience. A speech by Wang Chaowen, a Yan'an veteran and editor of the *Fine Arts (Meishu)* journal, set out the main objective:

> The speciality of the propaganda poster is that it attracts attention the moment it is seen, and gives people a clear and deep impression at a glance. But it should also have the capacity to make people want to look at it for longer. It is not enough if one look suffices. It should yield more on closer study.[7]

By this time a number of younger artists were specializing full time in propaganda poster art. Unlike older artists who regarded it as a less serious art form, they professed to find complete satisfaction in it on both social and artistic grounds. Ha Jingwen was a Hui-minority artist who had joined the People's Liberation Army and become a full-time art propagandist. Looking back on this period, he would later recall that the art workers never asked for extra payment when they worked overtime to meet a sudden demand for propaganda; they regarded themselves as engaged "on the battle front," and a successful poster was a sufficient reward.[8]

## Posters and Popular Art in the Cultural Revolution

Posters and those who made them were transformed, as in every other branch of art and culture, by the Cultural Revolution. The art colleges closed down with the rest of the educational system. Students and young art workers lent their services to the Red Guard and Red Rebel movements. But specialized production of posters continued; more senior artists who had been "struggled against" were sometimes brought back to give unacknowledged help. However, there was a much greater emphasis upon artwork that originated with nonprofessional groups, as had happened eight years before, when the country was swept by the Great Leap Forward. "Spare-time" *(yeyu)* art groups in factories and street communities and amateur peasant painters in the countryside flourished. Posters formed the most visible and explicit part of a continuum of art production whose themes and style were dictated by the new cultural authorities of the Cultural Revolution and which transformed equally "traditional" guohua, woodcuts, New Year pictures, cartoons, papercuts, and a whole range of art ephemera from alarm clocks and enamel mugs to children's toys. Posters produced in the early Red

Guard phase (1966–1968) and in the later revival of political activism (1974–1976) disregarded previous inhibitions against images that might appear to threaten those regarded as "the people," often crossing the thin line between exhortation and coercion. It has been described as the style in which "the fist was larger than the face." In one example from Beijing, probably dated 1967, the huge figure of a worker squeezes in his fist an assortment of U.S. imperialists and Soviet revisionists under the title *The Chinese people are not easily humiliated* (D6). This characteristic of "extremist" expression was much condemned after the Cultural Revolution. Disregard for other inhibitions sometimes had a more positive effect; posters illustrating scenes of popular activity were often packed with vivid detail and imagery —particularly in the countryside, which previous poster art tended to treat more routinely. Style was bolder and brasher; the cheerful faces and bright color contrasts of the New Year style were incorporated into many posters even if they were not labeled as nianhua. Poster art had received a similar but more short-lived stimulus during the Great Leap Forward.

Every village, factory, and street committee had its own propaganda artist *(meishu xuanchuan yuan)* or group *(xuanchuan dui)*. These amateur art workers were responsible for all visual propaganda from simple slogans hung outdoors to permanent displays in the work-unit headquarters. They contributed ephemeral work to the propaganda blackboards to be found in village squares and factory workshops, which carried a mixture of the latest political news, advice on health and similar matters, local propaganda, and handy tips on production technique. In these the text was usually more substantial than the accompanying artwork, but sometimes the balance was reversed. Themes were also conveyed through cartoons, either singly or in strip form. Lingering behind the guided tour, the visitor could often take advantage of such material to identify interesting local issues to raise to steer the next "brief introduction" into more useful territory.

The art workers also painted larger works on billboards or walls in work units, on rural meeting grounds, and inside schools and public halls. The veteran Dutch filmmaker Joris Ivens in one episode of his film sequence *The Foolish Old Man Who Moves the Mountains* (1976) shows such a work in progress in a fishing village being critically assessed by some passing villagers.[9] A similar scene appears in a 1974 poster from Shanghai, *Art comes from a life of struggle: the working people are the masters,* showing a peasant painter next to a mural (plate 1 [L17]). More polemically, a 1975 poster from Beijing entitled *Women shock troops* shows a group of women villagers putting up wall posters under the slogan "Women hold up half the sky." Although the material consists of written essays denouncing the philosophers Confucius and Mencius, the poster evokes the spirit of popular artwork. The smiling enthusiasm of the women is oddly at variance with the serious political nature of the exercise (Q5).

The amateur propagandists sought ideas and technique from cheap copybooks that offered different styles of characters, slogans, and model figures, which were often used as "masthead" decoration accompanied by text. Such books were in a familiar tradition dating back to classical art manuals such as the *Mustard-Seed Garden,* which gave instruction on how to paint birds, flowers, bamboos, and other stock subjects. These subjects give an accurate indication of changing political imperatives. A Shanghai copybook of 1970 contains militant images, mostly of workers, conducting "struggle" sessions against the main targets in the leadership, Liu Shaoqi and Deng Xiaoping, whose names are clearly indicated. (Posters for public sale referred to them less directly.)[10] These do not feature in a 1972 copybook from Beijing that gives instruction to worker-peasant-soldier "beginners." It offers a wider range of themes showing mass activities that include militia training, barefoot doctors, and students in the countryside. It also offers "headline decoration" for wall posters and other propaganda dealing with the revival of the Communist Party, which had almost disappeared from sight during the earlier period of political struggle.[11] Another volume, from 1973, offers outline sketches of figures ranging from heroes in the revolutionary operas to workers, peasants, and soldiers. Indicating a return to more normal life, it also includes athletes, doctors (engaged in an operation by acupuncture anesthesia), and public service employees such as mail carriers, hairdressers, cobblers, and shop assistants.[12]

Successful amateur compositions would appear in exhibitions and in newspapers or magazines, and a few would be converted into mass-produced posters. A 1975 album of "workers' art" from Shanghai celebrated the success of "spare-time artists" (*yeyu yishu zuozhe*) in overcoming "naturalism and formalism" to produce new revolutionary art based on their own everyday work. The frontispiece showing a worker leaping up a flight of stairs to fix his personal "pledge" (*juexinshu*) on the wall became a popular poster. This particular example—*At the pledge meeting* (*Shishi hui shang*, 1975)—is one where the foot, rather than the fist, is larger than the face (plate 3 [E20]).[13] Most of this work was technically competent—as would be expected of a collection produced in Shanghai—even when it had little or no artistic merit. A collection of various kinds of wall posters from the coal-mining town of Yangquan in Shanxi Province, which gained national publicity in 1976, is rougher but of more interest. It shows wall pictures (*bihua*) and "artistic big character posters" (pictures plus text, *meishu dazibao)* in their exterior locations. It is quite explicit about the need to substitute "revolutionary" for "revisionist" art, as in a wall poster showing a worker-painter with palette at the ready and a worker-singer in full voice above the slogan "We must occupy the [cultural] superstructure."[14]

Cartoon art had a brief vogue in the early and least disciplined months of the Cultural Revolution. It was particularly popular in the unofficial Red Guard magazines, which went much further and were more specific in their attacks on individual leaders than the officially controlled press. The most famous example was *A Crowd of Clowns* by Weng Rulan, a fifth-year art student in Beijing, which showed the entire cast of alleged anti-Party leaders in a grotesque procession, with Liu Shaoqi and Deng Xiaoping in sedan chairs. This circulated widely in Beijing and was even mailed to foreign purchasers of Chinese books and periodicals. But the satirical content of cartoon art made it politically riskier, and its use became rarer as the Red Guards were brought under control.[15]

More accessible and appealing—particularly to foreign visitors—was the school of peasant painting *(nongmin hua),* which was almost entirely identified during the Cultural Revolution with Huxian County in Shaanxi Province. Huxian was one of a number of areas that had joined in the rural art movement during the Great Leap Forward. Unlike most others, its interest in popular art had persisted, and it was selected by Madame Mao (Jiang Qing) in 1972 as her model art commune. Huxian paintings were displayed in an exhibition in Beijing in 1973 that was seen by over two million people, and a traveling exhibition went abroad in 1976. The catalogue produced by the Arts Council for its show in London spoke of "images which combine self-assurance with spontaneity, sweeping panoramas with a mass of precise detail . . . a new landscape being built up; well integrated in the use of its resources, its new roads and fields sheltered by newly-planted trees, its villages holding meetings and dances and studying at night under electric light." Enthusiasm has dimmed since then; the art historian Michael Sullivan concludes that the Huxian paintings of the 1970s, although technically more accomplished than those of the Great Leap period, were "often dull and lack the spontaneity of the crude early efforts." Yet Huxian still offered many works displaying genuine optimism and commitment to what remained of the ideals of the Cultural Revolution.[16]

Many Huxian paintings were reproduced as posters in cities far away. These include the famous *Commune fishpond* by Dong Zhengyi (plate 4 [A9]), with its swirl of fish caught in huge numbers that would have broken any real net. It was explained by the artist in these terms: "In our village the fishpond is not exactly like this: there's a wall around it. But in order to reflect the bright future I took out the wall. . . . The little fish are the new generation growing up."[17] In *New style shop,* barrows selling goods, sent to the villages by the central commune store, are framed attractively between two persimmon trees (plate 5 [C6]). A series of historical posters produced by Niudong Commune in Huxian was less idyllically rural. It showed the forced recruitment of peasant soldiers and the humiliation of landlords during land reform, before the village was able to celebrate with the famous Great Leap slogan, "The people's communes are good!" (E31, n.d.).

No discussion of the popular art of this period is complete without mentioning at least briefly the huge quantity of ephemera conveying similar images. Children's puzzle blocks carried scenes that depicted the downing of a U.S. imperialist aggressor's airplane over Vietnam and the humiliation of its pilots. Squeaky rubber dolls assumed the shape of young Red Guards. Handkerchiefs were imprinted with heroic figures. Enamel mugs, used by anyone working in an office, shop, or factory, were also decorated, usually with Mao's image and quotations. Papercuts in many sizes and styles form a large subcategory for this period. The largest ones depicted elaborate subjects such as Red Guard rallies, the sending down of students to the countryside, the construction of the Nanjing bridge across the Yangzi, and so on. In the standard sizes, scenes of revolutionary shrines *(geming shengdi)* and of workers, peasants, and soldiers were commonly found. There were also miniature cutouts of Mao and (less frequently) his wife, Jiang Qing, and "chosen successor," Lin Biao. These ephemera provide a rich source in themselves; so far only the ubiquitous "Mao badges" have received serious study.[18]

### Poster Themes in the Cultural Revolution

Chinese posters and similar art forms during the Cultural Revolution and afterwards were closely related to current political and social themes, which often had a very short life span. This means that the products can often be dated with precision. (Most posters for commercial sale carry the date—month and year—of production, as well as details of publisher, print run, and so on. But a number of items in the University of Westminster collection are one of a kind or were produced outside the regular marketing system and are undated.) Thus a poster bearing the slogan "Chairman Mao is the reddest red sun in our hearts" will belong to the earliest period (1966–1967). This iconic production shows a medallion of Mao radiating like the sun over a crowd of young girls with white tunics, red armbands, and black trousers (N1). So will militant references to the first struggles of Red Guards and Rebels to "seize power" from bureaucrats and managers. In a typical example—*The proletarian revolutionaries hold power* (E2)—from Hebei, a worker holding Mao's Selected Works strikes a brick marked "Political, economic, and cultural power," which in turn crushes two factory managers labeled "economism" *(jingjizhuyi)* and "one hundred yuan." This too must have been produced early in 1967 when senior leaders were accused of "economism" for offering material incentives to bribe the workers away from Mao's path (E2). Posters with themes of foreign struggle, referring to the Hong Kong riots (D11, *Our victory is certain, so is defeat of the Hong Kong English [Women bi sheng, Gang Ying bi bai]*, 1967?) or to Soviet revisionism (D7, *Down with Soviet revisionism [Dadao Su xiu]*, 1967) also date from this year. Designs consisting mainly of text were also confined to these first years, as in *Our literature and art is all for the masses,* in which figures from the model operas are appended merely as decoration to this quotation from Mao's 1942 Yan'an Talks (figure 6.2 [L5], 1967).

Mao dominates poster production in the Red Guard period of 1966–1968, and the most popular examples remained in print—unlike most other posters—through the ten years. (His image alone appears in semipermanent art form in statues and murals that, once erected or painted, cannot be removed.) He begins in the posters as an emblematic figure elevated above the rest of humanity or else as an affable companion of adoring Red Guards. He appears in military uniform with Lin Biao—before Lin's disgrace and death during flight towards the Soviet Union. Later, Mao is more often shown in historical settings, leading the revolution before 1949 or having heart-to-heart chats with the peasants after the Liberation. Two historical pictures of Mao achieved a special reputation at home and abroad. *Chairman Mao goes to Anyuan* (plate 6 [N35]), painted for a 1967 exhibition, became the defining icon of the Cultural Revolution with its quasireligious depiction of the young Mao, umbrella in hand, walking thoughtfully but with determination along a high mountain path. Much later, the artist responsible, Liu Chunhua, claimed to have been influenced in this composition by a Raphael Madonna. A very different type of historical painting, He Kongde's *Gutian Conference,* hung in 1972 in the first official art exhibition of the Cultural Revolution, was done in oils still showing the influence of the artist's Soviet training (F3, n.d.). Images of Jiang Qing are rare throughout; to display one would indicate adherence to the most radical strand of Cultural Revolutionary politics. In *Let new socialist culture occupy every stage,* she is shown in army uniform with cultural activities in the background—rather oddly including a man playing a cello (N28).

The late Premier Zhou Enlai, whose death in January 1976 led to a mass demonstration in April 1976 in Tian'anmen Square against the ultraleft leadership, was not regarded as a suitable poster subject until after the arrest of the Gang of Four. In *Premier Zhou shares our hardship* he is shown at a spinning wheel with a peasant and communist soldiers, invoking the wartime theme of self-reliance that also epitomizes Zhou's reputation for lack of ostentation (N27, 1978). The 1973–1974 campaign against Zhou by Jiang Qing had been disguised as a mass movement to criticize Confucius and repudiate the (by now disgraced) minister of defense, Lin Biao. It featured in posters depicting ordinary people who were allegedly enraged by the persistence of Confucian ideology in unlikely places. A scene entitled *Angry waves in fishing waters* (from a film of the same name) shows small boats full of fishing people with lanterns approaching a large junk for a nighttime "criticize Confucius–criticize Lin Biao" session (figure 1.1 [A40]). The campaign also encouraged a new witch-hunt against alleged subversives in all walks of life. The themes are linked in a rural poster, perhaps

Fig. 2.1 [N19]. *With you in charge, I feel at ease (Ni ban shi, wo fang xin).* Shanghai 1977.

based on a Huxian peasant painting, that shows a peasant training the village militia under the title *Furiously criticize [Confucius's doctrine of] "restrain the self and return to the rites" and grasp your gun firmly!* (J22).

Mao reappears as a contemporary figure after his death in a bizarre genre of posters that sought to strengthen the claim of the sycophantic Hua Guofeng to the succession. The most famous of these, *With you in charge, I feel at ease*, shows Mao and Hua talking in Mao's study (1977) (figure 2.1 [N19]). It refers to a conversation in April 1976 when Mao is alleged to have used those words to express confidence in Hua's succession. (The quotation may have been made up or embellished by Hua to convince the Party Politburo of his legitimacy.) A huge painted version of this episode hung for more than two years at the top of the escalator in the main hall of Beijing Railway Station, only to be removed when Deng Xiaoping returned to power in 1979. Most posters seeking to portray Hua Guofeng as a worthy successor were as inept in execution as in concept. Hua notoriously grew his hair long to appear more like Mao; in one painting I saw in 1977 he was shown looking poetic in a gown.

Jiang Qing and other members of the Gang of Four were by this time awaiting trial; however, they featured as targets of poster attack only for a short while after their arrest. There was a brief recurrence of slogan posters such as one demanding that the spectator "Thoroughly expose the monstrous crimes committed while attempting to take over Party power by the anti-Party clique Wang Hongwen, Zhang Chunqiao, Jiang Qing and Yao Wenyuan" (E43, 1976). Cartoons, otherwise confined to the first Red Guard struggles, also reappear in the anti-Gang propaganda campaign where the Gang members are lampooned in a style similar to that employed ten years previously against Liu Shaoqi and Deng Xiaoping.[19] Mao's first wife, Yang Kaihui, unmentionable while Jiang Qing controlled the cultural world, now made a brief poster appearance in *Comrades-in-arms (Zhanyou),* a gentle composition that shows the young couple together by the banks of the Yangzi (N42, 1977).

Two mass-production campaigns featured prominently in poster art, "In agriculture learn from [the model brigade of] Dazhai" and "In industry learn from Daqing [oil field]." Though championed by the ultraleft, the Dazhai campaign managed to project a more general appeal to the millions of Chinese peasants who sought to improve their life by hard work on the land. Popular views of Dazhai showed the village foreshortened from an aerial perspective to include all its famous features: the new blocks of housing, the large hotel for visitors, carefully terraced fields, an electric hoist up into the hills, aqueduct, and reservoir. One undated color print shows groups of pilgrims proceeding counterclockwise around the standard viewing circuit, each group behind a leader with a red flag (plate 7 [A7]). Dazhai is also frequently cited in titles to pictures that otherwise have no reference point, such as *Hold high the red banner of Dazhai and reap a rich harvest* (A36, 1976), which depicts a woman working in a grain silo with the harvest heaped in the background.

Rural themes raised few problems of political orthodoxy. In *The brigade's ducks* (A11, 1974) an everyday scene—two girls tending some ducks in a pond—is devoid of any message except that implied in the caption, that collective ownership at the brigade level is desirable. It may be compared with the post–Cultural Revolution *The people rejoice as the fish jump* (A34, 1978), in which two girls in a boat at sea are catching huge fish. The theme of the industrialization of the countryside was also politically less explicit. Pictures in the harry n. abrams style combined rural landscape with symbols of progress, such as dams and power stations, continuing a style already developed from the Great Leap onwards. It might be called the "pylon school"—electric pylons are raised, often in implausible locations, to indicate the speed of progress (A4, *We can certainly triumph over nature [Ren ding sheng tian]),* n.d; A41, *The new song of the Huai River [Huai he xin ge],* n.d.).

Industrial topics are less common in poster form except when linked to the Learn from Daqing campaign, perhaps because of the risk of being interpreted as attempts to preach economism. The Iron Man of Daqing, Wang Jingxi, famous for plunging into a pool of cement to prevent it from hardening, was offered for emulation (E23, *The Iron Man spirit will be handed down from generation to generation [Tie ren jingshen daidai xiangchuan],* 1974) (plate 8). But Shanghai steelworkers were more likely to be shown studying Mao's philosophy at the workbench than to be seen actually at work (E19, *Study and use Chairman Mao's glorious philosophical thought on a large scale [Da xue da yong Mao zhuxi guanghui zhexue sixiang],* 1971)—although the message was that Mao's Thought was the key to increasing production. Factory workers would be shown at the blackboard, copying out slogans to denounce the pernicious doctrine of putting production in first place (E24, *Spread revolutionary criticism in a deep-going way [Shenru kaizhan geming da pipan],* 1971). They were prominent,too, in condemning Confucius and Lin Biao (E35, *Continue to carry out the campaign to criticize Lin Biao and Confucius in a penetrating, widespread, and enduring way [Ba pi Lin pi Kong yundong shenru luoji, chijiude jinxingxiaqu],* 1974) (plate 9 [E35/E36]). A 1971 poster from Beijing with the title *Develop the economy and guarantee supplies,* showing two women in a textile factory holding bolts of cloth, was a rare exception for the time (C10, 1971).

## From Arts College to the Countryside

In the field of pictorial art as in every other department, the Cultural Revolution turned the traditional establishment upside down. Established artists suffered harsh treatment in the early period of greatest violence or were sent to the countryside. Some of those who were brought back in the early 1970s worked on state commissions in an initiative that stemmed from Premier Zhou Enlai to produce paintings, mostly in the national style (guohua) for hotels, railway stations, embassies, and similar government buildings and for sale to foreigners. The painter Li Keran was even commissioned to decorate official buildings used for the path-breaking visit of Richard Nixon in February 1972. Zhou sought to distinguish between "outer" art intended for foreigners and "inner" art, which should display political content for the Chinese. This led to further trouble in 1974 when, as part of the ultraleft (Gang of Four) counterattack upon Zhou, a series of exhibitions of "black paintings" was held in which such works were condemned for portraying counterrevolutionary or revisionist sentiments, for formalism, or for catering to foreign buyers. It was during this period that the popular painter and cartoonist Huang Yongyu (nephew of the banned writer Shen Congwen) was denounced for painting a winking owl: the subject was alleged to slyly imply disrespect for socialism. This denunciation would become a symbolic memory in post–Cultural Revolution years for this period of vengeful artistic politics.[20]

Yet the Cultural Revolution also created new opportunities for a generation of younger artists who largely superseded the veterans. Many were fired with enthusiasm by the new policy of seeking inspiration from everyday life—or at least those positive aspects that were approved—of taking art to the masses, and of encouraging popular artistic creation. These principles also provided opportunities for career advancement. By the mid-1970s, many of the youngest artists in art schools or studios were genuinely from the "worker-peasant-soldier" background that was favored in college recruitment. Others were the offspring of intellectuals.who used their artistic talent to escape from the countryside where they had been "sent down." Some established artists were "restored" (huifu) to teach the new professional artworks and to tutor amateur groups in city evening classes or on missions to the rural areas. The students themselves spent long periods in factories or villages, in line with the general policy for education that it should be "combined with labor and serve proletarian politics."

This mass-based artistic activity in the early and mid-1970s was regarded as one of the "new achievements of the Cultural Revolution" (xin sheng shiwu). To some extent it did represent a new outlook that was still being formed when Mao died and the Cultural Revolution was reversed. It naturally reflected the social composition and experience of the young artists involved: the themes of "going down" (xiafang) and making a "new home" (xin jia) in the rural areas dominated a large percentage of the output. The same themes were characteristic of much poster art of this time. At its best it displayed a sense of vitality and innovation reflecting some of the original enthusiasm of the student movement. This was in marked contrast to pictures with a more formal political content—such as portraits of Chairman Mao or scenes from the history of the revolution—by which young artists could make their reputation, although they also risked criticism if the result was later criticized.

A visit to the fine arts department of the Nanjing Art College in April 1976 found a well-developed curriculum designed to instill "socialist culture" and to produce art that would be appreciated by the masses. The images on display within the college were almost entirely within the range of what could be seen outside on the walls in everyday life; the continuum between academic art and the propaganda poster was unbroken. Two principles of the "revolution in education" *(jiaoyu geming)* governed work in the department. First, the students were "selected from society"—that is, they came from at least nominally *gong nong bing* (worker/peasant/soldier) backgrounds. The college divided its quota of student places for its three departments (fine arts, music, and drama) for the coming year among the districts in the city and adjacent rural areas. These vacancies were then subdivided to lower units and filled (at least in theory) by "recommendation from below." I met students studying "national painting" (guohua*)* from a printing factory, others from a fertilizer factory. One boy studying woodcuts was a crane-driver; a young peasant artist sat with a copy of a sketch by the revolutionary German expressionist Käthe Köllwitz pinned to his worktable. Other students had come straight from school where they had completed three years of "lower secondary" education.

The second principle was that of "open-door schooling" *(kai men ban xue),* which meant that academic work should be integrated with real-life work. Both teachers and students "returned to society" periodically, and it was intended that upon graduation the students should go back to the countryside or industry for good. During their three-year course, it was explained, the students "went down to be tempered by reality" (*bei xianshi duanlian).* They were not merely artists attached to a particular rural production team or urban factory. They spent half their time actually working in the fields or on the shop floor. The system required a placement of three months in the first year, four months in the second, and as much as six months in the final year. Teachers were supposed to spend one year out of three "out in society." Subject matter for art composition was chosen after much discussion and was based upon the practical labor that the students performed at their place of work. One student was observed preparing a factory scene, a complex composition showing two workers sitting on a girder with a construction site behind them. He would take an early cut back to the shop floor "for discussion by the masses," then return to the studio to incorporate the workers' suggestions, then go back again—perhaps to a total of three or four visits.

Pride of place in the college's exhibition room went to a painting with the title *Welcome Spring Teahouse.* This was executed in the New Year style and intended for reproduction as a poster. The lively scene was set in a village hall where peasants and sent-down students drank tea to celebrate the Spring Festival, entertained by two musical performers from a propaganda team on the stage. A village party official and the local teacher (wearing glasses) were easily identifiable. Lanterns, banners, character slogans, and pictures hung from the walls or ceiling, framing the scene, which was presented to the viewer as if the actual hall were onstage. Symbols of rural activity—wooden buckets and a carrying pole, baskets, a pair of loudspeakers, and a small generator—lined the foreground.[21]

This may be compared to a poster in the University of Westminster collection with the title *New Year's Eve in a collective household* (plate 10 [Z29], 1977). Also in the nianhua style, it shows a group of cheerful sent-down students preparing for a party in the hut where they live together. A villager—probably the production-team leader—

has come to see their preparations. The ceiling is densely hung with paper rosettes and tasseled balls and is traversed by an elaborate, continuous papercut decoration. The team leader is ushered in smilingly; the students' welcome to him symbolizes their commitment to rural society. This is reinforced by an antithetical couplet *(duilian)* being pasted on the wall: "Train your red hearts in the vast world of life. Make revolution by sinking your roots in the countryside." The couplet frames a large propaganda poster showing students heading out to work on a rubber plantation—no doubt on Hainan Island—above a similar slogan about making a new life in the vast world. (It is fascinating to discover that this "poster within a poster" was a genuine work that was reproduced elsewhere.)[22] In less revolutionary times, similar red strips of paper, bearing auspicious mottoes, would have framed a portrait of the kitchen god on New Year's Eve in a rural home, with food set before it. In this composition, bowls of fruit, a kettle, and steaming food placed on the floor indicate that the committed students are intending to have a good time too. Through the entrance, where a female, barefoot doctor has drawn back the curtain, the night sky is depicted in a decorative style, studded with innumerable stars.

Another picture in the Nanjing exhibition bore the familiar title *New family (Xin jia),* indicating the close relationship that was, ideally at any rate, formed by students when billeted in a peasant household. It is self-referential, showing a student who has brought art to her new family. A mural has been painted, apparently by a local young woman under the student's guidance, on the wall of an oven. The picture, of a girl driving a tractor, has been copied from a manual that is just visible on a bench. The result is being surveyed smilingly by a group including two more young women (one of them a student resting after carrying in water), the peasant mother of the household, and two young children. A map of the world, pinned nearby, suggests another way in which the students have brought knowledge to their "new family."[23]

Several posters in the University of Westminster collection offer a similarly rosy view of student life in the countryside and of the contribution that students can make. *We are determined to settle down in the countryside* (plate 11 {A25}, 1974) depicts an army officer in a peasant family's yard, sitting before a table laden with ripe corn and with a huge pumpkin at his feet. Equally impressive melons hang from a vine above. He is congratulating the family on its achievements that, it is implied, owe a great deal to a student who lives with them and has presumably contributed some valuable innovation to help improve the harvest. She sits next to the officer, holding a copy of Mao's *Quotations* to which she points with one finger, indicating that these were the real source of her inspiration. The picture is redeemed from banality by three local youths peeping at the scene through the courtyard gate. The symbol of authority is military because students were first sent down under the supervision of the People's Liberation Army, when the period of Red Guard violence (1966–1968) was brought to an end.

Posters on the theme of the new family may have been particularly encouraged in Shanghai, where many students had been sent to the remote northwest of China to work in harsh conditions, causing considerable unhappiness to their (old) families. The exiles began to return, some illegally, to the cities in the late 1970s to air their complaints. A sketch of rural hardship displayed on a Beijing wall in 1979 by a returnee from Yunnan would show a very different image, one in which the exiled students squatted miserably on a barren hill to eat their meager food.[24]

## The End of the Cultural Revolution

Posters offer a reliable guide to the shifting policies after Mao's death that led to the repudiation of the Cultural Revolution. The New Year poster, which had suffered a near total decline, gives a particularly sharp indication. During the Great Leap Forward, traditional themes and techniques (door gods and papercuts) had been successfully modernized to celebrate the People's Communes. Some traditional themes portraying the popular "fat baby" *(pang wawa)* continued to be acceptable. A child carried a basket of peaches to signify longevity; an accompanying cockerel crowed to frighten away evil spirits (Z32, early 1960s?). The problem once the Cultural Revolution began was not just with subject matter but with the occasion of New Year, a festival whose very celebration might be regarded as evidence of feudal thinking. Sometimes it could only be treated indirectly, as in *The spring wind brings warmth,* showing a New Year delivery of extracts from Marx, Engels, and Lenin (Z28, 1975/76). A 1973 volume of reproductions could only be identified as nianhua by its title. It did include a girl holding up a papercut that spelled out "Long live Chairman Mao."[25]

A more explicit example updated the traditional door gods *(men shen)* to be pasted on both outer wooden doors of a peasant dwelling. It was titled *A new flowering of village culture: the use of scientific farming methods will result in great fruits* (plate 12 [Z27]). Good luck was conveyed through the contemporary images of—on the left-hand side—a rural propaganda team with two actresses preparing to perform the Red Lantern opera, and—on the right-hand side—a peasant agricultural research team. (This continued a long line of adaptations of the *men shen* theme from the 1940s onwards.)[26]

As the Cultural Revolution began to fade, traditional elements reappeared, though modestly at first. Lanterns, firecrackers, and lion dancers mingled among workers, peasants, and soldiers in *This year there will be much rejoicing* (Z30) for the 1978 Spring Festival. A year later, the full range of fat babies, peony and lotus flowers, carp, and goldfish were again available (Z25, *Welcoming the spring [Ying chun],* 1979; plate 13 [Z26], *Goldfish baby [Jinyu wawa],* 1979). Studios at the Gugong Museum in Beijing, the Yangliuqing workshop in Tianjin, Weifang in Shandong, and Fengxiang in Shaanxi resurrected original blocks to produce wholly traditional Eight Immortals, red-faced warriors, white- and black-faced door gods, ghost catchers, imperial officials, and the philosopher Laozi himself (Z17–18).

The rapid shift in political culture at the end of the Cultural Revolution (1976–1979) produced interesting posters in other subject areas. Leftist slogans mingled uneasily for a short while with new exhortations to increase production. Uighur peasants were urged in 1977 (A5, 1977) to "go full steam ahead and speed up the building of Dazhai-type counties." Henan peasants were told to "Criticize and work hard" with the same aim in mind (A2, 1977). The proclamation by Hua Guofeng of the goal of "Four Modernizations" (in agriculture, industry, science and technology, and national defense) a year later clarified the situation. No poster was now complete without trains, planes, ships, power stations, space rockets, or satellites—and sometimes all of them—somewhere in the sky or foreground. The new heroic figures were holding walkie-talkies and oil cans, operating computers or complex machinery. "Good news travels ten thousand miles and warms ten thousand families," proclaimed a poster showing two women operating the control room in a TV station (figure 2.2 [B9]).The interest of the

Fig. 2.2 [B9]. *Good news travels ten thousand miles and warms ten thousand families (Jiebao chuan wan li, xixun nuan wan jia).* Shanghai 1978.

consumer appeared for the first time in poster form. "Promote high-quality goods, wholeheartedly serve the people," exhorted a picture of a woman selling kitchen equipment in a department store (1978) (figure 2.3 [C9]).

Science and education could now be presented as primary targets for achievement. A picture of Marx gesturing toward a large space rocket as it was launched was titled *Science is a productive force* (B5, 1979). A portrait of a girl student, pen in hand, was done in the style of the woodcut artist Huang Xinbo, who himself had been much influenced by the fine line drawings of the American 1930s painter Rockwell Kent. Entitled *The future summons us,* it showed the student in a night scene of brightly lit buildings with aerials, radar dishes, chemical flask designs, and the statue of a girl reaching out— a common symbol for educational endeavor (plate 14 [B10], 1980).[27] The Four Modernizations were summed up memorably for me on a large roadside billboard photographed outside the Shengli (Victory) Oilfield in Shandong in 1978. This showed a soldier, a worker, and a student looking determinedly ahead against the figure 2000 (for the year by which China would be built, according to Hua Guofeng, into a Powerful Socialist Country among the Most Advanced in the World). Space rockets passed through the figures, over an array of modern factories and a large satellite dish.[28]

### Conclusion: The Posters' Decline

My visit to Huxian County in 1980 showed that a significant change in popular art-making was already under way. Huxian was no longer a model for art, just as Dazhai had lost its model status for agriculture, and Chinese visitors had stopped coming in

Fig. 2.3 [C9]. *Provide high-quality goods and wholeheartedly serve the people (Tigong youzhi chanpin, quan xin quan yi wei renmin fuwu)*. Beijing 1978.

large numbers. However, Huxian had one advantage: its reputation abroad. The large exhibition hall was filled with *nongminhua* of all descriptions from the mid-1960s to the present day. Art groups continued to produce work, but increasingly with a view to sale. All the pictures on show were available for purchase, priced more according to size than to artistic value. Teams of art-sales representatives were also sent to Beijing to seek customers among foreign residents in the apartment blocks and the Friendship Hotel. In the village streets faded wall paintings of the 1970s with images of commitment and selfless labor were still visible. Much of the new peasant art celebrated the new images of economic reform. Their subject matter included new-style hairdressers, a furniture shop, the construction of new housing—and even a winter scene with children building a Father Christmas snowman (perhaps taken from a foreign magazine picture).

Huxian and other centers of peasant painting were able to adapt to—and profit from—the new entrepreneurial world emerging in China. The new art that this generated could be very attractive, although some of it was poorly executed for quick financial gain. Poster art did not have the same commercial stimulus to reform, and it was used much less for propaganda; it had begun to appear politically old-fashioned, and there was a general revulsion against political "movements" (yundong), which had inspired so much poster work in the past. The theme of commitment to science and education did inspire some striking work in the early 1980s; national festivals still required posters celebrating unity and harmony across the land. However, most posters were produced for less emphatic purposes. Apart from those intended for use in schools (mostly portraits of famous historical figures) and for hospitals (health education and medical charts), these were mainly intended as decoration in the home. The standard themes included portraits of children and animals, pictures of Laozi and other mythological figures, colorful national minorities, and traditional Chinese New Year images. Many people preferred the large-scale calendars now on sale with photographs or pictures of landscapes, traditional opera characters, fairies and other mythological figures, and fairly modest female pinups.

After 1984, poster art began to receive less attention in the main national journal, *Meishu*. Posters were no longer so widely on sale in general outlets. They were used for more specialized purposes with localized distribution, to commemorate sporting events, promote health campaigns against smoking and similar targets, encourage savings, and advertise exhibitions. A survey on poster art published in 1996 singles out cinema posters as one of the main achievements of recent years, devoting more space to them than to posters of the Cultural Revolution.[29] By the late 1980s, the poster sites that once carried huge billboards displaying quotations from Mao or images of revolutionary struggle were used to exhort the passer-by to drink Coca-Cola or smoke Marlboro cigarettes. More recently, with not unexpected irony, original posters and paintings from the Cultural Revolution have begun to fetch high sums in an art world: they appeal to the patriotic sentiment of Hong Kong businessmen—and to collectors of quality kitsch. In 1995 the China Guardian auction room in Beijing sold *Chairman Mao goes to Anyuan* (plate 6 [N35]) for nearly US$700,000. There is some market resistance to paintings with overly forceful political slogans from the 1966–1968 period: Red Guards sent an uneasy message. But revolutionary landscapes and Huxian peasant paintings command high prices; papercuts and stamps are also salable items. The China Guardian 1998 stamp sale included mint blocks of *Chairman Mao goes to Anyuan* in its 8¢ denomination.

In real life the type of popular didactic art discussed in this chapter survives visibly today only on propaganda blackboards controlled by an organization or work unit. (Almost all public display sites are now occupied by commercial advertisements.) Blackboard newspapers (heiban bao) are found quite widely outside urban neighborhood committee offices and in factories, schools, and other institutions and are used to publicize socially desirable issues such as planned parenthood, safety in the home, and measures against crime. Copybooks with model compositions continue to be published to help depict such themes.[30] However, the full-scale poster for individual purchase has almost disappeared. In May 1998, I searched for posters in the state bookshops of several large cities and one small county town. Only a few were to be found—the odd Marx or Engels, a fading photograph of Mao, one or two traditional New Year themes such as Laozi, and some crude traffic-education posters for children. Poster art is hopelessly dated now both in its political values and in its social implications. The originals have some commercial value as a form of revolutionary kitsch with patriotic overtones. Otherwise, it has nothing to offer a very different age, which wants to see some less old-fashioned—and more expensive—decoration on its walls.

## Notes

1. "Soldiers' art," *China Reconstructs*, August 1976, 42.

2. Edgar Snow, *Red Star over China* (London: Gollancz, 1937), plates 9–11; Harrison Forman, *Report from Red China* (London: Pilot Press, 1945), unnumbered plate.

3. Beijing Art Gallery, 1982 New Year pictures exhibition, reproduced in *Meishu* (Fine arts), no. 1, 1984.

4. China Revolutionary Museum, *Kangri zhanzheng shiqi xuanchuanhua* (Propaganda pictures of the anti-Japanese War period) (Beijing: Cultural Press, 1979).

5. Deng Liqun et al., eds., *Dangdai Zhongguo meishu* (Fine arts of contemporary China) (Beijing: Contemporary China Press, 1996), plate 217.

6. Tsai Jo-hung, "New Year Pictures: A People's Art," *People's China* 4, nos.1, 2 (February 1950): 12–18; "New Year Pictures," in *Folk Arts of New China* (Beijing: Foreign Languages Press, 1954), 23–29 and pictures.

7. Deng et al., *Dangdai Zhongguo meishu*, 226.

8. Deng et al., *Dangdai Zhongguo meishu*, 230.

9. "A fishing village," in the twelve-part documentary filmed from 1972 to 1975: see *Joris Ivens and China* (Beijing: New World Press, 1983).

10. *Mao Zedong sixiang xuanchuan lan: baotou ziliao* (Mao Zedong thought propaganda column: masthead selection) (Shanghai: People's Press, 1970).

11. *Meishu cankao ziliao 2: baotou xuanji* (Art reference material 2: masthead selection) (Beijing: People's Arts Press, 1972).

12. *Renwu hua cankao ziliao* (Figure painting reference material) (Shanghai: People's Press, 1973).

13. *Shanghai gongren meishu zuopin xuan* (Selection of workers' art from Shanghai) (Shanghai: People's Press, 1975).

14. *Yangquan gongren meishu dazibao bihua xuan* [Selection of art: big-character posters and wall paintings by Yangquan workers) (Beijing: Peoples' Arts Press, 1976), 14.

15. Julia F. Andrews, *Painters and Politics in the People's Republic of China, 1949–79* (Berkeley and Los Angeles: University of California Press, 1994), 335–37; see also cartoons of Liu Shaoqi in John Gittings, *A Chinese View of China* (New York: Pantheon, 1973), 154–55.

16. Press notice accompanying *Peasant Paintings from Hu County* (London: Arts Council, 1976); Michael Sullivan, *Art and Artists of Twentieth-Century China* (Berkeley and Los Angeles: University of California Press, 1996), 148. For a fuller discussion of the Huxian paintings, see Ellen Johnston Laing, "Chinese Peasant Painting, 1958–1976: Amateur and Professional," in *Art International* 27, no. 1 (January–March 1984): 2–12.

17. Dong Zhengyi, quoted in *Peasant Paintings from Hu County*, 12.

18. Robert Benewick and Stephanie Donald, "Badgering the People: Mao Badges, a Retrospective, 1949–1995," in *Belief in China: Art and Politics, Deities and Mortality*, ed. Robert Benewick and Stephanie Donald (Brighton, England: Royal Pavilion/Green Foundation, 1996). For discussion about papercuts, see Andrew Bolton, "Chinese Papercuts from the Cultural Revolution at the Victoria and Albert Museum," *Arts of Asia*, November–December 1997, 79–86.

19. *Manhua xuanji: quanguo meishu zuopin zhanlan* (Collection of cartoons: national fine arts exhibition) (Beijing: People's Arts Press, 1977); Ralph Croizier, "The Thorny Flowers of 1979: Political Cartoons and Liberalization in China," in *China from Mao to Deng: The Politics and Economics of Socialist Development*, ed. Bulletin of Concerned Asian Scholars (Armonk,

N.Y.: M. E. Sharpe; London: Zed Press, 1983), 29–38.

20. For this period, see Ellen Johnston Laing, *The Winking Owl: Art in the People's Republic of China* (Berkeley and Los Angeles: University of California Press, 1988); Sullivan, *Art of Twentieth Century China*, 152–53; Andrews, *Painters and Politics*, 368–76.

21. Transparency from the Nanjing Arts College in the author's possession.

22. *New shoots are thriving in the wide world,* poster by Guangzhou Municipal Propaganda Department Arts Group, in *Zai guangkuo tiandi li: meishu zuopin xuan* (In the wide world: selection of art works*)* (Beijing: People's Arts Press, 1974), 12.

23. Photograph in the author's possession.

24. Photograph in the author's possession.

25. *Xinnianhua xuan* (Selection of New Year paintings) (Beijing: People's Arts Press, 1974).

26. Pre-1949 examples in *Kangri zhanzheng shiqi xuanchuanhua,* 34, 102.

27. *Huang Xinbo banhua xuan* (Selection of woodcuts by Huang Xinbo) (Beijing: People's Arts Press, 1961).

28. Reproduced in John Gittings, *China Changes Face* (Oxford: Oxford University Press, 1989), plate 17.

29. Deng, *Dangdai Zhongguo meishu,* 216–40.

30. *Tu an ji: banbao changyong baotou* (Design collection: commonly used mastheads in blackboard newspapers) (Beijing: China Illustrated Press, 1995).

# 3

# Souvenirs of Beijing: Authority and Subjectivity in Art Historical Memory

*Craig Clunas*

When I first saw these pictures matters, but it is not what art historians normally write about. Such self-positioning is confined to the oral examination, the curriculum vitae, the occasional postcareer memoir; it is not an issue put in the foreground of writing art history. And it operates rather differently again in another sort of academic discipline within which I was situated in 1974 and 1975, that of "Oriental Studies," the title of the university faculty that I left to spend a year in Beijing under the auspices of the British Council.[1] However, this was not the way I spoke about my studies then. If anyone asked me, within the university or in my provincial Scottish hometown of Aberdeen, I answered that I was "doing Chinese," just like "doing maths" or "doing history." The classical and modern Chinese language (which certainly absorbed a very large proportion of my studies) was central to that conferral of authority to speak about "China" that *is* the underlying feature of orientalist pedagogy, and has been since the nineteenth century. However, Cold War geopolitics made the situation rather distinctive with regard to "doing Chinese" in the early 1970s; they certainly made it different from "doing Arabic" or "doing Japanese." Many members of the faculty by whom one was taught had either never been to China or had left it as refugees in the preceding decades. Their authority (and hence the authority they were conveying to the small cadre of their students) did not derive to any large extent from "being there," or even from ever having "been there," from experience "in the field" as anthropologists would call it. This gave "going there," as I did in October 1974, a particular piquancy, imparted a sense of superiority even, certainly a sense of ethnographic authority that not all one's teachers enjoyed.

For me in 1974 pictures played very little part in doing Chinese. We were firmly told that the Chinese script was *not* in any sense pictographic and were quick (as budding authorities) to enlighten anyone who made the mistake of calling it so in conversation. We all took an introduction to Chinese art history, taught by a distinguished Chinese archaeologist whose interest visibly waned once one reached the last two thousand years. He convinced me, in a series of early-Tuesday-morning lectures conducted in the traditional darkened room with its Hegelian twin projectors and screens, that art history was boring and a subject of no intellectual content whatsoever. My aspirations for scholarly advancement were concentrated more on the social and political history of the last imperial dynasty, largely because of personal sympathies with the American graduate students who taught me about it.

At an earlier stage in my life, however, pictures, visual culture, "Chinese things" had played a large part in getting me into the study of China at university level in the first place. There were no family connections with China, and I doubt that I met many Chinese people in 1960s Aberdeen (although my father did have students from Malaysia). But I did, as a regular part of middle-class childhood, visit museums, the Aberdeen Art Gallery and the university's ethnographic museum. I remember the eighteenth-century Chinese porcelain punch bowl in the former's granite halls, painted with the city's coat of arms, the same coat of arms that appeared on the breast pocket of my school-uniform blazer. And from the latter, a museum that even in the 1960s was stuck in a much earlier phase of curatorial practice, I remember above all the mutilated bound foot of a Chinese woman, preserved in a bottle beside the tiny shoes. It stood on a shelf at the end of a long run of cases, and it made me slightly sick, but not sick enough to overcome the scopophilia that (I didn't know at the time) bound me in complicity into a whole history of orientalist gazing and fetishization of the East long before "doing Chinese" became a practical possibility, and even longer before the professional scopophilia (the pleasures of looking) of the art historian became part of my life.

Doing Chinese already was a distant practical possibility by the time I first set eyes on the sorts of pictures reproduced throughout this book. It was the first years of the 1970s and I was about sixteen or seventeen when the local Maoist cell (a Maoist cell? in Aberdeen? perhaps they were a propaganda team from elsewhere) staged an exhibition of books and posters from China in a church hall very close to school. How I learned about it I don't know, but it must have been at very short notice, for I went immediately after school without taking any money, only to be overwhelmed by a desire to possess it all: the distinctive-smelling books, some with their plastic covers, all speaking of difference from the world I lived in. Also the posters, and though I can't recall examples, I have a sense above all of their clarity. Clear colors, clear gestures, clear relationships between good and bad, between licit and forbidden. At that age, I wanted above all to have a life of difference and of clarity, and I wanted to have these things, to possess that difference for myself. But what was *not* clear was the terms on which these things were to be had from the few youths who stood behind the tables on which they were laid; were they for sale, or were they free to those interested in the world revolution of which those same youths rather desultorily spoke? Others from my school were there, the curious and the scoffing and the bold, openly contemptuous of the youths, and beginning to take or steal the books and the posters even as I ran (I rarely ran) home to get my money. I ran back and the hall was shut. All gone. I obtained nothing. I had looked without possessing.[2]

The next time I saw such posters in quantity, I was in a position to possess all I wanted, but I chose not to do so. By then I was a student of Beijing Languages Institute, one of a tiny number of Western Europeans (there were eight British) who had the privilege of a Maoist Beijing almost to themselves, as it seemed, moving like ghosts among its population of the living. We sat in small classes drilling grammatical constructions out of Deng Xiaoping's speeches to the UN General Assembly. We ate lavishly in restaurants without any need for the ration coupons real people had. We bicycled as spectres through a city where anyone who spoke to us spoke immediately afterwards to the militia or the Bureau of Public Security. (In these conditions, it is not surprising that much of my engagement with the city was strongly visual.)

We accepted with lofty condescension the generous hospitality of the small British diplomatic community, drinking their beer, sleeping on their floors, accepting picnic and dinner invitations. In 1974 and 1975 Mao Zedong still lived to receive the cries urging him to live for ever, and the tiny British student community ranged itself along a spectrum of skepticism and hope regarding the ideal new civilization portrayed in the posters that could be had for pennies in the bookshops and embodied with less immediate clarity in what we saw from buses and bicycles. I didn't buy such posters. Perhaps their charge in the land of their manufacture was less weighty. Perhaps I was unsure how my successive Chinese roommates (men much older than me, learning English for scientific or pedagogic purposes) would take them. They were presented to us so openly, these bold pictures with their bold subjects, that they held no frisson of alterity, instigated no desire. Instead, I looked half-guiltily for the visual traces of the imperial past, haunting the Palace Museum on days off class, buying the seemingly randomly published classical texts that appeared without warning in the bookshops, usually by virtue of their association with the then febrile Movement to Criticize Lin Biao and Confucius (see plate 9 [E35/E36]). The only picture I brought home with me was a version in hanging-scroll format of the famous poster *Chairman Mao goes to Anyuan*, one that deserves the title of "icon" as much as any, showing as it does a begowned and youthful Mao Zedong off to foment his first worker's uprising in 1921 (plate 6 [N35]). It was anonymous then, although now art history can tell us it had been painted in 1967 by Liu Chunhua, who made a fortune in the Mao fever of the late 1980s by selling the original.[3] I pasted no Chinese posters on my wall when I returned to Britain, despite the fact that images like *Commune fishpond* (plate 4 [A9], 1974) were rather fashionable at the time in the milieu in which I moved. I had other souvenirs.

The relationship of the faculty of memory to the academic practice of art history is a lopsided one. On the one hand, the art historian is supposed to be able to remember what things look like, where they are, and the specifically visual relationship they bear to other approved objects of study. Although discredited by modern neurology, the notion of the mind as a filing cabinet, in which the looking subject rummages to match up images and thereby solve problems of connoisseurship and identification, is still deeply ingrained in professional as well as popular notions of what it is to "do" art history.[4] That is how it was understood at any rate by Giovanni Morelli (1816–1891), the nineteenth-century Italian patriot whose work did as much as that of anyone else to make art history possible as an academic discipline in Europe, in addition to its earlier (and indeed continuing) roles as polite accomplishment, marker of social status, index of cultural capital, and enabler of market transactions in works of art. But one kind of memory is almost never raised to the level of consciousness in art historical practice. That is the memory that inserts the art historians themselves into the recollection, that talks about occasions of viewing, that says, "I remember when I saw this first." Before the age of extensive mechanical reproduction, such originary moments of viewing must have seemed clearer, attendant as they were on journeys to Jiangnan or to Italy, access to the collections of the great, social negotiations in which the positions of the lookers were nicely and precisely judged before looking could take place. Since the nineteenth century it is no longer so. Although I can remember when I first saw Guo Xi's *Early Spring,* one of the major paintings of the art historical canon, "for real" in the Palace Museum, Taipei, I have no notion, and no way of recovering, when I first saw a reproduction of this most celebrated and most published of early Chinese landscape paintings. Similarly with a Rembrandt self-portrait or a Gilbert and George conceptual piece. The shock of the new is dulled, at least in memory, even if I take issue with Walter Benjamin's celebrated claim in "The Work of Art in the Age of Mechanical Reproduction" that reproduction damages the aura of the original; arguably it has acted instead to enhance it.[5]

But the visual culture of the Great Proletarian Cultural Revolution stands in a very different relationship to my memory from that of *Early Spring*, in that the viewing of it now is inseparable from recollections of time as a student of Beijing Languages Institute. The problem for me, nearly a quarter of a century later, is that art historical language has very few ways of validating, or even acknowledging, this experience, predicated as much of the discipline's practice is on ideal Cartesian viewings, which are outside time and certainly divorced from the viewpoint of the art historical observer (a position rarely acknowledged to exist at all). Over those twenty-five years there has been a great shift of disciplinary interest by scholars from what artists do to how audiences receive it, and there has been a corresponding willingness to study for the first time how those audiences were socially and culturally constituted. Fewer and fewer professional art historians have any problem with the notion that "meaning" is not something inscribed into material culture at the time of its manufacture, which remains invariant in time and place, but that it is instead a product of the interaction of the viewer and the thing viewed, which not only can change but which can be contested at any one given moment. However, this interest by art historians in contexts of viewing does not in general extend to a self-reflexive attention to their own viewing. Book prefaces continue to situate the writer socially and professionally by thanking funding bodies, partners, children. The very eminent may write memoirs in which they are allowed to talk about when they first saw what. But for the professionally active a taboo of some sort operates with regard to discussing where, when, and how the writer encountered the works to be discussed. The same taboo operates with respect to what the writer thought about them on first viewing. Partly this may be a professional distancing from an older sort of connoisseurly practice that was very explicit in its parading of the author's credentials to be believed: "I have seen it. I know." These credentials often made an issue of the social status of the viewer/writer and the expert's privileged access to works not seen by the common herd. Morelli, for example, embeds his explanation of his scientific method of connoisseurship in a narrative of easy travel between Russia and Italy and of access to private, princely collections of old masters that makes it clear that it is a methodology only deployable by those with enough of the right kinds of leisure, money, and social position. As fewer academic art historians enjoy private incomes, private collections are absorbed into public or quasi-public institutions, and travel becomes something to be funded by employers and grant-giving bodies, the kind of reminder of art history's drawing room origins and the associations of dilettantism conveyed by personal reminiscences become less and less visible.

But a larger problem to do with art history's methodological coherence is embedded in the refusal of self-referentiality. These weaknesses are trenchantly laid out by Donald Preziosi:

> If every methodology is construed as oriented towards some domain of attention, every perspective equally implicates a near side or inside of the analytic window. It incorporates a viewing from somewhere, a perspective whose apex is at the locus of the ana-

lyst, the wielder of tools. It is not without significance that this view is characteristically occluded or taken for granted in art historical or critical writing. The position of the analyst, in this panoptic regime, is a tacit space (that may be filled by similarly equipped or invested persons)—an ideally neutral Cartesian zero point, as divested of its own history, sociality and conditions of investment and establishment as its analysand.[6]

Art historians are belatedly coming to recognize a problem that anthropologists have had to engage with for some decades now, namely, that of the "politics and poetics" of their practices.[7] Anthropological writing now is as likely to be an engagement with the practices of Margaret Mead or Evans-Pritchard as it is to be an account in some unproblematic way about Western Samoa or the Nuer. Or rather, it is widely recognized that no such immediate access to "Western Samoa" or the "Nuer" is possible, and certainly not through the medium of some transparent ethnographic written account. Representations are taken to be "social facts," as the title of an influential essay by Paul Rabinow puts it,[8] and the creators of those representations are now legitimate, even essential, objects of study. This issue has forced itself to the fore in anthropology for a number of complex reasons (including the issue of colonialist complicity), but one of them is that the traditionally authentic ethnographic account is based on the bodily presence of the observer in the culture he or she is purporting to describe. Margaret Mead went to live in Western Samoa, "in the field," as it is traditionally described, and so her account must be authentic. She went there, she saw it, she knows. This manner in which, in rather the same way, presence generates authentic accounts is occluded to a much greater degree in art history.

I have referred above to the notion of the souvenir, and these pictures are certainly souvenirs for me now, in the full sense of the term laid out by the American literary critic Susan Stewart.

> The souvenir must be removed from its context in order to serve as a trace of it, but it must also be restored through narrative and/or reverie. What it is restored to is not an "authentic," that is, a native, context of origin but an imaginary context of origin whose chief subject is a projection of the possessor's childhood.[9]

I have only to look at the posters, or scan a list of their titles, to feel the years in between my first encounters with them and a professorship in the history of art collapse in on themselves. I cannot write about them without reflecting on the processes that give me the authority to do so. And I cannot see them without thinking, "I know what this means," decoding without thinking their assemblage of signs, their collected signifying, *even though* I am well aware that I do not believe in fixed meanings in a visual work of art. They challenge me personally and professionally. They are very hard to write about.

I was *there*, I *know*. But a complication ensues when I consider the question, *when* was I there? Any book will tell you that I was a student in China during something called the Great Proletarian Cultural Revolution, which lasted from 1966 until 1976, the year of the death of Mao and the arrest of the Gang of Four. These are the periodizations of modern Chinese history that journalism repeats and that beginning students are taught. Yet I have a very clear memory of being told, in answer to a question, that the Cultural Revolution had been "victoriously concluded" *(shengli jieshu)* and that the very current Movement to Criticize Lin Biao and Confucius represented a new stage of the political struggle, initiated and led personally by Chairman Mao.[10] Now my year at the Languages Institute is retrospectively absorbed into the "Ten Years of Chaos" that is the accepted, official verdict on those years. It is as if my native informants in the ethnographic sense have turned against me, risen up to say, "No, that is not it at all," just as happened in the end to the doyenne of the ethnographically authentic account, Margaret Mead.[11] Nervous laughter is mostly what the words *Pi Lin pi Kong*, "Criticize Lin Biao and Confucius," will evoke from my Chinese contemporaries now. Now "everyone knows" it was the camouflage for a power struggle intended to secure the downfall of Premier Zhou Enlai, Mao's ostensible number two and the bitter enemy of his wife, Jiang Qing, the soon-to-be-demonized "Madame Mao," the White-Bone Demon herself. Authority to speak, to "do Chinese," is severely damaged to the point of incoherence when the objects of the gaze gaze back with such impertinence. Memory is dethroned.

The pictures, on the other hand, remain, as part of a collection at the University of Westminster. Susan Stewart has had plenty to say about the politics and poetics of the collection, the anti-souvenir par excellence:

> In contrast to the souvenir, the collection offers example rather than sample, metaphor rather than metonymy. The collection does not displace attention to the past; rather, the past is at the service of the collection, for whereas the souvenir lends authenticity to the past, the past lends authenticity to the collection. The collection seeks a form of self-enclosure which is possible because of its a-historicism. The collection replaces history with classification, with order beyond the realm of temporality. In the collection, time is not made something to be restored to an origin; rather all time is made simultaneous or synchronous within the collection's world.[12]

These pictures exist for me in a tension between the souvenir and the collection; the former is the figure of a sense of self that is personal and based in memory and orality, while the latter arranges them less obviously chaotically under headings: Agriculture; Four Modernizations; Industry and Commerce; Politics; Revolutionary History up to 1949; National Minorities; Health, Education, and Society; Military and Sport; Art; Children; Leaders; Personalities; Women; Film Posters; *Nianhua*.[13] These are the raw materials of my professional, disciplinary, and public life. Such categorizations are contingent but necessary, not least to make the posters treatable in a pedagogic sense; stories of "when I was in China," even if told from the most impeccably self-reflexive of motives, will glaze students' eyes over faster than anything. But negotiating between the personal and the professional has proved hard.

What would happen if one turned some of the traditional methodological tools of art history on a body of material that was selected purely because it was all produced in the year the art historian writing about it lived in the country where it came into being? These tools are often about inflicting some sort of coherence on the chaos of material life, through labels like "artists," or "iconography," or "style." Groupings based on "places I went to when I was a student in China" (like the revolutionary pilgrimage sites of Shaoshan, Dazhai, Yan'an) are less common, or at least less frequently made explicit.[14] What happens if they go nearer to the front, not the back, of the explanation? What follows, then, is a necessarily tentative attempt to engage some of the methodologies of art history with a group of pictures from the University of Westminster collection that have in common only their production during the years 1974 and 1975, to make myself write about these things in a manner that allows for the personal and the contingent. I want to retain a deliberate indeterminacy here, a sense of possibilities rather than of closure, a refusal to be the authority.

One of the oldest and still flourishing practices of art history, in China as much as in Europe, is connoisseurship, defined as "the ability to deduce simply from a work of art alone its period, aesthetic merit and possible relationship with other works."[15] In both of these places the sixteenth century was the era when a growing commodity market in works of art led to a conscious expression of the need to discriminate true goods from false and to evaluate quality of execution in a manner that would allow a canon to emerge. The notion of a connoisseurship of Chinese posters of the years 1974 and 1975 may initially jar, but the posters are now themselves valuable commodities in China, the object of sales within a burgeoning art market.[16] The original designs for posters change hands now for large sums, and it is surely only a matter of time before unsigned objects begin to be ascribed to the hands of named artists. We know that *Commune fishpond* (plate 4 [A9]) is publicly associated with the name of Dong Zhengyi, identified at the time as "Representative of the Poor Peasants Association of Nanguan Production Team of Chengguan Commune," one of the "peasant painters" of Huxian County, Shaanxi Province, who formed one of the "new socialist things" *(shehuizhuyi xin sheng shiwu)* of the 1970s.[17] *Art comes from a life of struggle; the working people are the masters* (plate 1 [L17]), depicts the kind of scene in which a work like this was ostensibly created. When I visited Huxian on 1 August 1975 my enthusiasm for this work, recorded in my notebook at the time, was fulsome to the point of severe embarrassment today: "This stuff is just the antidote to most Chinese art. When you see what the peasants are actually painting, your faith revives." As part of the demythologizing of the post-Mao era, we are now told that the peasant painters of Huxian were extensively supported in their work by rusticated professional artists, and it seems likely to be only a matter of time before, driven partly but not wholly by the logic of the art market, an investigation of who did what, a connoisseurly sorting out of attributions, gets under way seriously. At that point, the University of Westminster collection, with its impeccable provenance, becomes an important resource for the art market, whatever other issues academics wish to engage it with. We may even see the necessary invention of artists, "the Master of the *Commune fishpond*," as has often happened in other areas of the artistic production in the past. Similarly, and unless the art market loses interest, it is only a matter of time before blanket terms like "socialist realism" (a Russian term scarcely used in the mid-1970s in China) or "revolutionary romanticism" (Jiang Qing's preferred locution for the style of most of these works) are refined by regional categories, in the attempt to isolate a Beijing School, a Shanghai School, and to affiliate the less productive Henan School (see figure 3.1 [H15]) with one or other of these larger metropolitan centers.

Such a practice would separate *We are determined to settle down in the countryside* (plate 11 [A25]) from *Return to the countryside after graduation to make revolution, vow to become a generation of new peasants* (figure 3.1 [H15], 1975) on grounds of the different centers of their production. An iconographical approach, the close attention to subject matter as bearer of meaning, would, on the other hand, force them closer together, as exemplifying one of the great policy drives of the late Maoist years, that of sending or returning "educated youth" to the rural areas. While connoisseurship has an equally long pedigree in art historical practices of China and Europe, iconography, the study and identification of subject matter, has less of a written history in China itself, as the result of a decisive turn by elite artists of at least the last

Fig. 3.1 [H15]. *Return to the countryside after graduation to make revolution, vow to become a generation of new peasants (Biye hui xiang gan geming, shi zuo yi dai xin nongmin).* Henan 1975.

seven hundred years in favor of manner rather than subject matter as the proper substance of creation and criticism in the visual arts. Text after text in the classical tradition hammers home the message that it is above all vulgar, and the kind of thing done by children, eunuchs, and other marginalized groups, to ask what a picture is "of," what "the story" is. European art has by contrast been enthralled by the pronouncements of theorists like the fifteenth-century Italian Leon Battista Alberti (1404–1472) for whom the Aristotelian concept of *historia*, "plot, story," was the central element of artistic success. This does not mean that all Chinese art of the past seven hundred years is antimimetic, only that a position against mimesis, against transcriptional renderings, enjoyed a hegemony in China during centuries when European painting saw representation as being its central theme. This has nothing to do with "realism." The identification of subjects, of scenes from Greek and Latin literature or the Old and New Testaments, was crucial to an understanding of art that made no pretensions to transcribe reality and whose practitioners and patrons were often dismissive of painters (like Caravaggio) who were believed to do so.

The kinds of traditional art historical skills developed to engage with an allegorical ceiling painting of baroque Rome—and these are to a large extent skills of iconography—are not dissimilar to those that can be used to look at *We are determined to settle down in the countryside* (plate 11 [A25]), *The main lesson (Zhu ke)* (plate 15 [E27], 1975), or *The pines and cypresses of Shaoshan (Shaoshan song bo)* (figure 3.2 [Q16], 1975) in a certain way. The (controversial) appropriation by art historians of

Fig. 3.2 [Q16]. *The pines and cypresses of Shaoshan (Shaoshan song bo)*. Hebei 1975.

ideas from semiotics has led to much use of the term "reading" in connection with images like these, for in both cases they are clearly collections of signs, often requiring initiate knowledge. Like the attributes of saints, the details of these works are marshaled in support of their larger ideological program, and the clarity of gesture and posture is as marked as it is in the art of the Catholic Counter-Reformation of four hundred years ago. The aesthetic principle in the 1970s Chinese case is that of the *san tuchu*, "three prominences," in which the good are more prominent than the bad, the very good are more prominent than the merely good, and one outstanding figure is most prominent among the very good. This program was laid down first for the reform of opera, to create the "revolutionary model operas," which were to provide a common template for all cultural forms. As well as the hierarchy of figures they contain, the iconographies and settings of these pictures are themselves clear to the extent that an audience can be expected, through incessant repetition of a few key images, to know that the pines and cypresses are in Shaoshan, the childhood home of Mao Zedong, while the inscription "Long March" on the red banner to the left alludes to the late-1960s practice of Red Guards engaging in extensive route marches to revolutionary sites of pilgrimage, journeys that reenacted and restaged the epic retreat of the Red Army to Yan'an, the setting of *A yangge troupe comes to the Date Garden (Shu yuan laile yangge dui)* (figure 3.3 [N38], 1975), in 1934 and 1935. There is much nice judging of what an audience for these works can and cannot be expected to know (the scenery of Shaoshan was reproduced in countless formats, while in the *Date Garden* the "period" and regional costume is enough to signify Yan'an). However, *The main lesson* (plate 15 [E27]) is as impenetrable as any Tridentine hagiography, unless you understand that its title refers to the idea of a continuous historical struggle between the two ideological entities of Confucianism and Legalism (metaphors for "revisionism" and "Chairman Mao's revolutionary line"). The adult, significantly a worker and not a professional teacher, instructs his class in the heroic deeds of Hong Xiuquan (1814–1864), the leader of the nineteenth-century millenarian movement known as the Heavenly Kingdom of Great Peace, and a man seen in the 1970s as a revolutionary forerunner of correct Legalist thinking. In the picture within the picture to which the teacher gestures, Hong is shown smashing a series of

Fig. 3.3 [N38]. *A yangge troupe comes to the Date Garden (Shuyuan laile yangge dui)*. Beijing 1975.

tablets with Confucian inscriptions, the most readable of them bearing the motto, "Restrain the self and return to the rites" *(Ke ji fu li),* a tag associated incessantly in the official discourse of 1975 with the traitor Lin Biao (on 27 December 1974 we were told in class he was supposed to have had it by his bed). What is being represented here is a kind of ostensivity, the picture as an integral part of a showing, incomplete without a commentary. Inside the picture the worker/teacher is showing, but we are to assume that the whole thing, the framing picture, is also subject to such overdetermination in contexts where it is used as a teaching aid on the classroom wall or in the course of the study session. The poster is thus a kind of commentary on itself, but one that relies on oral support at the moment of viewing, or at least on knowledge derived from "outside" the image itself.

Another kind of information supporting the image is in the form of written text within the picture; thus, as in figure 3.1, there are crucial textual clues to a correct reading that are independent of the title, *Return to the countryside after graduation to make revolution, vow to become a generation of new peasants.* The returning student carries on her satchel the inscription, "My resolution is in the village," while the badge on her jacket identifies her as a university graduate, and the slogan "Agriculture learn from Dazhai" in the background situates the scene spatially and temporally. This ubiquity of the written word is on one level "realistic"; such badges were worn, such slogans were painted on many walls. But on another level it serves to overdetermine interpretation by anchoring the image very firmly in a world of verbal formulae to which the audience was exposed on a daily basis. While it might be tempting to comment on the seeming survival of traditional Chinese elite patterns of image making in this imbrication of word and picture (the most prestigious traditional paintings all have words in or on or near them), this may be to misunderstand the way picture and words work in the imagery of the mid-1970s. The latter, the words, have a fixity and stability that is guaranteed by the close attention the central organs of the Communist Party paid to the relatively small array of formulations *(tifa)* and slogans authorized for dissemination.[18] Rather than enabling the complex word-image interactions of traditional elite painting, they reduce the risk of unauthorized readings of the visual component, of indeterminacy.

The practices of academic art history in the English-speaking world in the course of my career have seen some of these older types of analysis (whether formalist or iconographical) challenged above all by a feminist critique. This has situated itself as being not so much an "approach" to art history as a challenge to its very epistemological foundations in the Western notion of artistic genius embodied in works like *Lives of the Artists* by Giorgio Vasari (1511–1574). I arguably owe my current professional status to this development, since it is largely the feminist assault on the canon of "great" artists that has created the space within university art history departments in Britain for research into, and teaching on, work other than the "Giotto to Cézanne" canon. Much of the published scholarship in English on Chinese art since 1949 is by women writers (the academic politics of this are themselves a fit issue for further study). Gender, whether of viewers or subjects, is another category of analysis providing a mesh in which these images might be held, as Harriet Evans explores in her chapter. The Maoist rhetoric of "Women can hold up half the sky" is certainly embodied in these images to a considerable extent and seems to me to be particularly prominent in work from 1974 and 1975, but few would now think that the presence of lots of women in pictures (even if they are driving trucks and scaling telegraph poles) is an index of the actual performance of gender roles within a given culture. The penetration of art history by psychoanalytic and differently gendered concepts such as "the gaze" has scarcely been considered in relation to Chinese material, but neither has serious attention been given as yet to the presence of women artists and art administrators in the 1970s. The director of visual arts for the culture group of the State Council, Wang Mantian, remains, in Julia Andrews's words, "a shadowy figure."[19] The fall of her political patron, Jiang Qing, in 1976 not only precipitated her suicide but also set off a wave of misogynist rhetoric that makes a revisionist account of her hegemony through the early 1970s a near impossibility, at least for the present. Putting these works of art from 1974 and 1975 "in their context," as almost all art history rather naively claims to do nowadays, is a project that demands to be met with the question, whose context is that exactly?

Along with authorship and iconography, "style" has been one of the traditional Western art historical tools, flourishing in both formalist and cultural history guises for well over a century. More recently, one of the most influential paradigms in the dominant art history of the Anglo-American academy has been that of the "period eye," a term coined in the 1970s by Michael Baxandall and subsequently developed in the direction of the study of differing "regimes of visuality," often by scholars working with a psychoanalytic inflection. It is not hard for anyone to see that *The new look of Dazhai (Dazhai xin mao)* (plate 16 [A46], 1974), a view of the terraced fields of the model commune of Dazhai, does not "look like" *Criticize Lin Biao and Confucius* (plate 9 [E35/E36]) and that neither of them really "looks like" the *Date Garden* (figure 3.3 [N38]). "They are in different styles" is how it might be put, but work has not yet begun on what that might have meant to audiences, how it might have conditioned the reception of images at the time. It might also be noticed that none of these "styles" really "looks like" traditional Chinese art, and notions of "influence" or "Westernization" might be invoked here, all of these rather innocuous terms concealing within them a large amount of epistemological and interpretive baggage, some bits of it more dangerous than others. As Homi Bhabha has pointed out in the context of a discussion of colonial mimicry in imperial India, "to be Anglicised is *emphatically* not to be English."[20] So it is in art that the notion of Westernization is rarely invoked except to stress that the phenomenon so categorized is absolutely *not* really Western, to challenge in a real sense its authenticity. There can be no doubt that these works have been doubly marginalized within a Western discourse of art history that makes "modern Chinese art" something of an oxymoron; the truly Chinese cannot in this account be modern, just as the truly modern cannot be really Chinese.[21] This critique of these works seems to have all the more force in that it juxtaposes the "Westernized," the hybrid, the impure, with some notional "Chinese art," a canonical standard represented chiefly by ink painting, and by the painting of landscapes above all. This canon is not purely an orientalist construction read onto artistic production in China; rather, it is one that gains all the more force by being derived from standards generated within China itself over a very long period of time and that has derived renewed vigor in the 1990s from nationalist inflections of an essential Chinese art embodied in the brush-and-ink manner. This is not the place to recap more than a century's worth of polemics about the essential nature of Chinese art, but what those polemics share, whether they are in the end pro- or anti- the ink painting tradition, is a view of Chinese art as not being about narrative, about figuration, about signs that tell stories. When in the early part of this century the Paris-trained artist Xu Beihong (1895–1953) attempted to invent a tradition of history-painting in oils for China, painting immense works with themes like "Tian Heng and His Five Hundred Retainers," his enemies and his friends accepted that he was doing something unprecedented, making a rupture with the tradition for better or worse. The historical part of art history would tend to see something like the works of the mid-1970s as being in a line of descent from these innovations of the 1920s, as representing an irruption of the outside, of non-Chineseness into the traditional visual culture of an earlier period.

Yet what in the end could look more Chinese? Or rather, what in the end looks more Chinese to *me*? I do not wish to suggest that these posters do not somehow "look Chinese" to Chinese audiences; their art-market success and the appetite for Cultural Revolution nostalgia absolutely prove the contrary. But like the ethnographer, and in spite of the work done "in the field," I as an art historian have no access to "China," only to the constructions of it immanent in the way I was taught a language, in the memories I carry of my first lengthy (and subsequent shorter) sojourn there. My presence as an author in this volume, my desire to engage in the act of looking at, and writing about, these images is inseparable from the context in which I first saw them. Is there, however, not a darker side to this? Two things trouble me. First, where is the boundary between self-reflexivity and the claiming of orientalist authority to speak for, and on behalf of, that subaltern that cannot speak? Am I really claiming in all that I have written above that my training, a bundle of social and linguistic competencies, grants me an access to what these pictures really mean? And, second, there is an ethical issue, namely, where does self-reflexive reverie become complicity? The extreme unpopularity of the "educated youth to the countryside" policy is now a staple of Chinese memoirs of the period, and it was one of the first policies to be reversed by the post-Mao regime. For those who lived the Maoist project, the collecting and display of its imagery must evoke memories very different from mine. This is not a question of a simple binary opposition between undifferentiated "Chinese" viewers and equally undifferentiated "foreigners." The image in *Revolutionary friendship is as deep as the sea* (plate 17 [D12], 1975) cannot but remind me of my own visit as a "tourist of the revolution" (the phrase is Hans Magnus Ensenzberger's) to the Luoyang Tractor Factory on 18 February 1975. But it also reminds me of the barely suppressed racism with which the Tanzanian students who lived on our corridor were served (often not served) in restaurants around the Languages Institute. These were men for whom "doing Chinese," as a preliminary to degrees in other subjects, involved a very different type of experience.

Issues of my own identity were very much in my mind as a student in China, since my presence there immediately deprived me of the singularity of being someone who "did Chinese." I wrote in my diary on 1 December 1974, "a sinologist cannot exist in China," and was aware at the time that I was performing "being Scottish" with a particular enthusiasm as a compensatory factor. "Foreign friends" from Western Europe had no presence in representation in China in 1974 and 1975, unlike the Africans and the Albanians with whom we shared the Languages Institute. Part of my own fascination with these pictures may therefore indeed lie in my *absence* from them (unlike the generic "Africans" of *Revolutionary friendship*, an absence that allows me to place myself at the "ideally neutral Cartesian zero point" of which Donald Preziosi complained, an absence that allows these pictures of the Other to carry on constituting the untroubled art historical self.

Is it therefore the case that I am disabled from saying anything about these posters other than the self-reflexive? Is the stark choice between a sort of maudlin reminiscence and Cartesian detachment? One art historical paradigm, already invoked, that may perhaps enable a more open negotiation between the subject and the object is that of "visual culture," where looking itself is seen as a social activity, hence one in which the social positioning of the looker must of necessity be taken into account. The specific visual culture of the Great Proletarian Cultural Revolution would then become an object of investigation in a way that situated my student experience without privileging it. It would also facilitate the search for a language in which to convey the experiences of the Chinese bearers of the look at these objects, while also giving the objects themselves and their makers a position in the account. A true history of looking in the Cultural Revolution would have to take into account so much more than posters. Not just obvious things like film but also clothes and the objects of life, body language, and the shape of the crowd at a demonstration would all have to be part of it. That history would have to go alongside an attention to what has been called "the biography" of the object, in an approach that stops fetishizing the moment of production of the posters, as seeing them as somehow embodying the Cultural Revolution in their very substance, and takes seriously what they, and their various Chinese and Western audiences, have been up to *since* 1976. This changing and conflicted pattern of interactions between lookers and looked-at is what a sufficiently rich visual history of the period must be about; there is a lot to be done in creating it.

## Notes

1. I was in Beijing from 18 October 1974 to 27 August 1975.
2. "Gazing up into the darkness, I saw myself as a creature driven and derided by vanity; and my eyes burned with anguish and anger," the final words of James Joyce, "Araby," in *The Dubliners*.
3. Julia F. Andrews, *Painters and Politics in the People's Republic of China, 1949–1979* (Berkeley and Los Angeles: University of California Press, 1994), 338–42. Andrews points out that, unusually, the artist was publicly credited at the time, but my version bears no acknowledgment of authorship.
4. Hayden B. Magginis, "The Role of Perceptual Learning in Connoisseurship: Morelli, Berenson, and Beyond," *Art History* 13, no. 1 (1990): 104–17.
5. Walter Benjamin, "The Work of Art in the Age of Mechanical Reproduction," in *Illuminations*, by Walter Benjamin, edited and with an introduction by Hannah Arendt (London: Fontana, 1992), 211–44.
6. Donald Preziosi, *Rethinking Art History: Meditations on a Coy Science* (New Haven: Yale University Press, 1989), 39.
7. James Clifford and George E. Marcus, eds., *Writing Culture: The Poetics and Politics of Ethnography* (Berkeley and Los Angeles: University of California Press, 1986).
8. Paul Rabinow, "Representations Are Social Facts: Modernity and Post-Modernity in Anthropology," in *Writing Culture*, ed. Clifford and Marcus, 234–61.
9. Susan Stewart, *On Longing: Narratives of the Miniature, the Gigantic, the Souvenir, the Collection* (Durham, N.C.: Duke University Press, 1993), 150.
10. This is what I wrote down in my notebook from dictation by teachers of the Languages Institute on 20 December 1974.
11. Derek Freeman, *Margaret Mead and the Heretic: The Making and Unmaking of an Anthropological Myth* (Harmondsworth, England: Penguin Books, 1996).
12. Stewart, *On Longing*, 151.
13. "University of Westminster Poster Reference Guide," unpublished typescript (n.d.). A Chi-

nese encyclopaedia to set beside that which made Foucault laugh. Foucault refers to a short story by Argentinian writer Jorge Luis Borges. Michel Foucault, *The Order of Things: An Archaeology of the Human Sciences* (London: Tavistock/Routledge, 1989), xv.

14. I and my classmates visited Shaoshan on 22–23 February 1975, Dazhai on 27–30 July 1975, Yan'an on 2–5 August 1975.

15. Shearer West, ed., *The Bulfinch Guide to Art History* (Boston: Bulfinch, 1996), 352. This was the first definition that came to hand, but there is a considerable literature on this.

16. See, e.g., the sale catalogue, *Important Art of New China, 1949–1979*, China Guardian Auctions, Beijing, 19 October 1996.

17. *Huxian nongminhua xuanji* (Selection of Huxian peasants' paintings) (Xi'an: Shaanxi renmin meishu chubanshe, 1974), illus. 55. This kind of art was a major part of Chinese cultural diplomacy of the period. See, e.g., the exhibition catalogue *Peasant Paintings from Hu County, Shensi Province, China*, Arts Council of Great Britain, 1976.

18. Michael Schoenhals, "Proscription and Prescription of Political Terminology by the Central Authorities, 1949–1989," in *Norms and the State in China*, ed. Chun-chieh Huang and Erik Zurcher, Sinica Leidensia 28 (Leiden: Brill, 1993), 337–59.

19. Andrews, *Painters and Politics*, 349.

20. Homi K. Bhabha, *The Location of Culture* (London: Routledge, 1994).

21. This is now widely identified within the field of art history as a central problem. For two collections of essays engaging with it in very different ways, see John Clark, ed., *Modernity in Asian Art*, University of Sydney East Asian Studies, no. 7 (Broadway: University of Sydney Press, 1993); and Cao Yiqiang and Fan Jingzhong, eds., *Ershi shiji Zhongguo hua: "Chuantong de yanxu yu yanjin"* (Chinese painting in the twentieth century: "Creativity in the aftermath of tradition") (Hangzhou: Zhejiang renmin meishu chubanshe, 1997).

# 4

# "Comrade Sisters": Gendered Bodies and Spaces

*Harriet Evans*

"Women hold up half the sky" was the slogan that dominated Party rhetoric on women during the Cultural Revolution. "Times have changed," pronounced Mao Zedong in one of his famous dicta on women, "women can do the same as men." The visual representations of women that accompanied this rhetoric were more expansive and vigorous during the Cultural Revolution than in the 1950s and early 1960s, but the main principles of this policy had been established by the Chinese Communist Party (CCP) long before it came to power in 1949. Since the Party's early years, CCP definitions of the goals of the women's movement were framed in classical Marxist-Leninist terms. Women's liberation *(funü jiefang)* lay in participating in the revolutionary struggle against feudalism and imperialism; it lay in contributing to the liberation of the people as a whole, as the Second Congress of the CCP, held in 1922, made clear. It stated that "the Chinese Communist Party thinks that women's liberation needs to be carried out through relying on the liberation of the laboring people as a whole, because only if the proletariat obtains political power will women be able to achieve full liberation."[1] In 1940, an editorial article in the New China publication in Yan'an commented that "In order to demand their own liberation, Chinese women of today must participate in all movements that benefit the state and nation."[2] By the early 1950s, with the CCP's successful consolidation of state power, the official approach to "women's liberation" had shifted to emphasize women's equal entry into the public sphere of production and labor. As Deng Yingchao, chair of the All China Women's Federation, indicated in 1953, "Ten years of practice has proven that mobilizing the masses of women to participate in production is the basic key to improving equality between men and women and to achieving the thorough liberation of women."[3]

One corollary of this approach to "women's liberation" during this period was the marginalization from official debates of all arguments that asserted the need for a specifically gendered approach to the "woman question." Feminism—in this context referring to the gendered analysis of women's position and representation in society—had long been rejected by the party as a bourgeois approach to women's problems. A limited femininity, in the assertion of a specifically female identity, was occasionally encouraged during the 1950s, particularly when pressures from rising urban unemployment resulted in official policies to encourage women to withdraw from the urban labor force.[4] By the Cultural Revolution, however, all overt signs conventionally associated with feminine appearance and conduct were denounced. As Rae Yang put it in her 1997 autobiographical account, "As Red Guards we could not and would not wear skirts, blouses, T shirts, shorts and sandals. Anything that would make girls look like girls was bourgeois. We covered up our bodies so completely that I almost forgot that we were boys and girls. We were Red Guards, and that was it."[5] Almost all the art, literature, films, operas, and ballets produced during the Cultural Revolution featured women in conventionally masculine roles and appearance as militant fighters or political activists. Though some posters of the mid-1970s indicated a slight, patchy refeminization of the images of the 1960s—in the use of patterned blouses, for example, pastel shades, and softer outlines to bodies and features—most images of women during this period featured what were, in the terms of U.S. and British feminist debates of the period, "positive" images of women, images that, by disrupting the conventional associations of femininity, were intended to position women in new roles and positions. Marilyn Young has used the term "socialist androgyny" to describe the reworkings of female gender during this period. She has also discussed the sense of empowerment that women associated with the possibilities represented by their new "image."[6] Emily Honig has talked about the "supposedly gender-neutral representation" of women during this period.[7] Whatever the term, and whatever the shifts in political meaning to the subject of the posters, as the Cultural Revolution decade progressed, these dominant public forms of female representation remained, for the most part, unchanged. The exceptions, maybe, were in the filmic representations of older, usually peasant, women.[8]

A number of fundamental assumptions about gender and gender difference framed the official discourse in ways that effectively limited the possibilities for women of exploring the new subject positions offered by these images. It is now well established that policy towards women during the period fell far short of living up to the promise of full gender equality in employment, wages, education, and political participation.[9] However, policy did not fail women simply because it put the needs of the revolution for all and class struggle ahead of those of women as a specific category, as some have argued, though this was certainly the case.[10] The party-state's understanding of women's liberation was not only limited by its own discursive definition. It was also bound by an essentialist construction of gender difference according to which biology determined that women were by nature weaker, less intelligent and creative, and more susceptible to emotional fluctuations and small-minded interests and so on, than men. Though the argument presented in this chapter is based on analysis of the dominant textual discourses of gender and sexuality between the early 1950s and the late 1970s, ethnographic evidence from the period and beyond, up to the present, suggests that these assumptions were widely, if not universally, held.[11]

The posters that we discuss in this book in the first instance owed their production and existence to political interests. Their explicit function was to transmit party policy through the presentation of "ideal types," or models, molded within an aesthetic framework shaped by Mao Zedong's reworking of socialist realism and borrowings from popular tradition. Their contents and style were subject to detailed scrutiny and editorial control to establish ideological correctness. Their public display also carried an automatic inference: that their public—those asked to interpret their visual contents—was addressed as political subjects, accustomed to reading visual images as carriers of political meaning. The main themes of the posters of course changed over time, emphasizing different priorities and objectives in conjunction with the fluctuations of central policy. Yet they constituted a particular and omnipresent aspect of the mechanisms used by the party-state to ensure the dominance of its discourse. The images and symbols they contained were part of everyday discourse; as a particular molding of cultural and political forms, they could potentially appeal to a vast and relatively uneducated public in perhaps more powerful ways than the staid narratives contained, for example, in official documents, newspaper editorials, and the like.

The explicit political purpose of these posters did not reduce their function to one of political education (control) alone. Images can be read and interpreted in a variety of ways; there are no semiotically innocent meanings.[12] Little in the production of these posters was left to chance; apart from the overall theme, their specific symbolic references, use of color, the spaces between and juxtaposition of images, and so on were subject to rigorous editorial scrutiny. However, the aesthetic qualities these posters demonstrated, the images they contained, the social relations they described, and the conduct they exemplified were all inscribed with a range of different meanings, which were not necessarily consistent with their explicit political message. Even if selected to correspond with the dominant ideological themes of the moment, the images they contained were not, and could not be, divorced from the cultural assumptions—both conscious and unconscious—molding their representation. Of course, what different readers read into these "additional" meanings depended on their own position as well as the context within which the posters were situated.[13] But from these perspectives they also functioned to produce normative structures of power and exclusion concerning gender as well as other social hierarchies.

The spatial and visual importance of posters during the years of the Cultural Revolution and their function as texts of cultural and social, as well as political, meaning make analysis of them as a key component of the official discourse of the time much more important than their categorization as mere propaganda would imply. The gendered images and spaces through which their political "messages" were constructed reproduced a series of hierarchical relationships that in many ways resonated with the broader discourse on gender. I do not in this chapter analyze how these posters were read by their contemporary public, but it is important to stress that the hierarchies in their images were a constant visual presence in the physical and optical spaces of daily life. Whether their viewers accepted or rejected the gendered messages encoded in them, the posters were an inescapable component of the cultural environment shaping ordinary persons' identification of self and others. An analysis of the structures of, and interrelationships between, their images and spaces suggests many possibilities for how this form of visual discourse intersected with, substantiated, and even possibly challenged the dominant rhetoric of the period. In these senses, the gendered figures in these texts were much more than metaphors affirming certain kinds of behavior and political position. Their juxtapositions and the ways in which these changed in different groupings and different spaces projected meanings that were not necessarily intended as part of their "model" value. One might also argue that the visual closures of the posters often contradicted the overt message contained in the dominant theme and its accompanying slogan.[14] Read in this way, the posters did not simply shed light on how ordinary women and men should behave or what, in the ideal socialism of the future, they should do—though in their most explicit rendering, this was their purpose. Rather, they were a specific visual site controlling the production of cultural assumptions as well as political interests. One might think of them as specific aspects of the "habitus," to use Bourdieu's term—that set of structuring principles and common schemes of perception and conception that generates practices and representations—contributing to assumptions about gender that not only informed the party-state's formation of a legitimating discourse but also was vital to popular understandings of gender.[15]

## Men at the Margins?

A cursory glance at representations of women in the posters of the Cultural Revolution would suggest the foregrounding of a number of key images. Consistent with the intepretation of gender equality that was propounded by the Communist Party, images of women appear as a metaphor for the changing contours of debates about socialist struggle and modernity. Women appear doing things conventionally associated with masculine occupations and activities, demonstrating the principles and purposes of revolutionary struggle. They are young, healthy, strong, and invariably dressed in the same kinds of clothes as men. Whether they appear in the figure of the milita trainee in *Doing military drill at first light (Shu guang chuzao yan bing chang)* (plate 18 [Q17]), the electrician working on a high-voltage line in *Lofty aspirations touch the clouds (Zhuang zhi ling yun)* (figure 4.1 [Q4], 1973), or the inspired Red Guards in *The pines and cypresses of Shaoshan (Shaoshan song bo)* (figure 3.2 [Q16], 1975), they display sturdy features, robust faces, and shining eyes, denoting revolutionary commitment, youth, physical strength, and determination.

A first reading of these images would suggest that they fully exemplify the Cultural Revolution discourse of gender "sameness," defined according to the masculine standard. There is at first glance little in these images that distinguishes the activities and commitments of the women from those of men; women appear in the same kinds of spaces, against the same symbols of progress and struggle, dressed in similar attire, and displaying the same kinds of capabilities. As in images of men, they celebrate determination, commitment, physical health, and strength. On the surface, little can be distinguished in the form of their bodies that makes statements about gender identity and difference, unless it is to foreground the male standard. As the vehicle for messages defined by an external agent—the party-state—the female body in these examples seems to operate in much the same way as the male body. The particular form the female body takes in these posters makes it a powerful metaphor for a changing conceptualization of modernity, in which women are proudly displayed as creators and agents of history. Indeed, if, within this reading, the representation of the female has any affirmatively gendered meaning, it is to emphasize the distance from the past that socialism has forged for women.

Another look at these same posters produces different readings, which challenge the suggestion that women simply function as the same kinds of markers as men. Women and men may appear within very similar spaces, marked by symbols of industrial progress, revolutionary zeal, and cross-class solidarity. The gender and age composition of the group, however, women's physical positioning within the group, and their appearance and location in different kinds of spaces all introduce other possibilities into the dominant theme. Depending on her relationship with other gendered and social markers around, the female functions as a different kind of marker in different spaces and contexts.

Fig. 4.1 [Q4]. *Lofty aspirations touch the clouds (Zhuang zhi ling yun).* Beijing 1973.

First, the symbolic boundaries of authority and power— which include the power to be creative, to be the source of inspiration and initiative—invariably shift according to whether women appear on their own, either in groups or individually, or in groups with men. The boundaries also shift in the relationship between space, bodies, and symbols. Posters featuring groups of women on their own endow them with an authority that derives from their collective action and intercommunication as well as their domination of space. *Starting the game* (plate 2 [Q7]) foregrounds a group of young married rural women, dressed in bright red sports shirts, one in a patterned blue cotton jacket, under the red leaves and golden fruit of a persimmon tree. An abundance of yellow and red gives to the scene a mood of joyful celebration—in this instance, as the blackboard announcement displays, of the "iron maidens" of the "young married women's team." Men, both old and young, are displaced to the rear "row" as onlookers or spectators, neither participating nor challenging the women in the game. Here it is the women's turn to take center stage, and the men become enthusiastic but nonactive bystanders. Another poster evokes the same celebratory mood in even more vibrant terms. Painted in the unmistakable style of the Huxian paintings John Gittings discusses in his chapter, *New style shop* (plate 5 [C6]) gives an overwhelming impression of festivity, fecundity, red, and excited and happy female activity. (Red is the color of celebration, including of weddings, gifts, and births, in Chinese symbolic culture and, of course, was the color of revolution.) There are quite a number of children around, as well as a few men. The women who occupy center stage are looking at rolls of cloth and displaying eggs to sell. The men are engaged in conventional masculine activities, pulling carts, carrying sacks, even holding the scroll, but they are numerically in an evident minority and are visually displaced from the center. The same displacement of men occurs in *Women shock troops* (Q5, 1975), in which women, again in the same bright-colored clothing, are pasting a big-character poster on the wall to proclaim their own authority over "half the sky."

In these posters, women's numerical dominance is reinforced by the bright colors of their clothes, which effectively steals attention from the duller shades of the men's clothes. The subordination of the men in the visual hierarchy of these three posters appears not only through their physical displacement from the center of the picture but also in their status as spectators, bystanders, or viewers of female activity. Female authority here is constructed neither through the absence of men nor through positioning men as participants in an equal game but through showing men as spectators of activities from which, temporarily, they are excluded as actors.

Women's spatial dominance of the poster, however, is frequently counterbalanced by symbolic meanings associated with the male that diminish women's potential authority. In *Starting the game* (plate 2 [Q7]), the elder male sits behind the competitors facing south (on the axis of the poster); his position as a spectator is thus already privileged. His age also gives him an unmistakable authority that arguably conveys a greater status to the group activity than would his absence. A tension between the spatial and visual dominance of the women and the symbolic authority of the men again appears in *Women's Day channel* (plate 19 [Q23]). Here a team of women takes a brief rest from work on an irrigation channel named after 8 March, International Women's Day. The three men sit with their backs to the viewer, themselves spectators of another activity. Women conquer the world, they stand high up on the rock face where the irrigation channel emerges from the mountain. Yet the men's clothes indicate that they are cadres, men in positions of administrative and political authority who possess the power to "order" the women to take a rest from their work. *Vigorous and spirited; thriving and dynamic* (Q19, 1975) suggests a repositioning of women in relation to men in another way. This scene of an industrial space is almost completely occupied by a small group of women workers, standing talking to each other, center stage. Doubtless they are exchanging some important information in the line of duty, yet they could also simply be exchanging some piece of gossip as they pass each other in their work. A line of men is fitting some pipe to the right, smiles on their faces as they look over towards the women. The key juxtaposition in the picture thus changes. It is no longer only between the centered women and marginalized men but also between chatting and working, modifying the gendered meaning of women occupying center stage. Through this interpretation, the space the women occupy is also feminized, minimizing their potential challenge to male authority.

Images of women, either in groups or on their own, without the presence of men, by definition suggest an authority over the context and the skills and aptitudes that form the theme of the poster. There is no suggestion that the electrician working on high-voltage lines (figure 4.1 [Q4]) requires the assistance or knowledge of other gendered subjects to consolidate her control over the activity in which she is engaged (even though here, as Stephanie Donald points out, the Mao badge gleaming out from the central point of the poster suggests another mode of conferring masculine authority). Here woman's status as an agent of socialist modernity clearly echoes the male standard implicit in the Cultural Revolution's approach to gender equality. A gleaming Mao badge would also shine out from the chest of a male electrician. A look at some other images, though, shows that such professional, political, or physical authority is generally conferred on women when they appear on their own, in spaces from which the figure of the male, and of patriarchal authority, is absent.

Individual women also appear in contexts, activities, and roles that are associated solely with the female. Hence they appear as healthy and cheerful exponents of birth control (figure 1.2 [H8]) and as the diligent young peasant woman who burns the midnight oil as she studies at the side of her sleeping child in *Awake late into the night (Shen ye bu mian)* (plate 20 [Q18]). None of the posters featuring single men or small groups of men places them in domestic and servicing contexts such as these. Individual men are situated within the predictable contexts of industrial production and battle (C4) and of publicly displayed study (E19). In this poster, the combination of macho strength with political and intellectual status transforms the supposed philosopher of the poster into a kind of socialist pinup. The nearest to a domestic scene of men I have found in the Westminster collection is one of a group of People's Liberation Army soldiers squatting on the ground weaving baskets, a proto-industrial activity often associated with women's work in the household courtyard but here associated with the "production movement" of the Yan'an base area (J30, 1974); and one of Zhou Enlai, entitled *Premier Zhou shares our hardship,* in which the premier is shown at a spinning wheel with a peasant and communist soldiers (N27, 1978). In both these posters, however, women are noticeable by their absence, and men's "domestication" takes place in clearly public arenas, altering the gendered meaning of the activity invoked.

### Doing the Same Things

The possibilities and powers associated with the image of the female body clearly alter in contexts where groups of women and men are engaged in similar or related activities, regardless of the numerical balance between them. Posters group women and men together in a range of situations, from the oil fields of Daqing to the clinic of the rural barefoot doctor, from doing military drill in the early light of the morning to rushing through the waves of the sea to attack an unseen target on the shore. Women may be engaged in exactly the same kind of activity as men, physically positioned in close proximity to them, sometimes even touching them. However, in such groups, the presence of the male in itself seems to define the kinds of spaces represented. Hence these kinds of groups appear in the male worlds of industry, agriculture, and sometimes study, never in the feminized spaces of the household. It is significant in this context, for example, that the only adult male in *New family* stands outside the threshold, looking in on the women moving inside the house (figure 4.2 [H4]). Moreover, in contexts already associated with masculine activity, the spatial juxtaposition between female and male introjects further meanings. Women may be engaged in the same activity as men, but in contexts in which they appear together, doing the same

Fig. 4.2 [H4]. *New family (Xin jia).* Beijing 1974.

thing, neither women's position, their gestures, nor their gaze is seen to challenge male authority.

A good example is the 1967 poster of a small group of Red Guards, entitled *Revolutionary proletarian Right to Rebel troops unite! (Wuchanjieji geming zaofan pai lianheqilai)* (plate 2 [E37], 1967), in which the central figure is a young woman. Her raised arm and clenched fist give her figure a forcefulness and determination not shared by other members of the group. Her authority is further symbolically reinforced by the red band on her right arm. Yet at the same time that she appears as the key figure, the limits of her authority are established by the enormous portrait of Mao Zedong placed above her. The young woman's authority is conferred on her and ratified by the Great Leader; without his ratification she would be no one.[16] Another, rather different example is *With the sun in your heart, what is there to fear? Dare to sacrifice your*

胸怀朝阳何所惧　敢将青春献人民

Fig. 4.3 [E16]. *With the sun in your heart, what is there to fear? Dare to sacrifice your youth for the people (Xiong huai chao yang he suo ju? Gan jiang qingchun xian renmin).* Shanghai 1967.

*youth for the people (Xiong huai chao yang he suo ju, gan jiang qingchun xian renmin)* (figure 4.3 [E16], 1967). This features a group of young people acting as a human dam against a torrent; the slogan at the bottom exhorts spectators to "learn from the eleven educated youths of Shanghai's Huangshan TeaTree factory, who feared neither bitterness nor death." A young man and woman appear as the main figures, arms linked in defiance against the flood. He stands towards the edge of the frame, allowing the young woman to approach the center. She is also granted symbolic status by the "little red book" she holds in her hand. Nevertheless, her potential authority is offset by the strong right-arm gesture of her male companion. She also appears as the weak link in the chain who lets the water through the middle of the human barrier. In *Settle down in the countryside* (plate 11 [A25]), by contrast, the young woman's potential authority granted by her position and her possession of the "little red book" is offset by the main line of communication within the poster between the two men. Though seated on either side of her, these two men gaze intently at each other, implicitly pushing her towards the back (wanting her out of the picture?).

Other contexts in which these kinds of gendered juxtapositions appear refer to professional as well as political authority. In *Countryside medical station* (plate 22 [H5]) the three figures—one woman and two men—are all engaged in the same sphere of interest and expertise, Chinese medicine. The young woman is the barefoot doctor who brings a basket of medicinal herbs into the medical station. The foregrounded older man is probably the *lao zhongyi* (the old Chinese doctor); he holds a plant out for his companion to look at. The latter, standing at the center of the composition, holds up a book—maybe an encyclopedia of medicinal plants—in his hand as he looks with interest at the herb. All three characters here are placed within the same professional context; the context also suggests that they exchange and share their areas of expertise. Yet the young female barefoot doctor's position and stance clearly suggest other interpretations. Off center to the left, she bends down towards the basket as she looks over towards the two older men. They meanwhile, standing together, slightly apart from her, share the expert knowledge symbolically contained within the textbook of herbs. The men then seem to endow her activities with the authority of the text in their hand. The central figure may also be a local cadre, suggested by his cap and standard blue Mao jacket over his peasant shirt. Overall, the young woman's expertise is put on a different scale from that of her male elders; their mastery of the word gives them the authority to evaluate the fruits of her labor. In *Graduation report,* by contrast, the female figure at first sight appears as the most active and visually demanding figure (Q6, mid-1970s). She stands to the left of a table to deliver her report at the end of a period of open-door schooling to an assembled group of peasants, fellow students, teachers, and cadres. Directly in front of her is a group of three men, seated on the other side of the table with glasses of tea in front of them and listening with eager pleasure and maybe pride to her pronouncements. The men here appear as arbiters of the female voice; their already evident authority as teachers and cadres is reinforced by their ability to evaluate political language.

## Gender and Class

A notable aspect of the imaging of women and men in posters of this period concerns the representational features through which the female often becomes a marker of social as well as gender hierarchy. When we first started looking through the posters to prepare the material for this book, Robert Benewick pointed out to me that the "holy" triumvirate of worker, peasant, and soldier far more often than not—at least in the Westminster collection—is male. Together with the figure of the male leader (Jiang Qing, as John Gittings has pointed out, very rarely appeared in poster form), the major icons of socialist modernity are male. When a female figure is present in individual or collective representations of the triumvirate, she is invariably positioned as the "peasant." In industrial settings with male "comrades," she appears at the side of the main group as the textile worker, dressed in a white apron with a white mobcap; she sometimes also appears as a steelworker, protective helmet pushed back off her forehead, and standing behind or to the side of her male companions.

Throughout the 1950s and the Cultural Revolution, central policy oriented the rural sector and rural transformation as much to fulfilling the rapidly growing needs of the urban sector as to the needs of the rural population. The slogans of "taking agriculture as the basis" and "grain as the key link," upheld as key lessons from Dazhai, did not fundamentally challenge the hierarchical relationship between the town and the countryside. Discourses of gender and sexuality produced between the 1950s and 1970s paralleled this binary hierarchy by inscribing the rural woman with a whole series of "backward," "feudal," and "conservative" gender attitudes and practices, which awaited transformation by the urban-centered model of monogamous, free-choice marriage.[17] Women's social positioning in the particular visual form of the posters would seem to support the same kinds of associations. Through her visual identifications with the rural and, to a lesser extent, with the lower ranks of the urban labor force, the female's relative subordination in this particular grammar of representation was doubled. In terms of social class, as well as gender, she stood for the less privileged.

One might also argue that she was the less privileged in another sense as well. One of the curious features of the posters of the early and mid-1970s is the visual erasure of the "enemy," the target of criticism, attack, and transformation that the activities of the main characters frequently invoke by omission.[18] Of course, as we suggested in the introduction, the erased opposition is constructed, often forcefully, by its very absence. An apparent tension is created by the opposition between incorporation and exclusion of different kinds of politicized bodies, which reinforces the posters' ideological meanings. As Ann Anagnost wrote in her essay "The Politicized Body," "oppositional pairs have a deeply ideological function in all systems of meaning, and this is especially true in totalizing systems of meaning in which alternative coding is repressed or the intent is to obliterate prior coding through a revolutionary transformation of values."[19] The persistent rhetoric of class struggle of the period is visually described solely in affirmative terms; conforming to the principles of the "three prominences," emphasis on the "revolutionary" of the present and the future seems to necessitate the entire effacement of its "alternative." With the exception of the "big fist" images of the Red Guard years and the satirical, hand-drawn cartoon characters of big-character wall posters, the figures who appear in the posters, women and men, are all on the right (or left) side of revolution. They are presented as ideals, if not for immediate emulation in the present, then for aspiration. The female thus does not become a signifier of class difference, but of difference—not diversity—within class.[20] In posters where the female appears on her own, without men around, she represents the creative energy and initiative of rural and urban transformation, as do men. As soon as the male signifier appears, however, whether in urban or rural form or, in the case of the triumvirate, in military form as well, she is demoted to the lesser category. In this light, the figure of the female becomes a double signifier as the target (gender and social) of revolutionary transformation.

## Color, Age, and Ethnicity

Finally, a gendered reading of these posters suggests hierarchies of privilege and status through an analysis of color, age, and ethnicity. Poster images of national minority women, peasant, and, to a much lesser extent, worker women, and, in the case of *Revolutionary friendship* (plate 17 [D12]), African women (and to a lesser extent men) appear as the dominant sources of color, gaiety, and exuberance. At a time when an indispensable accoutrement of the female revolutionary was masculine dress, replete with the cloth shoes and cap (the leather belt and buckles were obligatory attire only during the Red Guard years), the association between women and color, often in the form of highly patterned blouses or scarves, could be read as a way of discounting women as serious revolutionary contenders.[21] Texts of the 1950s and mid-1970s repeatedly suggested that women were "by nature" drawn more to matters of sartorial interest and physical appearance than men.[22] Stories about women who had strayed from the socialist straight and narrow often started with references to their materialist interest in fine clothes. The same assumption lay behind the "prettification" campaign of the mid-1950s, which attempted to encourage women back into "the home" by appealing to their interests in fashion and bodily appearance. Of course, in a visual culture in which the figure of the male was denied direct association with color, the bodily focus of the *hong, guang, liang* (red, bright, and shining) principle could only be the female.[23] However, visual imbrication between the female, color, and clothing could also be seen as a means of reinforcing familiar hierarchical assocations. Drawing attention to women's bodily and sartorial features as the posters did was a symbolic means of perpetuating the impossibility of women's access to the serious world directed by male revolutionaries.

Though this chapter has focused essentially on images of Han women, analysis of the representation of the ethnic subaltern in the poster form would forcefully substantiate this argument. Painted in gay colors, dancing, waving ribbons, and always smiling, the ethnic woman emerges as the exotic embodiment of a range of imaginaries, fantasies, and sublimations that the dominant discourse denied in the representation of Han women. Of course, the association of women in general and color could have a range of possible meanings: the desire to escape the dull uniformity to which men were socially and politically bound, an attempt to inject an element of visual pleasure, even playfulness, into texts produced to publicize strictly defined codes of political and social conduct. Gaiety and color added to the potential appeal of the poster. In the form of the ethnic minority woman, however, these possibilities acquired additional significance, precisely because of the different power relations obtaining between the Han and the ethnic other. "Othering" the ethnic woman as all that the "true Han revolutionary" should not be functioned—and continues to function—as an orientalizing trope, in this case reinforcing the supremacy of the masculine Han center.[24]

Finally, poster representations of women during this period erase all but a single generational category. With very, very few exceptions old women simply do not appear, whether Han or ethnic minority, urban or rural. One of the few examples in the University of Westminster collection is *I accompany Grannie on her way to night school* (Q15, 1973), referred to by Stephanie Donald in her chapter. The oldest in the illustrations reproduced in this book is the woman studying at night by the side of her sleeping child (plate 20 [Q18]), yet she could not be thought of as old by any standard. By contrast, older men regularly appear: as the arbiter of the young woman (Q6, *Graduation report*), the potential head of the household in *Starting the game* (plate 2 [Q7]), the old doctor, and elsewhere the old peasant. The combination of age and authority gave the male leader claims to a particularly elevated position. With few exceptions, such status is denied to representations of the female, as Robert Benewick's discussion shows. As in Soviet posters of the Stalinist era, youth, whether male or female, was a dominant association of the revolutionary future. Youth signified health and strength, determination and courage, as well as the possibility of transforming the socialist ideals of the present into the reality of the future. Gender distinctions in representations of older people clearly suggested another layer of signification that derived as much from the cultural associations of age as from the revolutionary associations with the future. As the political leader, the village elder, or the doctor, the old man enjoyed extra status by virtue of his age alone. Images of Mao Zedong surrounded by young girls and boys functioned to affirm his authority as much by reference to his age as anything else. Conversely, the image of the old woman enjoyed no such privileged association, though as Margery Wolf's work showed long ago, the lives of older women could suggest a very different experience.[25] In texts of the 1950s, the older woman was frequently honored as the mother of revolutionary heroes or volunteers in the Korean war. She appeared in similar kinds of roles in some of the model operas and films of the Cultural Revolution. However, she did not enjoy any authority through her age alone. Respect based on her age was necessarily mediated by her relationship to a man, here to her son. The erasure of the "old woman" in Cultural Revolution posters, therefore, may be seen as an uncritical application of certain cultural assumptions about women in a visual form oriented to future possibilities.

## Posters and Gender Discourses

Given the quantities and visual dominance of the kinds of posters discussed in this book, it is quite extraordinary that so little has been written about them in analyses of the forms of political control deployed during the Cultural Revolution. As we pointed out in the introduction, on the few occasions when they have entered the debate, they have rarely been treated as anything more than instruments of party political propaganda, whose messages were either transparent to a mass audience or relatively simply coded.

This exploration attempts to take analysis of the posters much further. It is, though, very far from complete. I have not looked at spaces from which women are absent or from which they are excluded. Discussion about the use of color and color symbolism, the discursive function of the exotic ethnic woman, and age could be much fuller. My analysis has not looked at images of male leaders, such as Mao, Zhou Enlai, and Hua Guofeng, that are inflected with signs of femininity, such as chatting to small children, patting them on the head, and so on. Limited though it is, however, my exploration suggests that a number of things can happen when one applies a gendered reading to the posters. Images of women were projected to convey a whole series of ideological meanings and messages that were not centrally, even partially, explicitly concerned with gender. Indeed, the poster bodies of both women and men were inscribed with a relentless narrative of party politics, revolutionary transformation, and the collective and national good. Yet this analysis shows that the visual forms and arrangements used to transform supposedly gender-neutral bodies into vehicles for externally formulated political messages disrupted the possibility of inscribing a univocal meaning in the image. This analysis shows that there are always rhetorical and discursive elements at work that undermine the possibility of unitary meaning.

Enough scholars have now written about the inconsistencies between the rhetoric and the lived experiences of women during the Cultural Revolution for the arguments I have put forward here to be unsurprising. The images I have described also belong to a past that to many seems to be irrelevant to the problems and needs of current development in China. Yet revisiting the gender discourse of these years by looking at the posters is important for a number of reasons. For a start, it acknowledges this particular visual form as more than a colorful and graphic aside to the mainstream messages of written and spoken political discourses. This analysis recognizes a particular kind of cultural production as a powerful component of a broader, already hegemonic discourse that rejected a language of gender at the same time that it utilized symbols of gender difference. It also suggests—and this would be crucial for an analysis of public response to the posters—that the visual cues denying women the possibilities of becoming full subjects were often displaced from the bodies of women into the scene and the relationships contained in it.

Looking at posters in this way demonstrates not only just how much can be read from them but also the extent to which they contributed to the totalizing discourse of the period. The party-state and its leaders were the most visible components and instigators of this discursive turn, this way of thinking and saying and describing the present. Yet for a mode of thought, speech, and visual description to be paramount , all cultural forms, and all the consumers and producers of those forms, must in some way accede to its limitations and vocabulary. Of course, as we discussed in the introduction, these posters could be, and were, read in different ways, conscious and unconscious, depending on both the perspective of the reader and the context of production and display. Women who grew up surrounded by these images have referred to them with a certain nostalgia for an irretrievable past; they could represent multiple and inconsistent meanings, as Xiaomei Chen, in this collection, shows. Many younger women, by contrast, associate them with an unwanted and inelegant "masculinist" position, regardless of the hierarchical gender meanings they betray. Within the context of my interpretation here, the subject positions offered within them, whether in reference to women or to men, to young people or old, to workers, peasants, or soldiers, by incorporation or exclusion, were established within binary closures, in which the absence of the alternative, the "other," reinforced the structures and meanings that were present. As models of revolutionary aspiration, the gendered images in these posters projected, not possibilities and explorations of gendered subject positions, but positions fixed by an ideological authority deeply and uncritically attached to a set of assumptions about who and what women and men were. The posters, like other discourses of the period, established boundaries of gendered authority, which neither women nor men were permitted to transgress. In this sense, these images did not simply introduce new possibilities for women to accompany the dictum of women holding up half the sky—though this was, of course, central to their appeal. They simultaneously consolidated a discourse of women's unequal entry into a public in which male dominance—call it dominance of the Party, the patriarchal father, the male symbolic order—was unquestioned.

A final point refers to more recent representations of women in China. Many writers and scholars, both in China and elsewhere, continue to maintain the view that the "refeminization" of public images of women in the early 1980s signified not only a rupture with the gender constructs of the Maoist years but also a "redefinition of the image of women—as non-threatening to male activities and positions."[26] With reference to visual representations, I would suggest, on the contrary, that the resumption of conventionally feminine images in the early 1980s was facilitated by the many visual—and other public—cues of gender hierarchy that I have examined here. My analysis also suggests that, first impressions aside, the poster figure of the woman never appeared to "threaten" the male in any contexts in which men were engaged as participants. Rather, the images we have seen projected a dual message that was already prevalent in the 1950s and before, of encouraging women to engage in the traditional masculine sphere of public endeavor while simultaneously reinforcing within that sphere a familiar hierarchy of gendered authority. With the disappearance of the class-centered rhetoric of the Cultural Revolution, the introduction of an urban-oriented program of market reform, and the emergence of a series of socioeconomic difficulties including competitive pressures on the labor force, many of the former, barely disguised assumptions about gender rapidly and easily made their public reappearance.

## Notes

1. '"Resolution to the Second Congress of the CCP," 1922, in *Zhongguo funü yundong lishi ziliao* (Materials on the history of the Chinese women's movement), ed. Zhonghua quanguo funü lianhehui funü yondong lishi yanjiu shi (Research Department of the All China Women's Federation on the history of the women's movement) (Beijing: Renmin chubanshe, 1986), 1: 29–30.

2. "Jinian guoji funü jie guangfan kaizhan funü yundong" (Commemorate international women's day and widely develop the women's movement ), in *Shaan-gan-ning bianqu funü yundong wenxian ziliao xuanbian* (Selected materials on the women's movement in the Shaan-Gan-Ning border region) (Xi'an: Shaanbei sheng funü lianhehui, 1982), 80–82. Xiang Ying elaborated a bit more on this aspect of *jiefang* in "Our Female Comrades-in-Arms": "Women's liberation and social liberation cannot be separated, and it is inappropriate to seek women's liberation detached from social liberation. . . . Women must participate in the revolutionary struggle and must unite with all revolutionary forces to struggle for the victory of the revolution, for only with revolutionary victory can the victory of women's liberation be won. . . . Women's liberation is the glorious future to social progress and the progress of mankind." *Zhongguo funü yundong lishi ziliao* (Materials on the history of the Chinese women's movement) 3: 409–10.

3. Deng Yingchao, "Zai Zhongguo funü di'erci quanguo daibiao dahui shang de gongzuo baogao" (Work Report at the Second National Congress of Chinese Women), 10 April 1953, in *Zhongguo quanguo funü lianhehui sishinian* (Forty years of the All China Women's Federation) (Beijing: Zhongguo funü chubanshe, 1991), 381–94.

4. Harriet Evans, *Women and Sexuality in China: Dominant Discourses of Female Sexuality and Gender since 1949* (Cambridge, England: Polity Press, 1997), 136–37.

5. Rae Yang, *Spider Eaters: A Memoir* (Berkeley and Los Angeles: University of California Press, 1997), 213.

6. Marilyn Young, "Chicken Little in China: Some Reflections on Women," in *Marxism and the Chinese Experience: Issues in Contemporary Chinese Socialism,* ed. Arif Dirlik and Maurice Meisner (Armonk, N.Y.: M. E.Sharpe, 1989), 253–68.

7. Emily Honig, "Maoist Mappings of Gender: Reassessing the Red Guards," in *Chinese Femininities/Chinese Masculinities,* ed. Jeffrey N. Wasserstrom and Susan Brownell (Berkeley and Los Angeles: University of California Press, in press).

8. The model operas and the films produced during the Cultural Revolution featured a number of older women as mothers of revolutionaries. Paul Clark also discusses the trope of the "old woman" in films of the 1950s and 1960s.

9. See, e.g., Margery Wolf, *Revolution Postponed: Women in Contemporary China* (London: Methuen, 1985); Phyllis Andors, *The Unfinished Liberation of Chinese Women, 1940–1980* (Bloomington: Indiana University Press, 1983).

10. See, e.g., Elisabeth Croll, *Feminism and Socialism in China* (London: Routledge, 1978); Wolf, *Revolution Postponed*; Young, "Chicken Little."

11. See Evans, *Women and Sexuality.* See also Emily Honig and Gail Hershatter, *Personal Voices: Chinese Women in the 1980s* (Stanford, Calif.: Stanford University Press, 1988).

12. Dani Cavallero, *The Body for Beginners* (London: Writers & Readers, 1998).

13. In her comments as discussant on the panel where a first short draft of this paper was first presented at the 1998 Association of Asian Studies conference in Washington, D.C., Carma Hinton suggested that one of the most evident inconsistences in these different layers of meaning was between text, as manifested in the slogan, and image. We have pointed out in the introduction as well that these distinct "layers" of meaning also suggested different spectatorial modes.

14. In visual closure, the abstracted or aesthetic qualities of the image can foreclose on other rhetorical qualities. In this way, the overt rationale is undermined by symbolic or ideological compositional factors.

15. Pierre Bourdieu, *In Other Words* (Cambridge, England: Polity Press, 1990), 53; Henrietta Moore, *A Passion for Difference: Essays in Anthropology and Gender* (Cambridge, England: Polity Press, 1994), 78.

16. Maybe it is not coincidental that this poster is of a Red Guard rebel; female activism and violence in the Red Guards was a prominent, though still not widely analyzed, aspect of the turbulence of the early years of the Cultural Revolution. See Honig, "Maoist Mappings of Gender."

17. Evans, *Women and Sexuality,* 172–74.

18. Victoria E. Bonnell shows that this was characteristic of Stalinist poster representations fixed within a redefinition of socialist realism. See Victoria E. Bonnell, *Iconography of Power: Soviet Political Posters under Lenin and Stalin* (Berkeley and Los Angeles: University of California Press, 1997), 39–46.

19. Ann Anagnost, "The Politicized Body," in *Body, Subject, and Power in China,* ed. Angela Zito and Tani Barlow (Chicago: University of Chicago Press, 1994), 131–56.

20. I am thinking here of the distinction that Homi K. Bhabha makes between difference and diversity in "The Commitment to Theory," *New Formations* 5 (1988): 5–23. He suggests that by contrast with the plural equivalence of "diversity," "difference"contains notions of power and hierarchy.

21. Of course, the association of women with color is, was, and continues to be common in art and popular thinking and is reflected in such words as *hao se* (literally, "to like color," i.e., to be a womanizer, to lust for women).

22. Evans, *Women and Sexuality,* 134–38.

23. *Hong, guang, liang* was a common term used to describe post-1971 Cultural Revolution art. See Robert Benewick's chapter in this volume, 125.

24. In her article "Gender and Internal Orientalism in China," Louisa Schein puts this orientalizing of the ethnic other in a different context when she shows how ethnic peoples subverted the attempts to impose Han control through putting their orientalizing images to good commerical use. See *Modern China* 23, no. 1 (January 1997): 69–98.

25. Margery Wolf, "Child Training and the Chinese Family," *Family and Kinship in Chinese Society,* ed. Maurice Freedman (Stanford, Calif.: Stanford University Press, 1970), 37–62.

26. Stefan R. Landsberger, *Chinese Propaganda Posters* (Amsterdam: Pepin Press, 1995), 144.

# 5

# Children as Political Messengers: Art, Childhood, and Continuity

*Stephanie Donald*

> The child is the basis of the family, and the family is the basis of the State. Therefore, the question of children is not just a children's question but a social question which we must not underestimate.
>
> —Xu Xingkai, 1926

## Art for Children?

In this chapter I examine representations of children in the posters of the 1960s and 1970s. The posters illustrated here include art *for* children as well as art *about* children. The images are generally unambiguous, highly colored, and strongly composed (e.g., *Every generation is red [Daidai hong]* [plate 23 (M39), 1972]; *A new classroom [Xin ketang]*, [M42, 1975]; *I accompany Grannie on her way to night school [Wo song nainai]* [Q15,1973]; *Awake late into the night [Shen ye bu mian]* [plate 20 (Q18)]). The predominant images are of primary-age children with rosy cheeks, chunky babies' bodies, wearing red scarves, and waving copies of the "little red book."[1] These children seem healthy, happy, and, above all, positive in whatever action they are engaged in within the frame. I conceive of these images as public and therefore shared by large groups of the population. I discuss the ways in which children are pictured, what they are doing, how they are positioned in the image, and the ways in which they are made to *mean* by the caption. These issues are part of a larger question: why are there children in the posters at all? Is it simply a matter of addressing child spectators (many posters about children were pasted on school walls or were used as mise-en-scène in films made for children),[2] or does it have more to do with the potency of childhood in the public imagination? In exploring this last suggestion, I look not just at the *peculiarities* of the Cultural Revolution, but also at the *continuities* between its cultural formation and that of earlier and later periods. My analysis suggests that the use of children as symbols in political and social systems of iconography is of a different order from, say, the representation of women, men, or particular adult groups. Representations of adults are often coded to support social attitudes towards particular groups in the population. As Harriet Evans argues in this book, posters supposedly represent women as holding up half the sky, but an analysis of the organization of the images reveals that gender bias is still very much in operation. Images of children do not quite fit into this same paradigm of contradiction. The posters declare, visually and in the captions, that children are active components of the body politic, with the narrative implication that, as such, they need to be educated into its ways. The reproduction of society through education is not unusual. What interests me here is the status of children in such politically motivated art forms. The children are active, but they are also heavily constrained. Their contribution to the image is partly educative but also partly intended to address the fantasies of adults. The children in the posters are interestingly poised between innocence and effectiveness. They are connected to "real" children only insofar as the constitution of emotional affect in these pictures illustrates that children have no tangible political power in the adult domain.

Children occupy a prime spot in the cultural configuration of our daily lives. The way in which a society conceives of itself—its structures, its priorities, and its taboos—is intimately associated with the way in which it conceptualizes the meaning of its children and of childhood in general. These meanings are neither universal nor unmarked by context. Where politics and society are closely aligned, as was undoubtedly true of the People's Republic of China for several decades at least, it is arguable that children are also subject to conceptualization within the political imaginary. In a recent interview, the revolutionary actress, and latterly director of the Children's Film Studio, Yu Lan, told me that there was too much violence on television for children.[3] When asked whether she thought this was like the violence in 1950s films about revolutionary children, such as *Jimao xin* (Chicken-feather letter, 1954)[4] or *Hong haizi* (Red children, 1958), she was shocked. "But that is not violence, it's revolution, those children were fighting for their country." Yu Lan's distinction between revolutionary violence and the casual brutalities of Hollywood and soap opera is a clear articulation of a way in which children can be understood as both "really" vulnerable to culture and "ideally" constitutive of its political resonance.

In invoking film memories, I am writing about the *idea* of childhood not about the experiences of actual children. The importance of keeping these two concepts separate—as objects of study—must not be underestimated. This is not to argue that the experiences of children and adults are not invested in cultural material nor that they may not be painfully reinvoked by visual stimuli. It is, however, to say that there are qualitative differences between daily life and its cultural manifestations. Revolutionary films about childhood are not descriptive of most children's lives, but they incorporate their intended audience into the filmic body, which is also a public body, to share and legitimate their ideals and adventures, "fighting for their country." The most successful retain their popularity even now, through an appeal to adult nostalgia for ideal childhood. In the past couple of years, many of these films have been reissued by China Film and Television on videotape and video disk and are widely available in Beijing. It is perhaps significant that, when I watched (or tried to watch) some "typical" revolutionary films with a friend who had been struggled against in the years of the Cultural Revolution, she found that she could not in fact see them through. Even films of the 1950s and early 1960s, which she had looked forward to revisiting, were impossible for her to enjoy. Their passion was, to her eyes, always already betrayed and now meaningless in retrospect. In this case at least, even nostalgia failed to overcome the barrier of experience.

## Childhood, Families, and the State

In traditional Confucian societies, children represented the continuation of the conceptual unit of social organization, the family. Childhood was understood as the period of moral and intellectual development that would ideally transform the infant into a filial, respectful adult, desirous and capable of returning his/her parents' attentions in kind. This was a masculinized version of social morality, with the duty towards one's father—filial duty *(xiao)*—both a private and a public expectation. A mother's love was private and confined to the infantile period (children under six years old), but it was the duty towards the father that defined the family's coherence and stability.[5] As the philosophers David Hall and Roger Ames have pointed out, the family was and remains a historical *institution*. Notions of family love do not necessarily apply to the concept of filiality, which is understood as a social relationship. The filial relationship has been as much an agent in the production of family stability as it is an expression of the affection of close kinship.

> The various kinds and qualities of love that can be elaborated through the traditional institution of the family have an unquestionable richness: filiality *(xiao)*, paternal affection *(zu)*, fraternity *(di)*, camaraderie *(yu)*. . . . But even as an abstraction, . . . the family is perhaps best regarded as a contingent institution that could, under different conditions, be replaced by a different, more appropriate, more meaningful communal organisation.[6]

In modern Western societies, children have also been given—since the seventeenth century—something called childhood. At about this time European children began to be distinguished from adults by dress, material responsibilities, and language. This "discovery" of childhood, as Philippe Ariès describes it, allowed adults to distance children and "own" them not just in body but also in fantasy.[7] Ariès does not claim that pre-seventeenth-century mothers did not love their children, nor that women—and men—all over the world do not love their children. He simply suggests that at a certain point this love became available to fetishization, the child became an adored doll rather than a fellow worker. Of course, in this idea of the child, factors of class and gender play a major role in determining the availability of this discovery of childhood and of the possibility of Confucian or other modes of education. In the following quotes Ariès refers to a well-to-do eighteenth-century Parisienne, Madame de Sévigné:

> 'Our daughter is a dark-haired little beauty. She is very pretty indeed. . . . She gives me sticky kisses. . . . She kisses me, she recognises me, she laughs at me, she calls me Maman. . . . She blows a kiss, she shrugs her shoulders, she dances, she strokes, she holds her chin; in a word she is pretty in every particular. I watch her for hours on end.'[8]

Ariès's point is that a literary woman finds her child's childishness worthy of record. Childhood has become a legitimate spectacle for refined adult attention. If we compare this affectionate French child with the mother and daughter in a poster extolling the one-child policy; *One child is enough (Du sheng zinü yizhi hua)* (H17, 1980), we find another pretty, dark-haired girl, kissing her young, feminine mother, against a background of flowers. The flowers, which flutter prettily in the foreground also, echo the frilly dress worn by the child and the strands of loose hair that stray around the mother's face. This is a female and childish world, framed for our admiration and approval. We may watch it "for hours on end."

Watching children is a way of recapturing their privilege of youth. Part of that privilege is often characterized in memory as freedom from responsibility and a willingness to adventure. That freedom is, however, curtailed in cultural products by the demands of education and good behavior. This curtailment is due to the necessary limitations of being in public. Family life becomes part of the public domain by virtue of watching the one-child embrace of mother and daughter. Where parents are absent in the posters, then adult spectators, as well as the authority of the captions, take their place in the act of public spectatorship. The absence of parents or their absorption into the symbols of state authority draws the children into a direct relationship with the state, no longer mediated by intermediate figures in their ideological appropriation. In some posters, therefore, the apparent freedom of childhood is channeled into national concerns, "revolution," "fighting for the country," under the watchful eyes of those looking at the image. For them, the romance and "mischief" of childhood mitigate the brutality of the visual narrative, whereas their implied presence controls the anarchy of the children's actions.[9] Representations of childhood anarchy have not always been so mindful of public order. The 1930s cartoon character Sanmao (Three hairs) is a street kid with three hairs on his head and a bulbous nose. As the historian of Chinese children's literature Mary-Ann Farquhar has noted, he was extraordinarily popular. "As Xia Yan wrote in 1950, Sanmao was not just popular, he was loved: 'Sanmao is a most familiar creature in Shanghai; . . . children like him and pity him [as though he were] a real flesh and blood child of misery.'"[10]

Sanmao is still popular. His story has been retold in a television series on CCTV, and there have been sequels to the original 1949 classic film version of his sufferings, *Sanmao liulang ji* (Sanmao on walkabout, 1949). However, his endearing brand of needy mischief is almost entirely absent in the posters of the Cultural Revolution and the reform era. There is an echo of his mischief in one poster in the collection, but it promotes disturbingly violent patterns of behavior—for national ends rather than cathartic support for a child trying to survive an adult nightmare. *The Children's Corps thinks up a plan to kill devil [Japanese] soldiers (Ertong tuan zhi sha guizi bing)* (figure 5.1 [M35], 1978) was produced two years after the death of Mao and the end of the Cultural Revolution, yet its content is reminiscent of the violence of the Red Guard brigades. The poster is organized as a comic strip *(lianhuanhua)*. In the first illustration, two boys, whose red scarves identify them as members of the Children's Corps, stand arm-in-arm. They seem healthy, happy, and ready for action. The firmness of their stance is specifically *action* packed rather than *fun* filled. To their right, three soldiers walk miserably off frame. They are "Japanese"—but the iconography would also suggest Guomindang (Nationalists). The boys huddle together, plotting their line of attack. Our eyes are drawn to a large watermelon in the center of the poster. The hungry enemies are rushing to pick it up. It contains a grenade, cunningly placed there by our sweet young heroes, and the soldiers are blown to smithereens—in a way that only cartoon and animated drawings can really achieve. The boys then head off with the spoils: guns, ammunition, and a couple of backpacks. It is an extraordinary sequence. Its anachronistic nationalism, the Sino-Japanese war (1937–1945) being over many generations earlier, and its bizarre combination of cartoon comedy and murderous narrative motivation confuse playing life with real life, mimesis with anarchy, and here creates a sickening bastardization of the serial comic strip.

斗争生活出艺术 劳动人民是主人

Plate 1 [L17]. *Art comes from a life of struggle; the working people are the masters (Douzheng shenghuo chu yishu; laodong renmin shi zhuren).* Shanghai 1974.

Plate 2 [Q7]. *Starting the game: the Red married women's team, iron maidens, in friendship first and competition second (Shang chang: hong dasao dui, tie guniang youyi diyi, bisai di'er).* N.p., n.d. (slide only).

Plate 3 [E20]. *At the pledge meeting (Shishi hui shang).* Shanghai 1975.

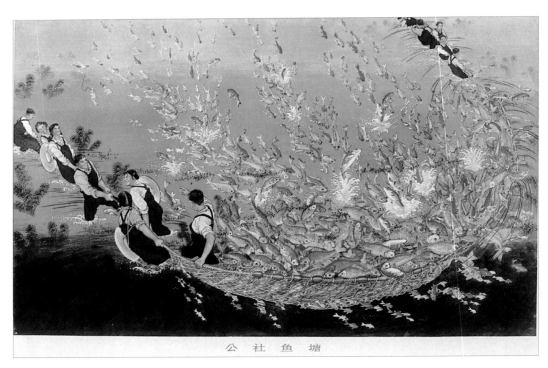

公 社 鱼 塘

Plate 4 [A9]. *Commune fishpond (Gongshe yutang),* by Dong Zhengyi. Beijing 1974. First printing, second impression, 1,000,001–1,370,000.

Plate 5 [C6]. *New style shop (Shangdian xin feng)*. Shanghai 1974.

Plate 6 [N35]. *Chairman Mao goes to Anyuan (Mao zhuxi qu Anyuan)*. Beijing ca. 1967.

Plate 7 [A7]. Dazhai aerial view. Anonymous. N.p., n.d.

Plate 8 [E23]. *The Iron Man spirit will be handed down from generation to generation (Tie ren jingshen daidai xiangchuan).* Heilongjiang 1974.

Plate 9 [E35/E36]. *Continue to carry out the campaign to criticize Lin Biao and Confucius in a penetrating, widespread, and enduring way (Ba pi Lin pi Kong yundong shenru luoji, chijiude jinxingxiaqu)*. Shanghai 1974.

Plate 10 [Z29]. *New Year's Eve in a collective houshold (Jiti hu zhi chuxi zhi ye)*. Shanghai 1977.

Plate 11 [A25]. *We are determined to settle down in the countryside (Zha gen nongcun zhi bu yi)*. Shanghai 1974.

Plate 12 [Z27]. *A new flowering of village culture: the use of scientific farming methods will result in great fruits (Nongcun wenhua kai xin hua, kexue zhong tian jie shuo guo)*. Shanghai 1974.

Plate 13 [Z26]. *Goldfish baby (Jinyu wawa)*. Tianjin 1979.

Plate 14 [B10]. *The future summons us (Weilai zai zhaohuan)*. Shanghai 1980.

Plate 15 [E27]. *The main lesson (Zhu ke).*
Beijing 1975.

Plate 16 [A46]. *The new look of Dazhai (Dazhai xin mao).* Beijing 1974.

Plate 17 [D12]. *Revolutionary friendship is as deep as the sea (Geming youyi shen ru hai).* Shanghai 1975.

Plate 18 [Q17]. *Doing military drill at first light (Shu guang chuzao yan bing chang).* N.p., n.d.

Plate 19 [Q23]. *Women's Day channel (San ba yin shui tong).* N.p., n.d.

Plate 20 [Q18]. *Awake late into the night (Shen ye bu mian).* Shanghai, n.d.

Plate 21 [E37]. *Revolutionary proletarian Right to Rebel troops unite! (Wuchanjieji geming zao fan pai lianheqilai)*. Jilin 1967.

Plate 22 [H5]. *Countryside medical station (Shancun yiliao zhan)*. Liaoning 1974.

Plate 23 [M39]. *Every generation is red (Daidai hong)*. Hebei 1972.

Plate 24 [M20]. *Joining the Young Pioneers (Ru dui)*. Shanghai 1980.

Plate 25 [M4]. *Presenting flowers to model workers (Xian hua song mofan).* Beijing 1978.

Plate 26 [M25]. *People's Liberation Army uncles are working hard (Jiefangjun shushu zai da gan).* Shanghai 1978.

立志做坚强的革命后代

Plate 27 [M40]. *Determined to be strong revolutionary successors (Lizhi zuo jianqiang de geming houdai).* Hunan 1965.

Plate 28 [H7]. *The sprouts are fat, the flowers big too, one plump baby's enough for you; girls are tough, boys are strong, it doesn't matter which you have (Miaor fei, huar da, zhi sheng yige pang wawa; nüer qiang, nanr zhuang, sheng nan sheng nü dou yiyang).* Jiangsu 1980.

这次无产阶级文化大革命，对于巩固无产阶级专政，防止资本主义复辟，建设社会主义，是完全必要的，是非常及时的。

Plate 29 [N8]. *For consolidating the dictatorship of the proletariat, guarding against capitalist restoration, and establishing socialism, the Great Proletarian Cultural Revolution could not be more necessary or timely. (Zhei ci wuchanjieji wenhua da geming, duiyu gonggu wuchan-jieji zhuanzheng, fangzhi zibenzhuyi fupi, jianshe shehuizhuyi, shi wanquan biyaode, shi feichang jishide).* Beijing 1976.

Plate 30 [N11]. *Chairman Mao's rural investigations in the Jinggang mountains (Mao zhuxi zai Jinggangshan nongcun diaocha).* Beijing 1971.

毛主席视察广东农村

Plate 31 [N51]. *Chairman Mao inspects the Guangdong countryside (Mao zhuxi shicha Guang-dong nongcun)*. N.p., 1972.

延安新春

Plate 32 [N13]. *New spring in Yan'an (Yan'an xin chun)*. Shaanxi 1972.

Fig. 5.1 [M35]. *The Children's Corps thinks up a plan to kill the devil [Japanese] soldiers (Ertong tuan zhi sha guizi bing)*. Shanghai 1978.

"Sanmao turns very nasty" or "Bart Simpson goes to South Park" might be a suitable alias for these boys and their melon.

## Models

It is not surprising that a revolutionary poster should engage the body of the citizen–political subject in its ideological rhetoric. The aim of direct ideological address is to confirm the subjects of the state as working components of the body politic. As I describe the posters of children, however, it seems that children are doubly subjected. Their bodies are symbolically called into the service of the state according to current requirements, while also carrying an emotional appeal to the adult spectatorship. They are in this way ascribed meaning that is firmly linked to political, adult prerogatives.

In all the posters, children are shown as every parent might want them, happy, healthy, and, above all, diligent in the cause of society and country. The bright colors, clean lines, and simplicity of the designs address children themselves but are also mindful of the general audience. The aesthetic is in part adapted from New Year posters (*nianhua*).[11] Nianhua are New Year pictures, woodblock prints made to celebrate each new year. They developed from symbolic "paper gods" and are essential to the public and private décor of the festival. Nianhua depict signs of youth, wealth, and good fortune, and children are an important part of that nexus. The legacy of nianhua style and content is strong in political poster art.[12] New Year prints encapsulate optimism from the perspective of the peasants, which translates easily into an expression of collectivity in a communist world.

> Much Government support was given to New Year's prints because they were a people's art, because they reached the largest percentage of the population, and because through them the new ideology and socialist goals could be quickly purveyed to the population at large.[13]

The posters in the collection bear heavy traces of the optimism and brightness of New Year pictures. From fat babies, surrounded by traditional icons of wealth and prosperity (*"Health, long life, and happiness are on the way [Jiankang changshou xingfu lai]*, M9, 1981), to a serious little girl placing a Young Pioneer scarf around the neck of a new recruit (*Joining the Young Pioneers [Ru dui]*, plate 24 [M20], 1980), these children epitomize the claims of the state and the desires of their parents. The perfect fit of such representation is due to an aesthetic that addresses the desire of the adult spectator, while fulfilling the iconic and discursive demands of the patron, the state. All these children are doing what is expected of them, and doing it prettily.

In *Presenting flowers to model workers (Xian hua song mofan)* (plate 25 [M4], 1978), a smiling girl holds out a huge orange chrysanthemum bloom. In the top of the frame, smiling heads of exemplary "model" workers look down on her. As with many posters, the flower fixes her childishness as a prettiness. The text is in the same shade of orange as the flower, which shades into the skin tones of the child's face. The color associates the child with the discursive parameters of the text and the decorative façade of the flower. She gains ideological meaning and context from this composition, but no space of her own.

In her work "Socialist Ethics" Ann Anagnost is careful to distinguish the disciplinary tactics of Foucauldian governmental discipline from "the willed consent of the people" inherent in Confucian and Maoist model-based educations.[14] The Foucauldian model imposes modern systems of surveillance through institutional organization. Models, however, are figures of influence rather than authority. They are associated with the discourse of power, in a symbiosis in which they return a moral legitimacy to the ideological source of their own preeminence. The long-established use of models in Confucian education has also given the method an embedded efficiency in revolutionary structures of mass reception. In the dynamics of everyday social life, argues Betty Burch, models provide four motivations to their fellow citizens: imitation, inspiration, competition, and emanation.[15] Their power comes from their status as "true stories" or, in local cases, as someone who might be your neighbor.

Model workers are incorporated icons of the body politic. They are ordinary citizens selected for public emulation because of their virtue.[16] National models tend to have died in serving the national cause. Even child models who featured as heroes and heroines in children's storybooks of the 1960s and 1970s die horrible, but noble, deaths.[17] Despite the early deaths of their protagonists, these stories establish the Party as a surrogate parent and ultimate protector of the new revolutionary family. Their actual parents are either killed or already absent when the narrative begins. In *People's Liberation Army uncles are working hard (Jiefangjun shushu zai da gan)* (plate 26 [M25], 1978), a smiling girl, against a background of flowers, is preparing water bottles for soldiers. The soldiers themselves are not in the image but are represented by their paraphernalia—hats, insignia, and water bottles. The most telling signifier is a booklet with a cover portrait of Lei Feng. Lei Feng was a model soldier whose iconic influence is still invoked when the government embarks on campaigns against spiritual pollution. The movement to learn from Lei Feng was first inaugurated in 1962, and he became nationally revered in 1963. His presence in the poster sublimates the girl to the anticipated presence of the revered, and literally avuncular, People's Liberation Army (PLA). Her value is in her emulation of the soldiers' inferred model behavior, just as the previous poster values the child for her appreciation of the model behavior of others. The domestic setting reemphasizes that her "family" consists of agents of the state, "PLA uncles."

In *Joining the Young Pioneers* (plate 24 [M20]), Young Pioneers are celebrated as models of children's behavior. (Many of the national child models are first introduced as Young Pioneers or join up just before martyrdom.) The occasion pictured is the formal acceptance of new recruits, standing brightly to attention, by older children who place a red scarf around the recruits' necks. The scarf symbolizes a corner of the national flag, stained red by the blood of revolutionary martyrs. The "conformist activist" interviewee in Anita Chan's study of revolutionary childhoods remembers her Young Pioneer scarf as an object that was endowed, in this very public world occupied by children, with almost sacred value. On one occasion, she mislaid her scarf and was first punished and then rewarded for her suffering by the ceremonial bestowal of a replacement scarf.

> 'It is a corner of the red flag. It's dyed red by the blood of the revolutionary martyrs. That's why we cherished it so much. If you dirtied it, they scolded you. Once I lost mine; the teacher asked me again and again, but I refused to tell how [she doesn't tell us either!]. The teacher punished me by making me stand. I stood for a long time. For several weeks I was not allowed to put on a new scarf. I cried and cried in front of the school office. At last they gave me another one, in a big and impressive ceremony. . . . Wow those enrollment ceremonies were so impressive.'[18]

The woman remembers herself as a small girl whose public status is dependent on a red scarf. Children commonly wean themselves away from the mother-child dyad by attachment to a transitional object, a scruffy soft toy or a piece of cloth. This child is trained to enter into another transition through an attachment to a quasireligious object. The scarf signifies her place in the designated public space for children. Her passion for it simultaneously allows her access to the privileged world of adults. Both spaces are determined by the reproduction of political agency and do not address the child's need to develop individual motivations and characteristics. Chan also interviews children who unconsciously subvert model behavior by being *too* good or *too* diligent in their public duties. These children's energies are not pictured in the posters I have seen. The Young Pioneers were replaced by Red Guard brigades during the Cultural Revolution. *Joining the Young Pioneers* and these reminiscences perhaps tell us more about an orderly childhood, desired by the post-Maoist state in its own nostalgia for the remembered simplicities of the 1950s. This poster organizes children, it does not unleash their energies into a political whirlpool of recrimination as happened in 1966 and 1967. It should perhaps be understood as a public antidote to the remembered anarchies of childhood in the period 1966–1968.

In *Joining the Young Pioneers* the children stand to attention on a platform hedged in front by rows of tulips, balanced by a set of steep vertical perspectives: children, flag, pine trees, aerial tower. The children are literally cut off from a domestic adult world by a crisscross of vertical and horizontal motifs. The space that they *are* accorded within the frame is highly organized and immobile. The tulips are particularly interesting. Flowers are often used to demarcate the space of the subject of a particular picture and in so doing soften the image as a whole. These flowers, however, are so tightly packed that they resemble the children standing in rows behind them. The children wear red scarves, the tulips are also red, and the text outside the frame *(ru dui)* is red too. The flowers strengthen the overall effect of discipline and order. At the same time, the youth of the protagonists is underlined by the presence of flowers. The effect is to ensure that these children encapsulate the optimism of the present and the hope of the future, while their incandescent innocence incorporates and sanctifies the revolutionary past.

Flowers are often pictured with or around the children—plates 24 (M20), 25 ([M4), and 26 ([M25) have already been mentioned—but in some the flowers are given additional symbolic status: *The flower of friendship blossoms (Youyi hua kai)* (M17, 1980) pictures Chinese and non-Chinese girls with flowers. Whether realistically or decoratively motivated, the flowers establish the childish world of the images, while serving as an important compositional aid to closure. (*Closure* refers to the way in which elements of the image, including human figures and space, are balanced and contained within the frame and how this encourages the spectator's understanding of the image.) Metaphorically, if the poster were a room with a single door, these flowers would stand in front of the door and prevent the children from "getting out" and the spectator from "getting in." The implication of closure in this context is that the visual cues contained in the text are so strong as to positively discourage an ironic, against-the-grain interpretation of the poster's intended message. Meaning in these posters is organized for the spectator, who may reject or question its political surface but who is expected to enjoy its mode of address. This is because these images are addressed to the fantasies of adults, as well as to the imaginations of children.

Despite the proliferation of images of children in the posters of the 1960s and 1970s, children's representational access to public space is, at best, ambiguous. Children are depicted to attract adult attention and also to offer models of behavior to real children. Any idea of representing children outside these limitations is absent. Conversely, the transfer of adult concerns into the symbolic world of children represents a disavowal of mature responsibility. It is as if the rationalities of political discipline produce an adult craving for the irrational wonderland of childhood. These contradictory drives to educate and escape produce a hybridized cultural product. In the case of the posters, this is characterized by a positively exuberant aesthetic, combined with a firm, occasionally brutal, political content. Hence the profusion of flowers is both a signifier of the natural and a configuration of visual control.

These representational practices are not confined to this particular political moment. There are parallelisms (visual expressions that vary in content but are close in form or style) that underline the importance of the relationship between childhood and adults, as much as between childhood and a particular national-political configuration, that is, 1966–1976. There are parallels between posters made during and after the period of the Cultural Revolution. Icons of political activism—Mao badges, "little red books," and weapons—are replaced with the paraphernalia of Deng Xiaoping's Four Modernizations: science equipment, symbols of wealth *(fu)*, reading books, hankies (clean ones to stress the need for hygiene in a modernizing society).[19] These motifs and patterns suggest certain symbolic changes in cultural practice. Nonetheless, the match of highly charged ideological investment with a similarly charged, although disavowed, adult attachment to childhood makes the images of children in the posters of the Cultural Revolution particularly powerful.

## Succession and Nationhood

Succession and nationhood are central themes of poster representations of children, sometimes constructed through direct reference to the authority of the word, at others through the foregrounding of symbols of leadership and revolutionary power. The continuities between these methods are such that the visual character of the written word is clearly apparent in the structure of meaning in the posters. Furthermore, the use of children as political messengers, carrying the power of the word, is refined to the point where their representation is itself a message of political optimism and revolutionary success(ion). This is perhaps unsurprising given the famously extended power of the word in Maoist China. Transferred to the printed political primer, it organized public and private consciousness around the *written* thoughts of the national leader, Mao Zedong.[20] So, how does the pictorial iconography of posters, along with the written slogans and descriptions that accompany the image, relate to the other language-centered aspects of the Cultural Revolution: the chanted slogan, the use of revolutionary language in everyday social communications and education, and the extraordinary status of Mao's written thoughts? It seems that the answer involves a very fluid approach to language and speech. The authority of the written text over the image of the poster seems clear, but that is not to deny the symbolic power, and even autonomous organization, of the pictorial composition. A poster that extols the potential of womanhood, *Lofty aspirations touch the clouds (Zhuang zhi ling yun)* (figure 4.1 [Q4]), is spatially organized around a Mao badge worn on the work clothes of a brave woman telegraph engineer.[21] The badge is tiny, but in compositional terms it is central to the image and operates as a fulcrum without which the structure of the painting collapses. So here there is tension between one text, outside the frame, and an iconic symbol within it. It is a tension that we can also understand as complementary. Women's aspirations may indeed be lofty, but the authority for their ambition comes from the person of the leader, Mao Zedong. In posters where children are the main protagonists, it is not so much a question of their status being fixed by iconographic trumps as that the figures of the children are themselves used as symbolic "fixers" of meaning. Their very presence in the frame gives legitimacy to the subject of the text. Thus in *PLA uncles* (plate 26 [M25]), the child stands in for the PLA soldiers, lending their work a picturesque credibility, which both charms and convinces.

The *sound* of language is of a different order from the written forms, which are used in the posters' inscriptions. Yet there is a connection between the two in an active revolutionary context. Mass mobilization among the whole population and the reproduction of revolutionary awareness in the young produce a symbiotic closeness between the revolutionary *body* of the citizen, the *voices* of the people, and the *texts* of revolutionary discourse. The depth of this association can be gauged by its pervasive endurance across the decades. Anita Chan's interviews in the 1980s showed that children of the Cultural Revolution generation could give voice to the *spoken* revolutionary word years after the events themselves:

> As an interviewee she is marvellous: her narration is the least tarnished by her current interpretations and feelings. In recounting her stories . . . *she got so carried away in her excitement that her voice broke into the same cadence as Peking [Beijing] radio; the same high-pitched, urgent, imposing, strong, gung-ho tone of voice*. I have become convinced she was able to do this so naturally only because she had internalized with the deepest conviction the same values propagated by the radio broadcasts.[22] (my emphasis)

In an early memoir/history of the Cultural Revolution, Liu Guokai also acknowledges the power of the voice: "People still cherish fond memories of the massive and solemn demonstrations, emotional mass rallies, deafening shouting, and writings sparkling with new ideas."[23] Both Chan and Liu acknowledge the sound of the voice. An association between body and word produces the voice, and these tones, shouts, and emotions are signs of the word's presence in the corporeal memories of the people interviewed.[24]

Chan and Liu's accounts show how the word is corporealized in speech. In the posters, written text is obviously present in the form of a caption, but its compositional alignment with the figures of children also produces an embodiment of the word. In conjunction with color and general composition, the word limits the representational space of the picture's object and thereby determines the meanings available to the spectator.

The written word is central to the spatial organization of *Determined to be strong revolutionary successors (Lizhi zuo jianqiang de geming houdai)* (plate 27 [M40], 1965). A boy and girl stand looking across frame towards the national flag, which mirrors their position. The boy holds the national flag, and the girl, her hand resting protectively on his shoulder, carries the *Works of Mao Zedong* clasped to her chest—but not covering the Children's Brigade badge pinned to her blue dress.[25] On the wall behind them is a painting of a revolutionary battle scene, the Dadu Bridge crossing during the Long March in the early 1930s. The caption, separate from the main image but noticeably large, tells us the thoughts of these children: "determined to be strong revolutionary successors." In their work on revolutionary discourse, David Apter and Tony Saich draw on Foucauldian theory and write of "exegetical bonding."[26] They describe the way in which an ideologically motivated discourse is tied to versions of history, the meaning of images, and the value of people, places, and political positions. Once that discourse achieves linguistic hegemony, it becomes almost impossible to conduct legitimate verbal dissent—or debate—outside the parameters already fixed. The association between the words, status, and image of Maoism with the children, the national flag, and recent history affords these words—both the caption and the inferred contents of the girl's precious book—great authority. It also deprives the children of any interest beyond their historical status as a bridge between the events of the past and the promises of the future. Their political status is identical with their public presence. As subjects of the ideological discourse of revolutionary inheritance, they are central to the image. As children on their own account, with immediate needs and priorities, they are invisible.[27]

Succession is also emphasized as a thematic bind on children's status in *Every generation is red (Dadai hong)* (plate 23 [M39]). Here, however, the depiction is more literal than in my other examples. The poster is organized to cram generations, location, and activity (class) into the frame. This poster shows children on a hillside. The girl in the center foreground is practicing her spear technique, and two boys stand waiting their turn. An old man is overseeing the practice. Behind the central group, peasants are harvesting fruit, and in the background is a standard depiction of the Great Wall and rolling hills. A thin strip of sky marks the horizon. The first obvious comment is that, although apparently enjoying themselves (the younger boy is smiling encouragement at his companion), these children are not playing, they are *in training*. Even in this image, straining under the representational demands of its subject, there is some sense of the continuity of the children's bodies beyond the immediate identification of the 1970s generation. The title of the poster, as well as the importance to the composition of the figure of the old man, places these children's bodies in a continuum of revolutionary activity and commitment, *every generation is red*. While the peasants in the background seem relaxed in their work—one turns to talk with the man behind her—the children are entirely concentrated on the task at hand. The generations are coded by red clothing, scarves, and, in the old man's case, a sword sheath. They are connected by the apparatus of struggle and the symbolic unity of pre-reform Communist iconography, national defense in the context of benign agricultural nationalism. The Great Wall positions "all generations" as defenders of the nation and national history. This strip of sky, in formal distinction to much traditional landscape painting—including the blue and green *(lanqing hua)* echoed in this color scheme—is extremely slight. Its tiny proportion to the Chinese nationscape and the Chinese revolutionary generations is unambiguous. There is nothing to be discovered on the horizon.[28] All generations are red, *and* all generations are in China.

In later posters, the themes that are so expertly tied together in *Every generation is red* (plate 23 [M39]) and *Determined to be strong revolutionary successors* (plate 27 [M40]) are still apparent but tend to be separated into discrete images. In *Babies look at a new picture (Wawa kan xin tu)* (figure 5.2 [M29], 1979), two babies (boys) look at a picture, "We love our homeland," which features children painting other children in front of Tian'anmen. The centrifugal arrangement of the image ties all the children in the multiple frames to the nationally significant space, Tian'anmen, in central Beijing. The baby boys have a few toys, books, and a wooden train and sit by an open window that looks out over ploughed fields. The foreground is broken by a bunch of flowers, by now a familiar reminder that these boys are part of a careful composition. Their focus, not on the toys nor out of the window, but on the "new picture"—and its text (which, presumably, they cannot understand)—situates the babies' interest in other children. This is refined to a statement of national sentiment both by the text "we love our homeland" and by the placing of those other children in the symbolic center of national power. Meanwhile, the view through the window positions them as babies in a broader, romantic vision of Chinese rural life. Finally, the books provide a link to the world of education, fundamental to the socialization of a new generation. As Bourdieu has

Fig. 5.2 [M29]. *Babies look at a new picture (Wawa kan xin tu)*. Shanghai 1979.

argued, the point of education is to reproduce society.[29] That theoretical perspective is neatly summed up in this poster. At some point these baby boys must learn to read the captions to their own representation.

Education is a developing theme on its own account in later posters. Spear practice, parades, agricultural work (as in *A new classroom [Xin ketang]*, M42, 1975—a picture of planting rice) are supplanted by scientific experiments. In *We love science (Women ai kexue)* (M33, 1978), children work with scientific instruments; in *Chart for preventive exercises for the eyes (Yan baojian caotu jie)* (H1, 1979), they do exercises to safeguard eyes when studying; and in *Isn't our life wonderful! (Women shenghuo duomo meihao)* (M8, 1980), they practice the violin; these are just a few of the injunctions to press forward in the service of the country's development. In these compositions, battlegrounds, rural scenery, agriculture, and the peasantry are replaced by computers and oil fields; sometimes there is also a textual transliteration to accompany the characters of the caption. A poster extolling science, *First experiment (Chu shi)* (figure 5.3 [M24], 1978), shows a girl using a microscope with two other children behind her. The continuity from earlier themes is marked by the absence of a parental figure. The authority of the written word binds the children into the intensity of the moment. They are young scientists, engaged on their first experiment, working against the background of national development. The frame is cluttered with references to the job of science and education. There is no unused space in these compositions. The meaning is determined by the clutter of signifying matter (also a hangover from the "busy detail" of the nianhua),[30] which fixes the children's context in the discourse of national regeneration. These children have no family, no history, and no secrets.

Fig. 5.3 [M24]. *First experiment (Chu shi).* Shanghai 1978.

## Playing

Growing up occurs in the imaginative excesses of play and baby speech. It is partly a question of discovering the meanings of the adult world and partly a process of making it your own. Playing insulates children against the full violence of adulthood, giving them time to try it out and reject it, *fort da,* again and again. The children in the posters do not seem to play, however. Everything is "for real." What then is the status of children as growing, developing human subjects in these highly politicized images? Where do children play? When can their attention wander out the window? This is not a plea—or not simply that—for children to have the right to stop listening and start fooling around. It is a serious questioning of a visual rhetoric that appropriates children's time and space and produces a symbolic public presence that leaves no room for anything (un)social or truly childish.

Children learn to embody themselves through copying the world in which, and the people among whom, they live. Playing, the beginning of mimesis, is the child's first and major form of communicated action.[31] Through fantasy or make-believe, children juxtapose personal psychic reality and the experience of control of actual objects. In this way they literally come to grips with the world around them. Play is disturbing when it is apparent that the adult world is not only informing the fantasy of children's play but also appropriating children's playful energy for adult ends. I would place *Every generation is red* (plate 23 [M39]) in this category. Play can also identify the moments at which adult activity is dangerously immature, insofar as the playful, mimetic version is *too* similar to its inspiration in form and content. There are examples of this below, in my descriptions of children on film. Play can also be most apparent by its absence, and that is the most significant category in the poster collection.

In an introduction to a special exhibition of children in art in Taiwan's National Palace Museum, the curator remarks, "Children are, by nature, simple and innocent. They express themselves spontaneously, and they love to play" *(ertong sheng er tian zhi huofa, xi'ai you wan xi zhan).*[32] The pictures included in that exhibition, from the Tang through to the Qing dynasties, a period spanning over nine hundred years, demonstrate that children do indeed love to play and that adults love to watch them playing. Their supposed innocence is less obvious and is better understood as an explanatory trope of the spectating adults—including the curators at the Palace Museum. Paintings of children at play *(ying-h'si t'u [ying xi tu])* and paintings of children engaged in physical fun *(hs'i-ying t'u [xi ying tu])* developed during the Southern Song (1127–1279). The genre soon became associated with festivals and general expressions of well-being. This tradition of children as icons of good luck continues in auspicious paintings, including, of course, the New Year decorative posters. Representations of children have also, however, long been tied to the theme of public duty, as opposed to private love, as the art historian Wu Hung has described in an analysis of funerary urn reliefs in the first and second centuries A.D.[33] These parallel histories are important if we are to appreciate the centrality of the figure of the child both in decorative popular art in China and in the visualization of children's public description in Chinese societies.

The paintings of children playing share formal features as well as a general feeling *(qi)* of energy and barely contained exuberance. In *Lantern Festival (Deng qijie),* late Qing, anonymous, album leaf, ink and color on silk), a large group of children is playing with lanterns, kites, and a lion-dancing mask. Some (the girls and younger boys) stand on a low balcony while older boys fool around on an open space two steps below them. The play area is framed above and to the left by a twisted pine that curls protectively around two thirds of the frame. The right-hand corner of the painting is left open, however, the children's movement curtailed by the formal method of having the child on the fringe of the action looking back at another child, their eyes locked in a secret game. The inscription on the painting is brief and minute in proportion to the figures and the tree. It is placed in the top left-hand corner, above the curl of the tree's furthest branch. It gives the merest context to the scene, *Lantern Festival,* without attempting to fix further the spectators' reception of the work. Other paintings and details that include children allow for a similar pictorial autonomy. Children are permitted to play by themselves. Adults, if present at all, peer through windows, or fan the children in the attitude of a servant, or simply ignore them. In one scene, *The Peddler* (Li Song, 1126–1243, Song Dynasty), a mother is present, breast-feeding her youngest child. Her other children, assuming that they *are* her children, cavort unheeded around the eponymous peddler.[34] It is as though for most of the millennium that preceded our own, adults unproblematically allowed children a representational space of their own. Playing is the child's contribution to her own development, and in these pictures it is valued through the allocation of pictorial space and compositional integrity.

If we look at filmic representations of young children in both Taiwan and the People's Republic of China, we see that they are still playing, with kites, cranes, shadow puppets, tortoises, and radio-controlled airplanes. The filmmakers of the 1980s and

1990s have identified play as *the* site of representation that will produce a narrative space for the child. In *The Ice Flower (Lubing hua)* (Yang Liguo, Taiwan, 1989), a film hugely popular on the mainland as well as in Taiwan, the plot revolves around contradictory value systems in the appreciation of children's art. Good draftsmanship and pedantic realism please the reactionary adults. The best artist of this type in the film is an official's son. The connotation is obviously that political organizations prefer images that are ordered and leave little to the imagination. Expression and genius, exemplified in the talents of the son of a poor tea grower, are encouraged by the free-thinking art teacher. In the end the teacher loses his job, the genius dies, and the reactionaries appropriate his talent in a stiflingly official ceremony, organized to apologize for ignoring the boy's potential.

*The Blue Kite (Lan fengzheng)* (Tian Zhuangzhuang, 1993) is a film that is almost unknown on the mainland—it was banned in 1993. It is a historical epic structured around the life of a boy between 1953 and 1967, and the finale is structured around the violence, immaturity, and anarchy of the Cultural Revolution, as well as earlier phases of China after Liberation. The film refuses to separate the Ten Years of Chaos from the rest of twentieth-century Chinese history. The violence of that history is made appallingly clear through play. In one fraught scene, the boy, Tietou, mimics adult violence by banging a drum, thus acknowledging the infiltration of political violence into his own domestic space, the family home.[35]

*The Blue Kite* is a self-conscious retelling of recent Chinese history. The posters were part of the cultural formation of that history. The film's acuteness lies in part in its central association between playing and politics. The concept of play is generally associated with toys—which we might call playthings. We need to be sure what is meant by that concept. Toys may be understood as objects specifically produced for a child to play with or as found objects that are mimetically transformed into playthings by childish attention. They may be used symbolically by adults to cut children off from the "real" world, or they may be appropriated by children to build a bridge between the worlds that they inhabit—fantastic, mundane, private, and public. Toys can be whatever promotes the inception and playing out of fantasies in a child's life and imagination. Toys may also function in adult fantasy as a metonym for childhood itself. In *The Blue Kite*, the kite is a metaphor for Chinese sociopolitical experience, while a toy drum helps the boy externalize trauma.[36] In the posters, there are very few recognizable toys, but there are objects, some of which might—for actual children—have offered the same panoply of fantasy and practicality as a baby doll. In the posters, however, the element of fantasy and privacy is absent. Children practice with spears, fill water bottles, read and wave Mao's "little red book." The child asleep as the mother studies is an exception, and the toy is an airplane (plate 20 [Q18]). But the toy is also a reference to Mao's reported desire for more airplanes and fewer Mao badges. In a post-Maoist poster celebrating a toy fair in Tianjin (*A happy generation [Xingfu de yidai]*, M28, 1978), a group of children stands in front a huge tower of playthings; they clutch some new possessions, but they still do not play with them. It is a strange image. The children look out front in a direct address to the audience, as though waiting for permission to play. The toys in the background bear the same spatial relationship to these young consumers as the oil fields to the budding scientist and the grape harvest and Great Wall to the spear warriors. These toys are still not there to be played with but to prompt a new generation to the duties of capitalist consumer culture. Cultural theorists Zhao Bin and Graham Murdock have written about the fad for "transformer toys" that hit urban Chinese children in 1989. Parents queued for hours to spend enormous sums on a toy that supposedly combined fun with educational value. For Zhao and Murdock, playing has marked out the new generation of post-Maoist China.[37]

> Is this the pattern of the future? . . . The children caught up in the Transformers craze in 1989 are now in their mid-teens. They were the first generation in modern [post-Liberation might be more accurate?—author's note] Chinese history to grow up in a culture of consumption, the first to play with the economic distinctions and imaginative landmarks of capitalism, the first to experience the sheer joy of possession and to grasp its ties to identity.[38]

It remains for future research to establish whether this is really the first generation "to experience the sheer joy of possession and to grasp its ties to identity." There are open questions on the relationship of children to their Maoist paraphernalia, Red Guard uniforms, or Young Pioneer scarves. Zhao and Murdock are perhaps too readily affirming the attraction of international consumer goods over the power of investment that young people bring to available objects. Nevertheless, the near absence of playthings in representations of children in the Cultural Revolution should not go unremarked.

Tian Zhuangzhuang takes the argument a bit further. He feels that children are treated as though they were toys themselves, entirely at the disposal of adults.[39] This opinion is borne out by posters about the one-child policy such as *Fat sprouts (Miaor fei)* (plate 28 [H7], 1980), in which the caption reads:

> miaor fei, huar da, zhi sheng yige pang wawa
> nüer qiang, nanr zhuang, sheng nan, sheng nü, dou yiyang
> The sprouts are fat, the flowers big too,
> One plump baby's enough for you.
> Girls are tough, boys are strong,
> It doesn't matter which you have.

A mother cuddles her little girl. They are surrounded by flowers and butterflies. The child holds a pen in one hand, but her arms are around her mother's neck. The mother looks at a book, maybe a storybook, maybe a book of her daughter's drawings. The poem, quoted above, is printed in pink, with soft fat characters. The flowers are pink or orange, and both mother and child have pink decorations in their hair. The poster celebrates femininity, girl children, the one-child policy, and maternal affection. Images such as this not only indicate the shift in ideological priorities from the Cultural Revolution to the reform period; they also indicate how easily visual strategies of address can be modified to suit new—or reemerging—themes. There were plenty of flowers in Cultural Revolution posters, but they were not there to extol the significance of maternal-child relations, or not explicitly. Posters depicting girls and women were also marked in ways that feminized the subject, as Harriet Evans discusses, with the effect of replacing gender hierarchies while insisting on material equality. Here too, while the mother-and-child genre does position two or more women as objects of mutual regard and emotional contact, it also identifies their space as apolitical and without any recognizable public signification. The mothers and daughters are generally surrounded—suffocated, one might say—by flowers. This sentimentality and deliberate lack of public signification could be taken for a strategy of trivialization. On the one hand, female viewers are asked to take the one-child policy seriously. They are persuaded by a child's rhyme, which reminds them of their love for children, which is immediately counterbalanced by the explicit instruction to value a girl as a boy and therefore not to want more—excess—children in the hope of conceiving a son. The message is underlined by the image of the comfortable delights of a loving daughter. The poster hints at the possibility of fulfilling her educational needs and at the internal coherence of the mother-child relationship. Here is a dyadic bliss uninterrupted by further pregnancies and the demands of other children. Yet in this appeal to the woman to comply with necessary public behavior there is no sense of her *public* place. She and, by extension, her child are suspended in a floral wonderland. The flowers do not simply feminize, they also implicate the mother in the negative public status of her offspring.

The appeal to childhood may have another, associated motivation. Authoritarianism teaches adults to fear maturity, as it brings with it responsibility, most pertinently, ethical and political responsibility. Talking to an adult *as an adult* becomes a truly dangerous exercise and perhaps an emotionally difficult one once the perceived danger is past. The cultural repercussion of this fear of maturity is an excessive reliance on the intercession of children. Images of children will tend to combine visual control with a rhetoric of innocence and sentimentality. The grown-ups indulge their desire for the political ignorance by activating nostalgic—or ideal—appeals to the child. The child becomes, perversely, a silent (and silenced) spokesperson for the curtailment of adult speech. This gives rise to children as models, as we have already observed, and also produces children as monsters. The children in the melon poster are monsters because the cuteness of their appearance belies the savagery of their imaginations. Model children are also cute, but their strength is generally displayed in direct response to attack or victimization. Models, and monsters, are produced by an adult desire for sweetness and a gentle expression of ideological limits. In the posters of Maoist China the child is represented as both a responsible actor in society's struggles and a symbol of society's denial of the harsh pervasiveness of political demands.

## Conclusion: Political Messengers?

The idea of children as political messengers is on one level quite literal. In posters and films of the Liberation and Cultural Revolution periods, children often carry secret information. In films, the adventure narrative is often structured around the child as messenger between the army and Party informers. In the film *Zhangge: A Little Soldier (Xiaobing Zhangge,* 1963), a boy actually forgets his message when he finally locates the Eighth Army agents—he is much more interested in getting his own gun. In *Jimao xin* a boy hides a message under a sheep to keep it safe from his Japanese captors. The story of the heroine Jiang Jie (played by Yu Lan), *Lian luo zhong yong sheng* (Living forever in burning flame, 1965) features a little child who carries messages between prisoners in a Guomindang jail, and the final message of hope arrives tucked into a baby's diaper: "Start to prepare—it is time to escape for the Liberation!"

In posters, the message is conveyed through a juxtaposition of the child, or children, with a didactic caption fixing whatever is "meant" by the organization of the image. The caption might carry "extra" information that is delivered by the children as messengers. In the posters in the Westminster collection, it is more a case of the children embodying a general message of optimism about any and all aspects of current revolutionary ideals. It is the presence of the children that determines the quality of the message. This is not a phenomenon reserved to revolutionary culture.

> Childhood is always a moment before, once it is contaminated it is lost. . . . It is as if the child serves to sanction that concept of a pure origin because the child is seen as just such an origin in itself. The child is there and the original meaning is there—they reinforce each other.[40]

Jacqueline Rose's analysis of the English children's classic *Peter Pan* includes an amazingly simple, yet pertinent, observation. She points out that *Peter Pan* was not written for children at all. Its classic status has much more to do with the way adult desire is satisfied by this tale of unending boyhood and girlish maternal instincts than it does with its address to children as readers. From this standpoint, we can argue that childhood is "contaminated" not (or not only) by the destruction of "innocence", nor by the exploitation of children's ideological potential, but by *representations* that capture a *version* of childhood that is both sweet and amenable to adult desire, whether that be sexually or politically motivated. The images of childhood in the posters of the Cultural Revolution and the reform era and in the enduring iconography of picture books and baby dolls address an adult audience through its desire for innocence, or ignorance, and through the actual sweetness of the young.

After all, children are, or are supposed to be, adorable.[41] They are often round cheeked, big eyed, and bouncy. If they are dressed in vibrant, "primary" colors, they stand out in our visual field. These attributes suggest themselves to the adult as a site for displacing and purifying the harsh realities of everyday existence. As political messengers, children work with a perverse neutral potency in political and social cultural production. They appeal to adults' nostalgia. They stimulate desire for, and a delusive belief in, the natural and sequential order of things. Children's bodies represent to the adult an imaginary state of plenitude. They are therefore valuable signifiers of a hopeful future, sullied neither by the complexities of mature political and social organization nor by the vicious simplicities of political suppression. Their symbolic presence is required to cleanse the adult imaginary world of its pervasive, necessary dirt. Yet their presence offers false hope. The problem lies in the toll it takes on the symbolic status of children as potential political agents. The linchpin of this version of the adult's image of a child is that it cannot progress, it cannot be heard to speak using the same dirty language as the adult political subject. In the posters of the Cultural Revolution and beyond, and arguably in many representations of children worldwide, their voices are stifled by textual determinism. Their transgressions are excluded from representation. Their energy is pictorially channeled into education and training for the reproduction of the social and political status quo. The real potential of children, their potential to develop into mature political and social agents, is lost in a bright, clean-cut symbolic servitude. The image of the child absolves the adult world of its failures by presenting a nostalgic present that is sweet, tenderly recognizable, and entirely fictitious.

In this chapter I have developed two arguments concerning the representation of children in the cultural sphere. The main focus has been on posters and the ways in which images of children are used to carry particular political messages to the public. I have primarily been concerned with an adult public and the nature of adult psychic investment in the figure of the child. The inclusion of children in revolutionary material represents their importance to the nation, as conceived within a particular political project of cultural totality. It is also an inclusion that aims to interpolate adult appropriations of the state of childhood for their own cultural pleasure in a strategic bid for their political attention in public space. My second point has been that, in order to make this first argument, it is important to look outside the bounds of the period, and the medium, under immediate discussion. The posters of the Cultural Revolution period do not reinvent art quite as thoroughly as might have been hoped by supporters of extreme change at that time. Nor, however, does the reform period move entirely away from models of representation that were explored in the programs of Jiang Qing and her apologists. Images of children continue to exemplify desirable patterns of behavior and to address adults. Posters are still available in Beijing that extol the "four loves": love your teacher, your classmates, your environment, and physical exercise. They are, however, subordinated to municipal photo-signage that shows children picking up litter on sunny, tree-lined avenues and to the backlit blandishments of Heinz foods to feed your baby on canned food. The baby on the Beijing subway system is a miniature Superman bursting with energy and almost busting through the picture. He wears a red stretch suit against an imperial yellow background, his color coding incorporating the energy of current national obsessions with Hong Kong–style advertising[42] and convenience food. He is auspicious, modern, and, in the cause of commerce, an effective call to adult attention. He is also alone. There are no parents in the image, just Superbaby and a can of Heinz food. I began this chapter with a pre-Liberation reference to the position of the child in the family. Posters of the 1960s and 1970s are organized around a notion of the revolutionary family, and the logical progress in the quotation, from child to family to state, is replaced by an elision of family and Party, and of Party and state. Whereas the images of mothers and girls-daughters counteract this practice, the Heinz baby reinvents it. John Gittings remarks that the poster died by the middle of the 1980s, making way for television and the advertisement. These new posters continue to employ children as messengers in Chinese public space.

## Notes

1. They are young "political activists" *(jijifenzi)* and, as such, are extremely important in the cultural landscape.

2. See, e.g., the animated film *Caoyuan yingxiong xiao jiemei* (*Little Sisters of the Grasslands*, 1964) and the classroom scenes in *Zuguo de huarduo* (*Flowers of the Motherland*, 1955).

3. Yu Lan, born 1921, joined the Communist Party in 1939, starred in *Lin Family Shop* (1959) and *The Flames of War* (1965), and started the Children's Film Studio in Beijing in 1981. *Zhongguo dianying da cidian* (Dictionary of Chinese film) (Shanghai: Shanghai Publishing House, 1994), 1248–49.

4. Letters "with feathers" were coded top priority during the revolutionary war and the war against Japan.

5. Wu Hung, "Private Love and Public Duty: Images of Children in Early Chinese Art," in *Chinese Views of Childhood*, ed. Anne Behnke Kinney (Honolulu: University of Hawaii Press,

1995), 96–97; Margaret Mead, "Monkey: A Chinese Children's Classic," in *Childhood in Contemporary Cultures*, ed. Margaret Mead and M. Wolfenstein (Chicago: University of Chicago Press, 1955).

6. David L. Hall and Roger T. Ames, *Thinking through Confucius* (Albany: State University of New York Press, 1987), 120–21.

7. Philippe Ariès, *Centuries of Childhood: A Social History of Family Life* (Harmondsworth, England: Penguin Books, 1973), 31 ff. First published in French as *L'enfant et la vie familiale sous l'ancien régime* (Paris: Librairie Plon, 1960).

8. Ariès, *Centuries of Childhood,* 47.

9. See Rudolph G. Wagner's notion of the "implied pilgrim" in "Reading the Chairman Mao Memorial Hall in Peking: The Tribulations of the Implied Pilgrim," in *Pilgrims and Sacred Sites in China*, ed. Susan Naquin and Chün-fang Yü (Berkeley and Los Angeles: University of California Press, 1992), 378–423.

10. Mary Ann Farquhar, "Children's Literature in China" (Ph.D. diss., Griffith University, Australia, 1983), 207. See also Mary Ann Farquhar's chapter "*Sanmao:* Classic Cartoons and Chinese Popular Culture," in *Asian Popular Culture,* ed. John Lent (Boulder, Colo.: Westview Press, 1995), 139–58.

11. See Stefan R. Landsberger's discussion of the adaptation of traditional pictorial models in *Chinese Propaganda Posters* (Amsterdam: Pepin Press, 1995), 21–24.

12. This summary is derived from Stefan R. Landsberger's very helpful website on the subject, "New Year Prints (and chubby babies)," *Stefan Landsberger's Chinese Propaganda Poster Pages,* <http://homepages.infoseek.com/-landsber/nh.html>. Accessed 23 October 1998. See also Joan Lebold Cohen, "Peasant Painting and New Year's Painting," in *The New Chinese Painting, 1949–1986* (New York: Harry N. Abrams, 1987), 144–49. For illustrations, an account of early influences, and transition to peasant-amateur art, see Ellen Johnston Laing, *The Winking Owl: Art in the People's Republic of China* (Berkeley and Los Angeles: University of California Press, 1988), 14–16, 18–20, 83–84.

13. Laing, *Winking Owl,* 20.

14. Ann Anagnost, "Socialist Ethics and the Legal System," in *Popular Protest and Political Culture in Modern China: Learning from 1989,* ed. Jeffrey N. Wasserstrom and Elizabeth Perry (Boulder, Colo.: Westview Press, 1992), 177–205, see 193. A repro primer from the 1960s (special collections, Murdoch University) still endorses the Confucian virtues through sage models: filiality, brotherly love, loyalty (*zhong*—often reinvoked on Mao badges in the 1960s), honesty, courtesy, righteousness, purity, sense of shame, justness (*gong*—a sense of public duty), uprightness, firm adherence to rites of order, candidness.

15. Betty B. Burch, "Models as Agents of Change in China," in *Value Change in Chinese Society,* ed. Richard W. Wilson, Amy Auerbacher Wilson, and Sidney L. Greenblatt (New York: Praeger, 1979), 122–37, 124.

16. The model citizen is also sometimes constructed through rule books—manuals of model behavior. One such was recently put together for the citizens of Tianjin and included a mishmash of political control ("don't put up unauthorized character posters or graffiti"), public hygiene ("don't spit"), and general guidelines on conduct ("love your country and native place and care about the collective"). Thanks to Michael Keane of Griffith University, Australia, for giving me this information.

17. All references to children's picture books come from a special collection held at Murdoch University Library. Models include Liu Wenxue, a boy martyr who died protecting communal property from an unjust landlord, and Huang Lianying, who survived the brutality of a landlord but lost her parents in the process of fighting him. Her story is a model version of "*shuo ku*" (speaking bitterness). Liu Hulan, a girl freedom fighter lauded by Mao, "A Great Life! A Glorious Death," had her story turned into a film in 1950 at the Northeast Film Studio. *Zhongguo dianying cidian,* 593.

18. Anita Chan, *Children of Mao* (Seattle: University of Washington Press; London: Macmillan, 1985), 28–29.

19. This has now developed into child-centered and mother-child images public information

notices on the subject of environmental hygiene, placed at bus stops in Beijing (1998).

20. Besides a reference to the three essential articles of Mao's Thought, the *lao san pian* (382), Rudolph Wagner describes how Hua Guofeng mimicked Mao's calligraphy—the phenomenal trace of Mao himself—as part of the symbolism of the Map Memorial Hall in Tian'anmen. Wagner, "Reading the Chairman Mao Memorial Hall," 398.

21. See Harriet Evans's discussion of this poster in "Comrade Sisters," chap. 4, this volume.

22. Chan, *Children of Mao,* 19.

23. Liu Guokai, *A Brief Analysis of the Cultural Revolution,* ed. Anita Chan (Armonk, N.Y.: M. E. Sharpe, 1987), 140.

24. Film scholarship also reveals an attachment to the word in Chinese cinema, either through excessive dialogue or through nondiegetic plot material—that is, material outside the world of the story, such as voice-overs, intertitles, commentaries, and so on. In her work on cinematic exhibitionism, Paola Voci suggests that conventions of Hollywood narrative, although present in Chinese films, are from the late 1930s onwards undermined by a direct address of the narrator. (Paola Voci, "The Aesthetics of Dissent in Chinese Cinema: Choosing Shots to Say What Words Do Not" [paper presented at the American Asian Studies Association meeting, Washington, D.C., March 1998]). Rey Chow and Xudong Zhang have also noted the significance of the written word in the film *King of the Children* (Chen Kaige, 1987); see Rey Chow, *Primitive Passions: Visuality, Sexuality, Ethnography, and Contemporary Chinese Cinema* (New York: Columbia University Press, 1995), 108–41; and Xudong Zhang, *Chinese Modernism in the Era of Reforms* (Durham, N.C.: Duke University Press, 1997), 282–85. On a slightly different tack, Cheng Jihua, a major voice in Chinese film criticism, speaks of the literary adaptation as the "walking stick" of cinema.

25. Michael Schoenhals points out that this badge alone dates the poster to no later than 1965, since after that date the youth movements were broken up and children reformed as members of a vast number of factional Red Guard brigades.

26. David Apter and Tony Saich, *Revolutionary Discourse in Mao's Republic* (Cambridge: Harvard University Press, 1994), 263–93.

27. Similar points are made, in reference to both revolutionary and contemporary China, in Ann Anagnost's article on childhood in a national context. I read this piece after completing my own research but would like to acknowledge here its clarity and helpfulness in considering childhood as a subject of serious analysis. Ann Anagnost, "Children and National Transcendence in China," in *Constructing China: The Interaction of Culture and Economics,* ed. Kenneth G. Lieberthal, Shuen-fu Lin, Ernest P. Young (Ann Arbor: Center for Chinese Studies, University of Michigan, 1997), 195–221.

28. For further discussion, see Stephanie Donald, "Landscape and Agency: Yellow Earth and the Demon Lover," *Theory, Culture, and Society* 14, no. 1 (February 1997): 104–6.

29. Pierre Bourdieu and Jean-Claude Passeron, *Reproduction in Education, Society, and Culture,* trans. Richard Nice (London: Sage, 1977).

30. Laing, *Winking Owl,* 20.

31. Stephanie Donald, "Chinese Cinema and Civil Society in the Post-Maoist Era" (Ph.D. diss., University of Sussex, 1996), 27–34.

32. Song Liyi, foreword to *Paintings of Children at Play* (Taipei: National Palace Museum, 1997), 2.

33. Wu Hung, "Private Love and Public Duty," 86–87.

34. This is also illustrated in Ellen Johnston Laing, "Auspicious Images of Children in China: Ninth to Thirteenth Century," *Orientations* 27, no. 1 (January 1996): 47–52.

35. Donald, "Chinese Cinema," 27–38.

36. In an interview with the author in 1998, the director, Tian, explained that flying a kite represented being part of Chinese society. One was always on a string, and freedom was limited by the length of the string and the unavoidable necessity to return to the ground or to be lost and tangled in a treetop.

37. Zhao Bin and Graham Murdock, "Young Pioneers: Children and the Making of Chinese Consumerism," *Cultural Studies* 10, no. 2 (1996): 201–17. Zhao and Murdock are looking at a

generation born after Mao's death. James Watson has written of a new cultural identity in a slightly older generation and makes the point that members of the 1989 student generation were too young to remember Mao as a "bad" authority figure. Hence his reemergence on the cultural scene through popular iconography. James L. Watson, "The Renegotiation of Chinese Cultural Identity," in *Popular Protest and Political Culture in Modern China: Learning from 1989,* ed. Jeffrey N. Wasserstrom and Elizabeth J. Perry (Boulder, Colo.: Westview Press, 1992), 67–84.

38. Zhao and Murdock, "Young Pioneers," 216.

39. Opinion expressed during an interview with the author, Beijing, 1998.

40. Jacqueline Rose, *The Case of Peter Pan, or the Impossibility of Children's Fiction* (Basingstoke, England: Macmillan, 1984), 19.

41. This comment is not so much a judgment on children per se as a summation of the many cultural depictions of children in European, American, and Chinese visual traditions. Or, more loosely, it is a comment based on a widely shared expectation that children "should" be adorable—a great problem for those who fall short of an arbitrary standard and interpretation of the word at any given time.

42. All the advertising on buses and metro systems in China's twelve largest cities and Hong Kong is managed by a coordinating agency, Top Result. Over a relatively short period of time, Top Result's access to public spaces across the PRC will challenge the memory of political visual campaigns of the revolutionary periods.

# 6

# Growing Up with Posters in the Maoist Era

*Xiaomei Chen*

How is the Cultural Revolution remembered? More to the point, is it remembered in a way that accords with its all-important role in modern Chinese political and cultural history? The official culture of the People's Republic of China (PRC) would erase it as an unprecedented "ten-year disaster," the darkest period in history, for which a previous political regime must be held accountable. It is this sort of amnesia that led to setting aside forbidden areas of national and local libraries for classified documents issued by former leaders of the Chinese Communist Party (CCP) during and after the Cultural Revolution. Recent studies by scholars in China, in spite of their advertised challenges to this state of affairs, only seem to ratify the official view; that is, they call for a shift from focusing on political events and the power struggle within the party hierarchy to examining the problematic mentality of the masses who carried out "the Great Proletariat Cultural Revolution." The negative national characteristics of the Chinese people and of traditional Chinese culture, for these scholars, touched off and intensified the massive violence, betrayal, cruelty, and indifference that characterized the Cultural Revolution. Other aspects of their inquiry, which emphasize the discursive metaphor of political power, the traditional concept of "loyalty to kingship" *(zhongjun),* and the national spirit of the Chinese, succeed in assuring that the Cultural Revolution will be remembered as a chaotic event, one without agency and in which no subjects were to be held responsible. These views expunge the connection between earth-shaking events as they occur in history and the mystified participants and collaborators, who cede their authority as witnesses to, and owners of, that history. Some scholars, for instance, judiciously point out that the Cultural Revolution is selectively remembered in the memoirs of former Red Guards, whose narcissistic gaze has the effect of incriminating others. In the process of explaining why they have "no regret for their lost youth" *(qingchu wuhui)* and "no regrets about the Red Guard experience" *(hongweibing wuhui),* they relegate the past to the past, present themselves as sacrificing their adolescence on the altar of duty, and construct themselves as glorious and charismatic, while portraying others as ignorant and reprehensible.[1] Relaying this perspective from the vantage point of the present, they enjoy assuming the guise of innocent idealists in order to deny their own role as partial propellers of the Cultural Revolution.

However, China no longer holds the copyright on this type of selective memory, nor is it the special property of a small circle of Chinese communities. Increasingly, American and other international best-seller lists host Cultural Revolution memoirs—written in English and geared to the interests of an English-speaking audience—that proffer horror stories of Maoist China in which the Orient is seen seeking salvation from an exalted Occident. The 1980s and 1990s saw a surge of this type of economic and cultural capital flowing from Asia to the West, carrying with it an East Asian subjectivity reconstructed for global consumption. In many of these works, a pattern emerges in which the narrators come off as heroic while they invest others with the role of persecutor. These memoirs read like stories of survival, culminating in the obligatory happy ending in America or Europe.

One of the interesting features of many of the dolorous accounts of China is the revelation of the tumultuous emotions surrounding the use of posters in the Cultural Revolution. In her very popular *Wild Swans*, for example, Jung Chang conveys the initial sense of chaos that posters created in her life. Following directly upon the initiation and spread of the Maoist cult in June 1966, signaled by the appearance in print of full-page likenesses of Mao with his quotations in bold letters, Chang, like many other people, started putting Mao's portraits up on the wall. Her action was prompted by a story she had seen in the *People's Daily* about a local peasant who had hung up thirty-two posters of Mao in his room, presumably so that he could be inspired from all directions at once. Chang took the posters down, however, when she learned that the journalist involved had been branded a counterrevolutionary, for it turned out that the peasant actually used Mao's portraits—printed on the best-quality paper—as free wallpaper.[2] Similarly, Chang's "surge of emotion"on beholding the large portrait of Mao in Beijing Railway Station was extinguished once it became clear to her that she could only catch a glimpse of his back from afar during his review of the Red Guards in Tian'anmen Square. Thus this familiar spectacle, represented in numerous posters of the Cultural Revolution, paradoxically smashed her hopes, once and for all, of ever getting a close look at Mao—after all the hardships she had been through, including "bursting trains," "blocked toilets," and the exhausting, long pilgrimage to Beijing from southern China.[3] Readers who lived through that period might well understand how the popular scene depicted on posters of passionate Red Guards being received by the benevolent Mao could end by highlighting, for many less fortunate Chinese people, the impossibility of their ever participating in such an act.[4]

If Chang's asexual treatment of the posters of the Cultural Revolution hinged on political horror stories, Anchee Min's use of posters in *Red Azalea* evoked a China whose politically demonic system kindled a steamy homosexual encounter in the countryside, where Min and another teenage girl struggled to survive hard labor and emotional trauma. To contextualize her intense bodily resistance to temptation, Min, in the early pages of the book, relates how she maintained her equilibrium with the help of posters of CCP heroines in model revolutionary operas: "I grew up with the operas. They became my cells. I decorated the porch with posters of my favorite opera heroines. I sang the operas wherever I went. My mother heard me singing in my dreams; she said that I was preserved by the operas."[5] Min nevertheless was consumed by sexual desire: "The restlessness overtook me like the growing back of the reeds, from nowhere. It was the body. That must be it. Its youth, the salt. The body and the restlessness worked hand in glove. They were screaming in me, breaking me in two."[6] So powerful was the "monster of desire" that it drove Anchee Min to chasing mosquitoes every night, pinching them "to death," playing with their "long legs," and watching one "insert its tiny strawlike mouth into" her skin, "feeling its bite."[7]

Her sexual body screaming out against her disciplined, heroic body, Anchee Min yields to the tender body of Yan, her lover. Until now, Yan herself had been a typical Maoist woman with no observable interest in sexual activity—in fact, she combined all the admirable traits of the model opera heroines, such as Wu Qinghua, represented in Cultural Revolutionary posters. Ironically, it is the message given off by their prison-like life on the farm that heterosexual love is forbidden—as symbolized by the death of their comrade Little Green—that brings about Yan and Anchee Min's lesbian experience, and it is that same life that eventually drives them apart. For Western audiences, the fundamental appeal of *Red Azalea* may be its negative depiction of a demonlike China, which prohibits any freedom of expression, including the freedom to show love, whether heterosexual or homosexual. At the same time, this politically bleak and culturally alien land of the other is exoticized with a forbidden erotic lesbian experience, reconfirming the hellish nature of China.

With such paradoxes of alienation and desire, posters played their part in cross-cultural constructions of the miserable other, placed strategically at the center of dramatic events, to be gazed upon by a global audience. I believe that the posters, along with the popular China-bashing memoirs, were useful during the post–Cold War era to enhance the nationalism of an America—and a West—whose hegemonic position was beginning to be challenged. In this manner the United States could uphold its role as "international policeman" by constantly replaying the record of the suffering other who needed to be rescued from the socialist camp, just as it remained perpetually fascinated by the stories of Holocaust survivors, toward whom it had acted in the role of savior. Such an enhancement of American neonationalism could also include at least the United Kingdom, where *Wild Swans* and *Red Azalea* were first published; both books reinforced, if not an exactly equivalent UK nationalism, at least a sense of the Cold War wisdom about the superiority of Western liberal values over those of the socialist camp.[8] The Cold War tension between China and the so-called free West—a persistent theme reflected by posters even before the Cultural Revolution—refers to a geopolitical landscape not really foreign to the post–Cold War era, whose spirit is traceable in *Revolutionary friendship is as deep as the sea (Geming youyi shen ru hai)* (plate 17 [D12]). This picture is complicated, however, by its problematic resonance with some approaches to cultural and postcolonial studies. The poster depicts an essential bond between the Chinese and the developing world, which assumes resistance to Eurocentric, colonial, and neocolonial world orders and hegemonies. The ideal of class, gender, and racial equality as pictured here could also describe the agenda of liberal arts in some intellectual institutions in the West. This is a complex situation for any adequate reading of this poster and the cultural and political environment climate in which it was produced. The question of how to avoid a conflation of Western preoccupations and recent Chinese perspectives informs my reading, and I will return to it at the end of this chapter. Furthermore, the countryside background of this poster, in which Chinese peasants pose with their African friends beside a tractor, might invite postcolonial scholars once more to construe Third World natives as the main force in history making. They would be peering through the very lens of Mao's theory of world revolution, which privileged the countryside as the vast seedbed of revolution that would eventually surround and overpower the isolated cities occupied by the rich and powerful few in the First World.[9]

Although they were primarily intended to represent the binary oppositions of good/evil, liberator/oppressor, China/superpowers, and past misery/present happiness, the posters of the Cultural Revolution lent themselves to more than one-dimensional readings. The intricacy of the visual form is best illustrated in some other poster stories, such as that contained in Gao Yuan's *Born Red*, one of the precursor texts of Cultural Revolution memoirs that shocked Western audiences with its depiction of the Red Guard–caused mayhem, which brought the country to the brink of civil war. As middle school students ardently throwing themselves into the Cultural Revolution, Gao Yuan and his classmates tried to decipher the counterrevolutionary slogan supposedly hidden in the wheat field in a painting (at the back of *China Youth* magazine) that depicted young people happily gathering a bumper harvest. This sort of vigilant search for counterrevolutionary art prompted one student to point out that the portrait of Mao in their classroom showed only his left ear, a "serious political problem" on the part of the artist who had thus dared to insult the great leader. Other students, however, defended the artist, saying he had merely pursued the kind of "artistic realism" that Mao himself promoted. Heated debates of this type provoked ever more frantic searches for class enemies, with one student declaring, for example, that a snake was to be seen on Lenin's nose, while another argued that it was only a shadow. One student even unearthed a sword hanging over Mao's head in a picture of the leader standing on the rostrum in Tian'anmen Square, although everyone else argued that it was "only a painted beam."[10] The feverish detective work spread from posters to novels, films, plays, and even to the nonverbal form of dance. The day after the performance of a recital, for instance, posters appeared on school walls denouncing one of the dances as having distorted the image of peasant girls. "Nothing was immune from suspicion,"[11] since people were merely following Mao's call to eliminate feudal, capitalist, and bourgeois culture, in keeping with the revolutionary spirit of the 1871 Paris Commune, commonly glorified in the fashion of *Long live the dictatorship of the proletariat (Wuchanjieji zhuanzheng wan sui)* (figure 6.1 [F1], 1971), a later variation of the earlier Red Guard posters around 1966.

These narratives illustrate the ignorance, confusion, and chaos constituting people's responses to posters, as well as their use as possible evidence for persecution. These stories also point up the posters' power in generating a multiplicity of meanings and subject positions, especially when scrutinized across time and history and through the labyrinth of memories and the changing of positions amid diverse cultural experiences and ideological backgrounds. To complement other essays in this volume, in the following pages I retrieve my own experience of growing up with posters, returning to the early 1960s before the Cultural Revolution, when I was touched, intrigued, and indeed constructed by the posters that offered me space to play in what seemed like a simple world of bright colors and thrilling events. I hope that my account of "growing up there in the 1960s" will set off a dialogue with other scholars, including those represented in this book, about their experiences of "going there in the 1970s." Yet as an insider looking *in* again from the *outside* seventeen years later, I want to ensure that an academic memoir such as mine does not become a privileged site for cultural representation of a past life; for I must admit that the memoir is at every turn narrated from my present subject position as a Western-trained academic struggling to find the most constructive and effective way to represent China in the diaspora. With that in mind, I recognize that a journey into my past can help me sort out the role I undertook in my own culture and clarify for myself the constructive roles I might like to take on in writing and teaching about my culture and that of others, both here and

Fig. 6.1 [F1]. *Long live the dictatorship of the proletariat (Wuchanjieji zhuanzheng wan sui).*
Beijing 1971.

in China. Using my own perspective on the story of posters, I hope ultimately to
address the question of what is at stake when memory is retrieved and represented in
cross-cultural and transnational contexts.

I grew up in a culture where posters remembered, talked back, and also constructed and reconstructed who I was and what was socially expected of me. Born into
a family of theater artists, I believed that, following the example of my parents, who
were devoted to representing workers, peasants, and soldiers on stage, I must learn
from these same cultural models in order to reform myself into someone who was
acceptable to them. Thus, from an early age, I willingly subjected myself to subalterns,[12] sharing "their" dream of building an ideal society in which men and women—
rich and poor, educated and uneducated—could, through their collective efforts, share
equally in wealth and happiness. Indeed, I first encountered the image of the subaltern
through my father, who was a determined, self-taught painter. A leader of the team of
stage designers handling the sets, costumes, and lighting of the China Youth Art Theater *(Zhongguo qingnian yishu juyuan),* my father was celebrated for his abstract,
imaginative blueprints for the theater's productions, which reflected the nation's cultural and political history.[13] My father believed, however, that he could become an
even better artist if he improved the practical skills that went into painting stage sets
and drawing dramatic characters. Aware of the vigorous training program he had
devised for himself, I became fascinated by the sketchbook in which he painstakingly
copied the subaltern figures portrayed in picture books such as *Great Change in a
Mountain Village (Shanxiang jubian),* which at that time was equally popular among

children and adults. Based on a well-known novel by Zhou Libo that was first published in 1958 and recounted the author's experience of living with the peasants and
their participation in the collective movement, this book brought me vividly in touch
with the remote and unfamiliar world of the simple and direct subalterns, whose
endeavor to forge a better society seemed so admirable. I remember gazing at the
healthy, attractive body of Pretty Plum (Deng Xiumei), a female Communist Party
worker from afar who had joined the revolution at the age of fifteen and who now lived
among, and worked day and night for, peasants she hardly knew. I wanted to grow up
to be just like her.[14]

The many images of the countryside contained in the picture stories that I perused
eased my adjustment when I made the shift from being a Beijing middle school student to being a farmer in the Northeast Wilderness *(Beidahuang),* so that it was not
as intimidating to me as it has been made to seem in Cultural Revolution memoirs.
Moreover, it was inspiring to believe (as Mao had instructed us) that in the vast arena
of the countryside, revolutionary youth could make full use of their talents and
enhance their prospects. Picture books, posters, and newspaper stories all helped to
bring home that message. Indeed, at the age of fifteen, a year younger than the min-
imum age required, I had to beg permission from my school to join my fellow classmates in what then seemed their exciting collective journey to the countryside. Growing up in the crowded city of Beijing (the northern capital), I detected a special allure
in Beidahuang: although still northern, and hence familiar, it suggested an enchanting
adventure composed of a blend of romance and successful harvest, in a space even
larger than the big city of Beijing. However, later years in the countryside brought dis-
appointing experiences for many, which resulted in my reading sardonically such
posters as *Return to the countryside after graduation to make revolution (Biye hui
xiang gan geming, shi zuo yi dai xin nongmin)* (figure 3.1 [H15], 1975) and *New
Year's Eve in a collective household (Jiti hu zhi chuxi zhi ye)* (plate 10 [Z29]). Both
posters forecast later attempts to reconstruct positive stories from a national movement that was already failing in the late 1970s, when large-scale strikes and public
demonstrations reflected the anger and frustration of millions of educated youth (who
were actually not so young anymore by then) still toiling in the godforsaken countryside.[15] I reacted to these kinds of poster images with a deep sense of guilt. A benefi-
ciary of the movement, I had by then by then already left behind in the wilderness
many of my friends, who continued to pay for a dream we once all shared, while I, the
"chosen one," was transferred back to the city. As a "worker/peasant/soldier student"
admitted to college by recommendation of the local subalterns in 1973, I masquer-
aded as one of them in order to reclaim proletariat control of higher learning on their
behalf, as we were expected to do. At the same time, I was passionately learning the
English language and the culture, history, and literature of our national enemy in a
cozy classroom amid the green sanctuary of Beijing's Foreign Languages Institute. I
felt like the vilest of hypocrites.

These, however, were later experiences and did not alter the buoyancy of my early
childhood up to the mid-1960s, before the Cultural Revolution, when I playfully imi-
tated what I took to be the spirit of the subalterns by doing good deeds for the common people. Beginning in the fourth grade, for example, I would get up at 5:30 A.M.
and hurry to school to light the coal stoves and clean the office for my teachers, who
were striving so single-mindedly to turn us into worthy standard-bearers of the proletariat cause. Many an afternoon after school did I linger at the New China Bookstore

to admire the beautiful bodies on wall posters, and, spending what little pocket money I had, I would bring some posters to my classroom so that my classmates might be equally inspired by them, in our mutual exertion to gain the honorary title of "five-distinctions class" *(wu hao ban jiti)*. Our classroom in Beijing's Jingshan School, it must be said, did not need wallpaper at all—much less a good-quality sort—since it was situated in a modern building and had walls that glistened with snow-white, fresh paint and large windows that let in brilliant sunlight.

I provided the posters for my class anonymously, in a manner that would have been approved by Uncle Lei Feng, the national hero from the People's Liberation Army who always urged us to do compassionate deeds for the people without seeking credit. The posters of Lei Feng and various picture books depicting his magical transformation from suffering subaltern in the old society to model soldier of socialist China had much to do with planting the seed of national pride in me and molding me into an aspiring young citizen of the young republic. I remember picking up especially the posters that related to our daily activities as schoolchildren; although products of the early 1960s, these posters resembled in spirit, in style, and even in terms of the actual events depicted their 1970s counterparts such as *The main lesson (Zhu ke)* (plate 15 [E27], 1975) and *Presenting flowers to model workers (Xian hua song mofan)* (plate 25 [M 4], 1978).

On weekend trips with my father to national and regional art exhibitions, the Beijing Art Gallery, the Museum of Chinese Revolutionary History, and others, I was exposed not only to oil paintings and ink drawings but also to the grand portraits of Chairman Mao, especially the one entitled *Chairman Mao traveling through the countryside (Mao zhuxi zoubian quanguo)*. Later on we purchased that poster and placed it in a central spot in our house, so that we could often view the amiable father figure Mao surveying the life of the subalterns, caring for them, and perhaps even joining in their physical labor, as suggested by his white shirt and stage-prop straw hat. Indirectly, the poster also provided an early lesson in traditional Chinese art, for it epitomized *guohua* painting (traditional Chinese painting with brush and ink) in the socialist realist style, which, according to Julia F. Andrews, was regarded in the PRC as "the best example of painting that is nontraditional in style but traditional in materials."[16]

From those days also surfaces my memory of the famous painting *The founding of the nation (Kai guo da dian)*,[17] which displays Mao on Tian'anmen's center stage, announcing to the nation that the long-suffering Chinese people had at last stood up to the entire world. Said to be influenced by European history painting while setting the standard for the realist style of oil painting, according to Julia F. Andrews, works of this sort—and the posters derived from them—were for me an introduction to European art. At that time the fact that there were at least nine founding fathers, but only one founding mother in the corner, did not prevent me from relating to the picture as a willing player of political theater. I was unaware, then, of the unequal gender relationship in the CCP hierarchy, which ran counter to its official claim that it strove for gender equality. Seduced by the enchanting blue skies, white clouds, and red flags of Tian'anmen Square delineated in the background of the picture, I longed to merge with the enthusiastic crowd in hailing the founding of the nation. From the vantage point of today, I can detect an intriguing discontinuity between a poster such as *The founding of the nation* (1952, revised in 1967)[18] and its 1970s successors such as *Closely follow our great leader Chairman Mao and go forward courageously (Jin gen weida lingxiu Mao zhuxi fenyong qianjin)* (figure 7.2 [N59]). Whereas *Founding* presented a

我们的文学艺术都是
为人民大众的．首先是
为工农兵的．为工农兵
而创作．为工农兵所利
用的。

毛泽东
·在延安文艺座谈会上的讲话·

Fig. 6.2 [L5]. *Our literature and art is all for the masses; in the first place it is for the work-ers, peasants, and soldiers; it has been created for them and is for their use (Women de wenxue yishu dou shi wei renmin dazhong, shouxian shi wei gong nong bing de, wei gong nong bing er chuangzuo, wei gong nong bing suo liyong de).* Beijing 1967.

real historic event, with Mao, although occupying center stage, still shown in relatively balanced proportion to other leaders and to the distant crowd, as seen from afar, the 1970s posters consisted of highly imaginative abstract scenes over which towered the idolized figure of Mao, the sole national leader, with the following masses portrayed in the background at a level almost below his waistline (figure 7.2 [N59]); this was the familiar, ubiquitous image carried in print media and on souvenirs and other emblems at the peak of the Maoist cult during the Cultural Revolution.

The shift to an ever shrinking representation of the masses relative to the ever larger icon of Mao is also symptomatic of the poster artists' loss of autonomy. Although the artists in other circumstances and cultures would have been endowed with power and knowledge by virtue of their literary and artistic skills, during the Cultural Revolution, their work communicates the powerlessness of their social status, which compelled them to pose as proletariat artists and subaltern characters in revolutionary model theater, as may be seen in *Our literature and art is all for the masses (Women de wenxue yishu dou shi wei renmin dazhong)* (figure 6.2 [L5], 1967). Bearing in mind the artists' dilemma, one might be similarly inclined to read ironically *China should contribute more to humanity (Zhongguo yingdang duiyu renlei you jiaoda de gongxian)* (figure 6.3 [N43], 1978), for the scientists with whom Mao and Premier Zhou Enlai are depicted chatting as though they were friends and respected citizens were in effect among the hardest-hit social groups during the Cultural Revolution. Furthermore, the revolution's central theme of promoting the Four Moderniza-

Fig. 6.3 [N43]. *China should contribute more to humanity (Zhongguo yingdang duiyu renlei you jiaoda de gongxian)*. Shanghai 1978.

tions, with scientists playing pivotal roles therein, was not seriously tackled until after Mao's death; Mao had abruptly ended such initiatives with the ouster of Deng Xiao-ping, who was blamed for the "counterrevolutionary" Tian'anmen demonstration on 4–5 April 1976. Although I had already become more than a little skeptical at the time these latter posters were around, I did not find them overly offensive. No longer cred-iting their spirit or content, I still, to some extent, appreciated posters as one of the few public artworks available in an era when there were plenty of sculptures of Mao but few art museums.

I have no doubt that in my unconscious, posters became indelibly inscribed as part of my childhood world of wonders, my wanderings, and the emotions associated with growing pains. My weekend visits to history museums in the early 1960s (before the Cultural Revolution when museums, libraries, and other cultural institutions were closed) included joyful bus trips to the architectural marvels known as the "ten great buildings" *(shi da jianzhu)*, which were constructed in a very short period of time to celebrate the tenth anniversary of the nation's founding. I do not recall whether spe-cial posters were printed to commemorate endeavors of this sort, but these edifices constituted the setting for many posters; the most frequently used was the Great Hall of the People. Surely there would also have been commemorative stamps *(jinian you-piao)*, souvenir badges *(jinian zhang)*, and postcards that would have found their way into the treasured space of my messy drawers. In this way painting, poster, artifact, museum, and national identities and narratives all become blurred, coalescing into the most valued memories of my childhood. One of the highlights of that childhood was the role I played as the enterprising diminutive leader of the Young Pioneers. In this capacity, I remember taking my class on a weekend outing in Jingshan Park, where we reenacted an ambush by Japanese invaders. Our military strategy entailed a charge toward the top of the hill to take over the enemy's territory, in the course of which we acted out familiar images from a *lianhuanhua* (illustrated strip) book, *Railroad Guerrillas* (1956–1958).[19] This activity afforded us at once game, sport, theater, and the ritual observance of Young Pioneers Day *(Dui ri)*, whereby we could renew our pledge to the sacred revolutionary cause. The top prizewinner of the first national lianhuanhua exhibition in 1963,[20] *Railroad Guerrillas*, which incorporated as many as ten volumes, held a special space in my memory, not only for its enjoyable collection of pictures to look at, but also, and more important, for the role models it contained that showed me how to courageously defend my motherland. With more than ten thousand lianhuanhua produced, and seven hundred million copies published by 1963, one can easily imagine the psychological, ideological, and cultural impact they had on the lives of millions of children in Maoist China.[21] The phenomenon has continued to have an impact, as evidenced by the sale, in 1996, of new editions of selected masterpieces of Maoist lianhuanhua originally published before the Cultural Revolution and now touted to the younger generation as a book series that "Our Mom and Dad Once Read."[22] Moreover, it has been an effective cultural buffer against the incursions by Japanese and American cartoons, which dominated the Chinese children's book market in the 1990s.

Perhaps, in my eagerness to contribute to the revolutionary cause, I, like the many youngsters portrayed in posters, was merely doing what was "expected" of me, as Stephanie Donald has pointed out in her essay in this collection—and "doing it prettily." In the process, I had my considerable share of fun and excitement, since playing it "prettily" had much to do with pleasing my parents and teachers and dealing with peer pressure in a way that would make me the best—or one of the best—in the unspoken but ever present competition among me and my friends—perhaps a universal experience for children. Posters, however, were not the only models children grew up to identify with in the early 1960s; in this sense, pictorial representations such as that of the pretty girl in *Presenting flowers to model workers* (plate 25 [M4])—which granted ideological meaning but no autonomous space to the girl—could not represent the multidimensional experience that provided me with a sense of freedom in the 1960s. I have discussed elsewhere the peculiar sense of autonomy that my background gave me as a child. This was a function of my being born into a celebrated family associated with a national theater and my feeling simultaneously attached to the subalterns that my parents both devotedly represented onstage and used as models of social behavior offstage. Functioning between this space of double identities (the "extraordinary" and the "ordinary"), I paradoxically enjoyed a sense of ease. For I knew I could relate to either or both groups at any given moment, depending on which was the least restraining, and this choice gave me a relatively balanced view of myself and the world around me.[23] In the following pages, I briefly address a different sort of ambiguous space, the one relating to gender identities, in which, by virtue of the androgynous play between a manly woman and a womanly man, I gained a similar sense of freedom.

From early on in my childhood I have a vivid memory of my mother's femininity, both as she expressed it onstage when she played the gorgeous Nora in Ibsen's *Doll's House*—dancing in her elaborate Spanish costume while desperately trying to charm her husband before scandal struck—and as she exuded it as a charming woman and loving mother at home.[24] A surge of pride would flow through me when I saw her come into the house after a performance, her arms filled with bouquets of fresh flowers pre-

Fig. 6.4. *Full of hatred (Manqiang chouhen)*. 1970. Library of Congress collection.

sented her by the admiring public. I longed for the day when I could shine as brilliantly as she did onstage and be the captivating woman adored by multitudes. To love my mother was to act just like her, to copy the feminine manner that came naturally to her. I revered her smile, her words, and the way she lowered her head with its lovely wavy hair to kiss me gently on the cheek—although, because of her busy schedule, not as often as I would have liked. My response to her feminine body was not unlike the ecstatic excitement I felt when, as a sixteen-year-old in the Northeast Wilderness, I received from her the birthday gift of a photo album with stills from the revolutionary model ballet *The Red Detachment of Women*. I was especially struck by a photo (which had become a very popular poster in the China of the Cultural Revolution) that displayed the elegant and shapely body of Wu Qinghua, the female revolutionary heroine whose long, straight legs and graceful body had resisted a vicious, oppressive landlord.

The example I choose for this chapter, however, reveals another aspect of the visual culture of the time. Entitled *Full of hatred (Manqiang chouhen)* (figure 6.4, 1970), it is an oil painting of Wu Qinghua that meticulously copied the stage photograph of the same image from the ballet performance. Wu Qinghua is in chains, tortured by the oppressive landlord who imprisoned her to prevent her escape. For Western audiences, her handcuffed hands, whipped body, long and braided hair, and torn red silk dress not unlike that of the teasing Victoria's Secret lingerie might invite sexual and perhaps even masochistic fantasy with or without any knowledge of China. For audiences within China in that period, however, the embodiment of youth, beauty, grace, passion, and energy that the model theater heroines featured on posters and other artworks was one of the rare decorations to be seen in public spaces and private homes, and as such the models could be gazed on with the same intensity as pictures of Marilyn Monroe, whose seductiveness had magnetized both the powerful few and the common people. Today, looking back, I am aware that my treasuring of these images was not unrelated to their voluptuous appeal and bodily beauty, which was securely disguised by the focus on an ideologically correct story and by equipping the womanly body with a "manly spirit," as it was traditionally defined. Thus did the androgynous nature of model theater account, to some extent, for some of the appeal of the posters of the period. The posters conveyed their political messages via the written word in captions and titles, while model theater did the same through script, lyrics, and dialogue. In both forms, however, the visual representation, comprised of body politics (whereby bodies carry meaning into the picture from sociopolitical external sources), color, light, and composition, might sometimes provide cues for other interpretations and for the sort of appreciation not necessarily endorsed by mainstream culture. The two forms also differed in that the shapely body of a female lead could be accentuated by elegant movement in model theater, especially in revolutionary ballet, whereas in posters, the female figure might be dressed in baggy clothing to hide its curves and, in any case, was fixed—a special feature of the art object—without benefit of the flow of movement, a property of performing art. In the context of the comparison between different genres of visual art, moreover, it is perhaps interesting to mention in passing that the appearance of the oil painting of Wu Qinghua in chains indicated a conscious attempt on the part of Chinese artists to integrate a different art medium into the creation of a new and revolutionary culture. As proclaimed in the preface of the collection of the oil paintings of *The Red Detachment of Women* from which the above-mentioned Wu Qinghua picture was taken, forty oil paintings of the main scenes and characters from the ballet (ranging from 89 cm x 93 cm in size, as in Wu's picture [figure 6.4], to 233 cm x 127 cm, as in *Changqing shows us the way* [*Changqing zhi lu*, 1970])[25] were completed within just three months, from June to September of 1970, as the result of the collective efforts of a group of painters who were determined to use this Western-imported medium to *re*-present revolutionary model ballet (itself also a Western medium). The paintings were finally presented as gifts to an exhibition in Shanghai commemorating the thirtieth anniversary of the publication of Mao Zedong's Talks at the Yan'an Forum, thus providing useful models for worker/peasant/soldier amateur artists to imitate revolutionary art on canvas.[26]

Given the values implied in my surroundings, the feminine attributes I adored in my mother could also become a source of embarrassment to me in front of my peers. At a time when every one in the nation was being urged to focus on the noble goals of self-reliance, thrift, and hard work for the sake of strengthening the country, how could I always feel proud of a mother who wore fashionable dresses and high heels? I remember worrying that my classmates might show up at my house when I was not feeling well. Visiting a sick classmate was praised as a good deed; it was one of the lessons we learned from Uncle Lei Feng, who demonstrated his concern for other people in countless ways. In the spirit of Lei Feng, it was thought even better to bring some candy or fruit, to help your classmates recover. But what if my classmates should run into my mother, who, rather than looking like a subaltern, dressed like the bourgeoisie?

I do not know with any certainty how my idea of a manly woman developed in my childhood, in that dynamic period when sexual ideology was always being reconstrued and revolutionary culture was defined in both traditional and nontraditional gender terms. Nor can I pinpoint when it was that I was ready to be drafted into serving the republic—I mean when I became the almost ideal Chinese "man," physically, morally, and spiritually strong, with no uncomfortable sense of the conventionally defined antipodes of man and woman. What I do remember is how intensely I tried to imitate Uncle Lei Feng and the energy I expended competing with both girls and boys in that effort. We all exerted ourselves to approximate his heroic masculinity (which was set off by his plain and simple lifestyle) and such endearing habits as his unwillingness to throw away a much overdarned pair of socks.[27] It became for me an important "fashion statement" to wear some much overdarned pants and, for that matter, pants handed down from my brother, the type made specifically for boys at that time, with an opening at the crotch. I went so far that my classmates began to tease me about my cross-dressing, but if they thought to win the teacher's support with their mockery, they were disappointed. She criticized *them*. Declaring that there was nothing wrong with wearing boy's clothing, she encouraged my androgynous act, claiming that it accorded with the simplicity exemplified by the subalterns. I then felt freer than ever to dress and act like a boy while trying to come out as the strongest and fastest at whatever we did, whether it was physical labor or phys ed exercises.

Much later I would be interested to learn that cross-dressing as a boy could, in the words of Margorie Garber, "affirm the reality of pleasure, sexual and cultural" and that clothing "constructs (and deconstructs) gender and gender differences, . . . power relations and career paths."[28] Furthermore, one of the most important aspects of cross-dressing is the way it challenges facile binary notions, calling into question the categories of "female" and "male," as in the simplistic rule of pink for girls and blue for boys, in effect "since at least the 1940s" in America, according to Garber. (In earlier years boys were dressed in pink, which was then considered "a strong, more decided color," whereas girls were in blue, the "delicate" and "dainty" hue.)[29] As for my precocious cross-dressing, I merely knew I enjoyed the freedom entailed in acting the tomboy and tough, youthful revolutionary. Playing in my neighborhood after school, I vied for the opportunity to parade as a male hero to be executed by the Guomindang nationalists before 1949, confronting death without blinking, just like the fearless heroes in movies and picture books. I would then gladly sit down at the dinner table with my graceful mother and listen to her soft, feminine voice discussing recent theater productions with my father. I remember my indignation when I overheard some people attributing my mother's femininity to foreign origin. After studying the photographs of my mother in the window of the China Youth Art Theater, one man said to his friend that my mother seemed too feminine to be Chinese. "Look at her shapely body," he said; "she was 'borrowed' from the Soviet Union to act in a play." Young as I was, aged eleven, I could not keep from yelling, "She is not Russian. She is my mother!" Before they had a chance to question me about *my* origins, I ran home, scared but very proud, to my mother and father, and to our warm house. Home was the place where femininity and masculinity did not have to be interrogated and where I could enjoy my mother for being both Chinese and Western. (She was the latter when she recreated the many characters from the classic European repertoire.)

Theater, however, was hardly confined to my family background. In time I indulged in additional role-playing, when the dark blue and gray of my boyish clothing gave way to "girlish" colors of various shades of red. On the eve of International Children's Day, 1 June 1964, I reveled in wearing a red hat, red leather shoes, and golden short skirt with white lace while playing the title role in our school's English production of *Little Red Riding Hood.*[30] I could not have known then, of course, what Margorie Garber meant by referring to *Little Red Riding Hood* as one of the most frequently interpreted stories in the West. It has been viewed by many literary experts as "the primal scene of narrativated cross-dressing," in which the wicked wolf dresses up as a woman, the benign grandma, who "terrifies and pleases, seduces and warns."[31] Nor could I have understood that *Little Red Riding Hood* belongs to the "very existence of transvestite theaters, from Shakespeare's cross-dressed 'heroines' to the contemporary drag show" that "testifies to the primacy of cross-dressing as spectacle, as that which purports both to conceal and to reveal."[32] What was revealed to me, however, was my culture's version of the story's moral: we should never be taken in by our national enemy, who could cross-dress as our best friend. This interpretation was infused with the same anti-imperialist spirit that informed so many posters, such as *The Chinese people are not easily humiliated* (D6, 1966/67). Although Mao used the phrase "paper tiger" to underscore the vulnerability of U.S. imperialists and reactionaries in other countries, these enemies seemed at times as frightening as the tigers and wolves in children's stories.[33] National myths emphasized their aggressive and vicious nature, as communicated by the phrase *meidi yexin lang* (the U.S. imperialist wolf with wild ambition) in the model opera *Raid the White Tiger Regiment* (*Qixi Baihu tuan*, 1972), which extolled the period when China came to the assistance of North Korea in the Korean War (1951–1953).[34]

I also remember that the stylish cape I wore had been made by my teacher from a red flag; after the performance, it was reconverted to its original shape, for further use in celebrating National Day and other festivities. Figuratively, my little red riding hood, like my red scarf, became "a corner of the red flag that had been colored with the warm blood of revolutionary martyrs"; this common saying was often heard in reference to the red scarves worn by the Young Pioneers, who were taught that their scarves should be as precious to them as their own lives. To this day, I can still identify with the boy solemnly holding the end of the red flag in plate 27 (M40), *Determined to be strong revolutionary successors* (1965), and plate 24 (M20), *Joining the Young Pioneers* (1980), as they dedicate themselves to the revolutionary cause. I did the very same thing many times over in the course of festivities, parades, and other public events. I have no horror stories to report from that period, and no sense of constraint to mar my heightened memories of seeing bright red everywhere around me. Red was my favorite color. Collectively and personally, it made the best sense.

It would be natural for me, as an academic interested in gender studies, to point out the unequal power relationship between men and women among the leadership and the masses in those days. With only one woman at each side of its scientist grouping, the poster *China should contribute more to humanity* (figure 6.3 [N43], 1978) reveals the same male-dominated society seen in *The founding of the nation.* Similarly, in plate 30 [N11], *Chairman Mao's rural investigations in the Jinggang mountains,* only two women are visible standing behind a group of male peasant supporters of the Red Army, gazing at Mao and the army from afar, playing a subordinate role even as eyewitnesses to a momentous episode of CCP history. Harriet Evans is thus correct when she asserts in her chapter that although the women appear to be participating in the same activities as the man, "neither their position, their gestures, nor their gaze is seen to challenge male authority." And yet I remind myself that on the level of personal experience while I was growing up, the male and female worlds seemed to me much more blurred. It may be that Mao's dialectical materialism, with the theory of binary class struggle as its centerpiece, inevitably promoted a process of change in which, for example, "good things can turn into bad and bad things can turn into good." Or perhaps, as my story of cross-dressing suggests, no matter how binary the society that was supposed to be in the making, there was almost always some room in between in which to transgress mainstream codes of behavior as they related to gender or other societal norms.

The story of Cultural Revolution posters must also include the perhaps surprising tales of the martyrs and saints who openly questioned the revolution in its heyday, when the great majority of the Chinese people still cheered it on and some others chose to remain silent and indifferent onlookers. To retrieve some of the lost memories of the Cultural Revolution, in 1989 a collection of twenty-one letters to Mao and other chief CCP leaders was belatedly published under the title of "A Humble Position Does Not Allow One to Forget One's Duties to One's Country" (*Weibei weiguan wang youguo*). The letters—preserved in sealed archives as criminal evidence that would facilitate the sentencing and execution of political prisoners—recover amazing stories of posters. In the process they reveal how, contrary to the poster creators' intentions, posters could function as seeds of rebellion, militating against the very icons and concepts presumably propagated by the poster.

In 1968, for example, Xiao Ruiyi, a twenty-year-old high school graduate in Hunan Province, mailed a letter to Mao to protest the Maoist cult, Mao's theories on class struggle and collective farming, and the party and state bureaucracy. While explaining to Mao what had motivated him to write, he disclosed that after following the initial events of the Cultural Revolution, he had found repugnant the sight of a hotel that hung on its walls as many as seventy different kinds of posters. Some of the scenes depicted included Mao's early journey from his hometown to the outside world on his way to mobilizing miners, Mao shaking hands with passionate Red Guards, Mao wearing a long raincoat on his national tour, Mao sitting, Mao standing; in all of the posters Mao was the central figure "who possessed the entire world."[35] Consequently, a hotel had been "remodeled" into a poster museum. After describing his own experience as a starving child in the barren countryside during the three years after the Great Leap Forward movement, Xiao expressed the wish that the youthful spirit that had once animated Mao would be rekindled and cause him to travel again among the subalterns, "umbrella in hand," "across mountains and rivers on foot"—a familiar image taken from the popular painting-turned-poster *Chairman Mao goes to Anyuan (Mao zhuxi qu Anyuan)* (plate 6 [N35]).[36] Were this to happen, Xiao believed, Mao would develop a much more realistic policy than he had now in regard to agricultural production in the countryside.[37] Xiao also showed that he was ahead of his time by proposing that farmland, although owned by the state, should be leased to individual peasants, to motivate them to work for their own benefit; this economic reform policy, which was undertaken in earnest only in post-Mao China, would radically change the landscape of much of the countryside.

Commenting on the much publicized event of Mao swimming across the Yangzi

万里长江横渡

Fig. 6.5 [N16]. *Swimming across the ten-thousand-mile Yangzi River (Wan li Changjiang heng du).* Beijing 1974.

River when he was in his seventies (figure 6.5 [N16]),[38] Xiao wrote of his disappointment that Mao did not apply his surplus energies to helping the subalterns with their strenuous physical labor. Xiao's comment reminds me of another popular painting, *Mao at Ming Tombs reservoir,* which commemorates the brief appearance there in 1958 of Mao, who worked side by side with workers. One might also recall Tian Han's play *The Imaginary Song of the Ming Tombs Reservoir (Shisanling shuiku changxiang qu),* performed by the China Youth Art Theater around 1959 to celebrate the heroic national spirit expressed in the Great Leap Forward.[39] In the play, my mother had the role of the schoolteacher who speaks enthusiastically to her students at this site about the Party's blueprint for a Communist society of uncommon promise.[40] Had Xiao seen this painting and play, it would probably only have served to emphasize for him the infrequency of such an appearance by Mao and would have confirmed his impression that these visual products had nothing to do with the reality they were supposedly representing, even though realistic imitation was the literary and artistic style Mao himself advocated.

Another story uncovers even greater complexity with regard to posters' paradoxical role in constructing cultural identities. From 1966 to 1979, Wang Rongfen, a nineteen-year-old college senior majoring in German languages and literature at Beijing Foreign Languages Institute, was imprisoned as a counterrevolutionary for having written a half-page letter to Mao. As a CCP member and a representative member of the Chinese nation, she asked Mao to consider what on earth he was doing in this so-called Cultural Revolution and in what disastrous directions he was taking the entire country. Wang declared that from the date of the letter, she was "excommunicating" herself from the China Youth League.[41] Interviewed years later, after having spent thirteen years in prison, she traced the birth of her rebellious spirit to 18 August 1966, when she was among the millions of Red Guards received by Mao in his mass review in Tian'anmen Square, a pivotal event of political theater much depicted in posters. "This country is finished. This world is too dirty," she thought.[42] She could not "go on living" without risking her life to speak her mind and to pursue the magnificent and heroic undertaking *(zhuangju)* of defending her political convictions.[43] As if driven by a "ghost writer" and against her own better judgment, she started writing letters addressed in turn to the CCP Central Committee, to the Chinese Communist Youth Central Committee, to the training school for youth leaders, and, finally, to Mao himself.[44]

Just before putting the last letter in a mailbox, however, she did exactly what posters of the time had taught her: she walked through the still sacred Tian'anmen Square, paying tribute to the revolutionary martyrs in front of the Monument to People's Heroes. She continued to walk toward the east, after having ingested four bottles of DDT, only to wake up in the hospital attached to the ministry of public security. She had intended to lay down her life in front of the embassy of the former Soviet Union, the enemy of the Chinese people, so that the news would be broadcast all over the world that she had thus sacrificed herself to protest the Cultural Revolution. She insisted that her so-called counterrevolutionary act was not motivated by a hatred of the CCP, as her accusers maintained. On the contrary, she said, it was impelled by a commitment to the Party cause so profound and so passionate that she was willing to offer up her life if doing so would awaken others to the need to rescue the nation before it was too late. She was indeed reenacting the same kind of rite as that delineated in *Joining the Young Pioneers* (plate 24 [M20]), the familiar scene in which young successors to the revolutionary cause pledge to keep alive a martyrlike revolutionary spirit. Wang was a Maoist woman par excellence, liberated and rebellious, yet, even in the act of rejecting it, never free of the cultural ethos that had constrained her in the first place. She was both the subject of the poster (by virtue of creating herself in the image of the saint) and a product of the poster, which urged the people to renounce orthodoxy (by virtue of the depicted Red Guards, whose role models were the revolutionary martyrs and political saints canonized after 1949).

To conclude this chapter, it might be useful to consider what is at stake in memory studies. What do we do when faced with conflicting versions of poster stories, some discriminating, some nostalgic, and some, like the last two, courageous and prophetic? In any case, what are the critical issues involved in arriving at such judgments to begin with? And how do those issues affect the way we teach Chinese culture in the diaspora when we assemble, relate, and disseminate these memories—and the knowledge and power they possess? I have often discerned at least two intellectual choices, both of which were equally honest at different moments in time and were consonant with my multiple—and often shifting—subject positions as I teach in front of different audiences. In my undergraduate classes at Ohio State University, for instance, I am eager to use "incredible" stories about China in order to stimulate in my midwestern students an awareness of the unfamiliar (to them), and hence fascinating, outside world. I would feel fulfilled if I could periodically convert a few students into Chinese majors, students whose most extensive traveling had heretofore been represented by Florida's Disney World. To achieve this goal, however, I sometimes end by recounting the same melodrama, in tone if not in factual detail, as that contained in the works *Wild Swans* and *Red Azalea*. Although I make sure at the end of my course to emphasize the difficulties of representing China in the diaspora, I am still concerned lest my own stories fall into the same traps as those I have been critiquing. Through good intentions, hard work, and persistence, I hope to recognize and hold myself accountable for any lapses resulting in my joining the chorus of postsocialist and post–Cold War China bashers in the diaspora.

However, my graduate seminar classes run another risk when I challenge the advocates of political correctness (PC) and demonstrate how the liberal agenda promoted by cultural studies in America, far from representing anything new, only inherited a legacy of Mao's pro-women, pro–Third World, and pro-subaltern approach (as clearly shown by many of the posters in this volume). The stance of political correctness, now taken in the American classroom and beyond, would be deemed politically incorrect in present-day China, where many have repudiated these aspirations as the failed experiments of thirty years ago. Under the circumstances, I think my strategy must be to pose questions about the problematic discourse of Third World and non-Western cultural studies and to inquire whether, in spite of the goodwill exemplified by their postcolonial and anticolonial agenda, they consolidate the mainstream Eurocentric tradition, buttressed as they are by Western theories that increasingly dictate the methods for examining culture.

Taking this approach, however, also worries me, because I simultaneously feel the urgent need, through my teaching and service in the university environment and the local and wider communities, to promote that liberal agenda as I drive home the obvious point that literary and cultural studies do not start with the *Iliad* and end with Derrida. I had the frustrating experience of having to argue for many years that a credible graduate program in Chinese studies required at least one specialist in classical Chinese literature, since the high (and the low) cultures of Tang (618–907), for instance, are at least as crucial to such a program as is the coverage of the medieval and Elizabethan periods to a graduate program in English literature.

Fortunately, there is a third way to proceed. It would set out to preserve both the constructing and deconstructing power of posters and to explore how posters present an ambiguous space where different meanings blur and overlap, without resorting to binary oppositions. In other words, this approach would seek to incorporate as many different voices as could be recovered.[45] This third way would also lead us to interrogate the troubling nature of both China bashing and PC bashing while delineating their dialectical and dynamic relationship to each other in time and space. Thus, non-Western studies entail not only examining unstudied cultures but also not limiting oneself to a single version of the "truth." By these means, it might be possible to circumvent the need to choose: if we conceded that Mao, with his concept of continued revolution to deter materialism, was introducing to China what he thought was missing, we could also see that the West is entitled to carry out Mao's pro-woman, pro-subaltern, and pro–Third World approach to create a space for what is lacking in contemporary America and Europe.

By such reasoning, I would hope to call into question the prevailing discourse of Cultural Revolution memoir literature and reevaluate the prevalent postsocialist and/or antisocialist discourses in the West. I am reminded of an alternative voice that came in 1996, on the occasion of commemorating the thirtieth anniversary of the inception of the Cultural Revolution, by way of a Taiwanese who had spent ten years in prison because of his professed belief in Mao's theory of continued revolution and class struggle.[46] Many years later, he still held that, despite the apparent victory of the capitalist system, which in the postsocialist era informed orthodox discourse in the West, one should not forget the Cultural Revolution, its durable impact on the Third World and the Chinese people, and the warning it issued against the imminent danger of capitalist domination. What I value in this individual's statement is not so much its redemption of the Cultural Revolution as cultural memory and history as its expression of "otherness" and hybridity, serving as a reminder of the ways in which the oppositional influence of that period transcended its immediate historical contexts. Across the Taiwan Straits one might hear this person's views echoed in the PRC. When asked about the impression they had obtained of the Cultural Revolution from their parents, young people described it as an era when people were sincere, passionate, and enthusiastic about their ideals.[47] The parents characterized the period as free, one in which drugs and prostitution were unknown, with low and stable grocery prices, a low crime rate, and more honest officials.[48] A senior high school student claimed that the days of the Cultural Revolution were surely better, that it would be great if she could see those arrogant millionaires and their shameless women escorts chastened through mass criticism meetings, in the same way the Red Guards used to humiliate former landowners and capitalists.[49] Others expressed a similar relation to the past, constructed with reference to what they saw as missing in the present: "The Cultural Revolution seemed to let politics take control, whereas right now money is everything"; "it would be nice if we could take half of each extreme and make a happy medium."[50]

The "imagined" world of the Cultural Revolution reconstructed through parental recollections helps us appreciate the surviving and struggling generation's dreams of the future; their best way of fulfilling their dreams is to survey history in the way most meaningful to them—and meaningful in different ways to readers like us who ponder those dreams. I would be content if, after reading this chapter, some readers could share with me a glimpse into an unfamiliar past and present through visualizing dreams that they would recognize as not being inappropriate to the spirit of their own times.

## Notes

My special thanks to Harriet Evans and Stephanie Donald for inviting me to write this chapter, something that I have found really compelling; for Harriet's timely help in sending me copies of the posters overnight; and for their valuable comments on the draft of this chapter.

1. Zhang Zhizhong, "Lishi zhi mi he qingchun zhi wu" (The mystery of history and the mistake of youth), *Zhongguo yanjiu yuekan* (China Research Monthly), August 1996, 64–70, 65.

2. Jung Chang, *Wild Swans* (New York: Doubleday, 1992), 276–78.

3. Chang, *Wild Swans*, 321.

4. For representative works of Mao receiving Red Guards in Tian'anmen Square, see fig. 110, *Chairman Mao's Heart Beats as One with the Hearts of the Revolutionary Masses* (1967), and fig. 111, *We Must Implement the Proletarian Cultural Revolution to the Finish* (1972), in Julia F. Andrews, *Painters and Politics in the People's Republic of China: 1949–1979* (Berkeley and Los Angeles: University of California Press, 1994), 322–23,

5. Anchee Min, *Red Azalea* (New York: Pantheon Books, 1994), 17.

6. Min, *Red Azalea*, 70.

7. Min, *Red Azalea*, 71.

8. I thank Harriet Evans and Stephanie Donald for reminding me of this more global picture of the post–Cold War mentality that is not limited to the United States.

9. For a development of the Maoist theory of the Third World, see Lin Piao (Lin Biao), *Long Live the Victory of People's War!* (Renmin zhanzheng shengli wansui) (Beijing: Foreign Languages Press, 1965). I elaborated on related issues in my paper, entitled "Global Transactions of Chinese Country and the City in the Formation of Transnational Cultural Capital in Chinese American Best-sellers," presented at the American Association of Anthropology, Philadelphia, 2 December 1998. A different version can be found in "Time, Money, and Work," *Journal of American Studies* (Seoul, Korea) 29, no. 2 , (Winter 1997): 414–21.

10. Gao Yuan, *Born Red* (Stanford, Calif.: Stanford University Press, 1987), 39–40.

11. Gao, *Born Red,* 40.

12. By "subalterns," I am referring to the Maoist ideology of viewing the workers, peasants, soldiers, and other laboring classes as the politically privileged ones, for they were supposed to be the masters of the socialist state after the CCP's overthrow of the nationalist government in 1949. Before this time the majority of these laboring classes were seen as having been politically and economically oppressed as the subalterns by the ruling class. Intellectuals and artists such as my parents were therefore expected to reform their bourgeois ideology by following the models of the laboring people so that they could accept their values and create literature and art that best served their interests. By using this specific term, I also intend to draw a contrast with the subaltern studies of the postcolonial approach. This was introduced by Indian scholars who interrogated the role of Indian intellectuals in constructing colonialist history from their elitist point of view in India, where the subalterns were the makers of history. As several China scholars have pointed out, in spite of its heuristic value in Western cultural studies to deconstruct an Eurocentric view of history, subaltern studies might present a much more complicated picture in contemporary China, where class categories crosscut each other and are continuously redefined by the ruling class for its shifting political agenda. In many aspects, the Maoist subaltern discourse emptied out the very agency and subject positions of the subalterns, who could not really speak for themselves. See Gail Hershatter, "The Subaltern Talks Back: Reflections on Subaltern Theory and Chinese History," *Positions* 1, no. 1 (1993): 103–30; Xiaomei Chen, *Occidentalism* (New York: Oxford University Press, 1995), 20–24. For Indian subaltern studies, see Ranajit Guha and Gayatri Chakravorty Spivak, eds., *Selected Subaltern Studies* (New York: Oxford University Press, 1988).

13. Chen Yongjing, my father, was the director of stage designers *(wutai meishu dui)* for the China Youth Art Theater until the start of the Cultural Revolution. He designed the stage setting and costume for eleven plays from 1950 to 1964. For a biographical account and theoretical analysis of his artistic achievements, see Cai Tilian, "Xinchao qifu yi quanquan" (Surging thoughts and emotions with a sincere heart), *Qingyi* (Journal of the China Youth Art Theater) 58, no. 2 (December 1994): 31–36. I have described the China Youth Art Theater as the national theater, since it was regarded as the *"guojia juyuan"* directly attached to the ministry of art and culture, whereas other nationally known theaters such as Beijing People's Art Theater (Beijing Renmin yishu juyuan) and Central Experimental Theater (Zhongyang shiyan huajuyuan) were attached to the local municipal government of Beijing.

14. For an elaborated reading of this and other lianhuanhua, see Xiaomei Chen, "Picture Stories of the People's Republic of China: Images from Popular Culture," in *Literature in Line: Lianhuanhua Picture Stories from China*, ed. Julia F. Andrews and Kuiyi Shen, exhibition catalogue (Columbus: Ohio State University Cartoon Research Library, forthcoming). For illustrations and background of *Great Change in a Mountain Village*, see Andrews, *Painters and Politics,* 246–50.

15. According to Deng Xian, 100,000 educated youth, then farmers in Xishuangbanna of Yunnan Province, staged their large-scale strike in November 1978, triggering a series of chain events such as demonstrations, lying across the railway tracks as a form of protest, and sit-in petitions in Tian'anmen Square. The irreversible national movement for the educated youth to return to their home cities reached its climax in the spring and summer of 1979. On 7 July 1979, government officials finally revealed to journalists of the *People's Daily* that in 1979, they promised to arrange for 7.6 million educated youth to relocate to the cities from which they had

been sent down to the countryside during the Cultural Revolution. See Deng Xian, *Zhongguo zhiqing meng* (The dreams of the Chinese educated youth) (Beijing: Renmin wenxue chubanshe, 1993), 172, 245, 351.

16. Andrews, *Painters and Politics,* 50.

17. For a detailed account of the political history and artistic style of this painting, and a copy of the painting itself, see Julia F. Andrews, "The Making and Remaking of a Cultural Icon: Dong Xiwen's *The Founding of the Nation,*" in *Painters and Politics,* 75–86, plate 1.

18. Andrews, *Painters and Politics,* 197, plate 1.

19. For lianhuanhua in general, and illustrations of *Railroad Guerrillas* and their role in political culture, see Andrews, *Painters and Politics,* 130–34.

20. Andrews, *Painters and Politics,* 130, 133.

21. Liu Zengrong, "Ganwen qianlu zai he chu" (Dare to ask where the future road leads), *Beijing qingnian bao* (Beijing Youth Newspaper), 23 October 1996, 3. I thank Professor Wang Jing of Duke University for sending me this article.

22. Liu, "Ganwen quianlu zai he chu," 3.

23. Xiaomei Chen: "From the 'Lighthouse': 'Mingdeng' and the Discourse of Celebrated Subalterns in Maoist China," in *Some of Us: Chinese Women Growing Up in the Mao Era,* ed. Zhong Xueping, Wang Zheng, and Bai Di (New Brunswick, N.J.: Rutgers University Press, forthcoming).

24. The most acclaimed dramatic roles my mother played for the China Youth Art Theater before the start of the Cultural Revolution included Yelena in Anton Chekhov's *Uncle Vanya* (*Wanniya jiujiu,* 1954); Nora in Henrik Ibsen's *Doll's House* (*Nuola,* 1956); Almaviva, the countess in the adaptation of Pierre-Augustin Caron de Beaumarchais's *Marriage of Figaro* (*Feijialou de hunyin,* 1962); and Amina in Wu Yuxiao's *Youth from Afar* (*Yangfang qingnian,* 1963).

25. It is interesting to note the implicit gender politics here. It was said in the print culture at that time that in the process of creating revolutionary model ballet, Hong Changqing, the party representative of the Detachment of Women, was constructed as the leading protagonist in order to foreground the Party's leadership role in the revolutionary war. This fact was eulogized as a key victory in transforming the bourgeois form of Western ballet, which always gave central roles to soft and weak female leads and assigned only supporting roles to male characters. See, e.g., Hong Chanying's essay, "Xiongwei zhuangmei, guangcai zhaoren" (The magnificent and brilliant ballet performance), *Jiefang ribao* (Liberation daily), 15 July 1970), reprinted in *Zan Hongse niangzijun* (Praising *The Red Detachment of Women*) (Guangzhou: Guangdong renmin chubanshe, 1970), 29–37, 31. Such a privileging of male over female lead also found its expression in the size of the oil paintings: the very first one of Wu Qinghua was among the smallest, whereas the one depicting Hong Changqing guiding her to the liberated areas was among the largest. The latter image was also one of the most popular, since it underscored, among other things, the significance of the Party in its role of educating and emancipating subaltern women.

26. *Youhua: Hongse niangzijun* (Oil paintings of *The Red Detachment of Women*) (Shanghai: Shanghai renmin chubanshe, 1972).

27. *Mao zhuxi de hao zhanshi Lei Feng* (Chairman Mao's Good Soldier Lei Feng) (Hong Kong: Chaoyang chubanshe, 1971), 83.

28. Margorie Garber, *Vested Interests* (New York: Routledge, 1992), 3–4.

29. Garber, *Vested Interests,* 1.

30. In 1960s China, English was not normally studied in elementary school. Beijing Jingshan Xuexiao, where I was enrolled, was one of the few elementary schools that offered English classes as part of its efforts to experiment with a ten-year educational system (from first to tenth grade) before college *(shinian yiguan zhi)* as opposed to the then conventional twelve-year system (with six years of elementary school, three years in middle school, and another three years in high school).

31. Garber, *Vested Interests,* 376.

32. Garber, *Vested Interests,* 389.

33. Mao Zedong's comments on "imperialists and all reactionaries are nothing but paper

tigers" were first put together by the editorial board of *Shijie zhishi* (Global knowledge), according to an essay by the editorial board of the *People's Daily* on 27 October 1957. The essay divided Mao's comments on "paper tiger" over the previous twenty years into comments on: (1) the inevitable decline of the decadent forces of imperialism no matter how strong they might appear to be at present; (2) the nature of imperialism as a paper tiger that is outwardly strong but inwardly weak; strategically, therefore, we should despise it, but tactically we should take it seriously; (3) the analysis of the basic characteristic of the 1960s international scene where the East wind was overpowering the West wind and socialism surpassing imperialism. See *Diguo zhuyi he yiqie fandongpai doushi zhilaohu* (Imperialism and all reactionaries are nothing but paper tigers) (Beijing: Renmin chubanshe, 1958), 5. See also *Xuexi Mao zhuxi lun 'zhilaohu'' wenxian* (Studying Chairman Mao's thoughts on paper tigers) (Hong Kong: Wenhui bao, 1958).

34. The year 1972 is the date for the revised edition of the opera as model revolutionary Beijing opera, published in *Hongqi* (Red flag) 11 (1972): 26–54. An English translation can be found in *Chinese Literature* 11(1970): 3–62. The stage line of "defeating the ambitious wolf of the U.S. imperialists," however, was a central image of the opera long before it was upgraded to the status of a model opera. See the 1964 performance script of *Qixi Baihutuan* by Beijing Opera Troupe of Shandong Province (Shandong sheng Jingju tuan), playwrights Li Shibin et al. (Beijing: Zhongguo xiju chubanshe, 1964), 6.

35. Xiao Ruiyi, "Wode shangshu huiyi" (Recollections of submitting letters to Mao), in *Weibei weiguan wang youguo* (A humble position does not allow one to forget one's duties to the country), ed. Yu Xiguang (Changsha: Hunan renmin chubanshe, 1989), 22–35, 27.

36. Xiao, "Wode," 25.

37. Xiao, "Wode," 25.

38. For another popular poster depicting the same event, see Andrews, *Painters and Politics,* plate 10, *Follow Closely Great Leader Chairman Mao, Ride the Wind, Cleave the Waves, Fearlessly Forge Ahead,* by Tang Xiaohe and Cheng Li, 1972.

39. This play was premiered by the China Youth Art Theater on 19 July 1958, with a run of 212 shows, a record high in comparison to other plays of the same period. Jin Shan was the director, and Zhang Zhengyu and Mao Jingang were the stage, costume, and lighting designers.

40. For the painting and the story around it, see Andrews, *Painters and Politics,* 211–16.

41. "Wang Rongfen shang Mao Zedong shu" (Wang Rongfen's letter to Mao Zedong, in *Weibei weiguan wang youguo* (A humble position does not allow one to forget one's duties to the country), ed. Yu Xiguang (Changsha: Hunan renmin chubanshe, 1989), 52.

42. Dai Qing and Luo Ke, "Nü zhengzhi fan" (Woman political prisoners), in *Weibei weiguan wang youguo* (A humble position does not allow one to forget one's duties to the country), ed. Yu Xiguang (Changsha: Hunan renmin chubanshe, 1989), 52–74, 59.

43. Dai and Luo, "Nü," 59, 60.

44. Dai and Luo, "Nü," 60.

45. Garber made a similar point when she talked about a Third World approach as "a mode of articulation, a way of describing a space of possibility. Three puts in question the idea of one: of identity, self-sufficiency, self-knowledge." See Garber, *Vested Interests,* 11.

46. Chen Yingzheng, "Wo zai Taiwan suo tiyan de wenge" (My experience with the Cultural Revolution in Taiwan), *Yazhou zhoukai,* 26 May 1996. Reprinted in *Huaxia wenzhai (zengkan)* (Supplement to *China News Digest*), *Wenge bowuguan zhuanji* (Special issues on the Cultural Revolution Museum, no. 20), vol. 114, 13 March 1997, 14–16.

47. Feng Jicai, "Zhongjie wenge" (On the conclusion of the Cultural Revolution), in *Huaxia wenzhai (zengkan),* 6–9, 7. See also Feng Jicai, *Ten Years of Madness: Oral History of China's Cultural Revolution* (San Francisco: China Books & Periodicals, 1996).

48. Feng, "Zhongjie wenge," 9.

49. Feng, "Zhongjie wenge," 8.

50. Feng, "Zhongjie wenge," 9.

# 7

# Icons of Power: Mao Zedong and the Cultural Revolution

*Robert Benewick*

This chapter describes the centrality of the representation of Mao Zedong in the revolutionary iconography of the Cultural Revolution. Written and visual representations and venerations of Mao appeared in many forms. These included imposing larger-than-life statues dominating the entrance to public buildings and occupying prominent public spaces. Porcelain figures of Mao in different poses were manufactured to adorn homes, offices, and meeting rooms. A staged photograph shows a naval hero studying Chairman Mao's works, with a portrait, a porcelain bust, and two plaster of paris figures of Mao on the table.[1] Three hundred and fifty million copies of *Quotations of Chairman Mao Zedong* (the "little red book"), which was originally published in 1964 for the People's Liberation Army (PLA), were distributed. Quotations were extracted and, along with Mao's poetry and calligraphy, were reproduced for display in poster form. The PLA also created behavioral models for emulations and encapsulations of Mao Zedong thought.[2] Mao's portrait first appeared on postage stamps in 1944, as did Zhu De's in the liberated areas, replacing those of Sun Yat Sen and Chiang Kai Shek. By the time of the Cultural Revolution, stamps were replicating the posters and featuring Mao. Not content with visual and written representations, Mao's supporters also composed hymns and anthems.

While there is nothing unique in the promotion of a personality cult, the sheer volume, scale, and pervasiveness of this iconography, along with that promoting agriculture, industry, commerce, the Communist Party, the PLA, sports, health, education, the *new* culture, Chinese revolutionary history, and patriotism and that portraying workers, peasants, soldiers, heroes and emulation models, women, children, national minorities, foreign friends and enemies, are revolutionary.[3] No doubt visual representation was also expedient given the limited means of alternative communication, the people's limited literacy, and Mao's limitations as a public speaker. Consequently, there was no physical, let alone politically permissible, space to challenge Chairman Mao, thereby imparting meaning to the slogan "The whole country is red." This is totalizing power.[4]

The promotion of the cult of Mao's personality was characterized by the extraordinarily high, perhaps unique, degree of politicalization featuring mass mobilization, violence, and indoctrination; a symbiotic relationship between authority and rebellion serving the leader—a distortion of the Yan'an talks; the creation of mass insecurity aligned with the promotion of Mao as the symbol of stability and order; as well as the development and widespread use of revolutionary iconography. The strategy was one of upheaval, as reflected in the *People's Daily* headline: "There Is Chaos under Heaven—The Situation Is Excellent." Millions of Chinese were victims of the Cultural Revolution, particularly intellectuals—universally a symptom of a tyrannical regime. The chosen instruments were the peasants, workers, and in particular the eleven-million-strong Red Guards, who were instructed to smash the Four Olds: old ideas, old culture, old customs, and old habits of the exploiting class, while not only new ideas, new culture, new habits, new customs but also new icons would be created. To give just one example of the fanaticism engendered, the Red Flag Combat Regimental team of the Beijing Institute of Aeronautics and its counterparts in other cities attempted to turn China into a "Red Sea." Wearing Mao badges and carrying copies of *Quotations of Chairman Mao,* members painted everything in sight red. According to one account, "the stores, government offices, tea shops, noodle restaurants and various eateries were so completely covered that it was impossible to tell which was which." The Central Committee and State Council were forced to issue a proclamation at the end of 1966 entitled "Notice about Restraining the Indiscriminate Action of the So-Called Red Sea."[5]

This chapter will focus on portraits and posters as icons of the totalizing of Mao Zedong's power and on badges as individualizing icons of his power.[6] The choice of icons is commensurate with the levels of identity. Portraits of Chairman Mao identify him with the Chinese nation and *as* the party-state. Crowd posters identify Mao with the viewer; these and the portraits will be examined in the next section, "Poster Power." Badges identify the viewer-wearer with Chairman Mao and are the subject of the section "The Red Badge of Power." The commodification of Mao's identity and of icons of power is discussed in the concluding section.

**Poster Power**

The revolutionary iconography of the Cultural Revolution was multifunctional, with thin lines of demarcation and considerable overlap between functions. The list is imposing and includes education, propaganda, persuasion, communication, inspiration, contemplation (see John Gittings's chapter), ideology, exhortation, promotion (personality cult), catalyst, interpretation, visual presentation, design, decoration, art production, technology, and representations of socialist realism and revolutionary romanticism. Above all they were expressions of power, and no more so than in the representations of Mao Zedong. He was officially characterized as "Great Leader, Great Teacher, Supreme Commander, and Great Helmsman." And as Chairman Mao he was all four at one and the same time, reinforcing his identity with the nation and as the party-state. What was intended, of course, could give way to the unintended, so the viewer might perceive him as revolutionary hero or tyrannical dictator.

The portraits and posters can be classified into those that feature Mao directly and those that represent him indirectly. In the first set, Mao either fully occupies or shares poster space and may be depicted in different poses and settings and at different ages. In the second set this domination is indirectly and symbolically represented, by what Stephanie Donald describes as icons of political activism. The figures may be wearing Mao badges depicting Mao or carrying *Quotations of Chairman Mao* or copies of the

*Selected Works,* or they may be Red Guards, presumably acting on Mao's behalf, wearing armbands and mouthing slogans, while the captions may repeat his quotations. They may appear in combination and in nonpolitical settings to promote production, education, or health, for example. In every poster, however, these figures are expressions of power.

Chinese Communist revolutionary art had been given a new twist. The original formulation and legitimization of this art dates from Mao's talks at the Yan'an Forum on Art and Literature in 1942. Yan'an was the revolutionary base in west-central China, established at the end of the Long March, which served as the headquarters for the communists during the anti-Japanese and civil wars. Mao ordered artists and writers to "go among the masses and serve the people." They were to discover and promote the revolutionary consciousness of the Chinese peasantry through all art and literary forms—the *old* was to serve the *new*. The campaign was also to broaden people's involvement in whatever was seen to serve as art.

The outcome was a series of symbiotic relationships: artistically between (revolutionary) realism and (revolutionary) romanticism; ideologically between the party and the state; culturally between Mao as leader, the nation, and the Chinese people. The Cultural Revolution and the promotion of the cult of Mao's personality, however, came to signify both Mao's authority and people's rebellion in the service of the leader against what appeared to be the party-state. Portrait and poster art expressed totalizing power, while badge art, which combined an optimistic aesthetic with political functionalism, expressed individualizing power. Traditional art forms (the old), rather than being made to serve the people and promote the new, were branded "poisonous weeds."

Domination and power are most explicit in the 2.2 billion poster portraits of Chairman Mao.[7] They signified deification, distance, and omnipresence. He may appear as a young scholar, as in *Chairman Mao goes to Anyuan (Mao zhuxi qu Anyuan)* (plate 6 [N35]), or asking "Who is in charge of the universe?" (*Asking who is in charge of the universe [Wen cangmang dadi shei zhu chenfu],* N41, 1978); as a young revolutionary in an army uniform (see below); as one of the immortals with Marx, Engels, Lenin, and Stalin;[8] as well as the omnipresent Chairman Mao.

Great care could be taken in presentation. Posters were reproduced from oils, watercolors, and photographs. The principal standards for painting Mao after 1971 were "*hong, guang, liang*"—red, bright, and shining—a fact that was precisely confirmed by the leading Sichuan landscape artist Li Huasheng. For the red flag and for the star on Mao's cap, only the purest red pigment could be used. And one couldn't use any gray for shading.[9] In 1997 Men Songzhen revealed how the photographic department of the New China News Agency touched up photos. Her most famous work was a makeover of Edgar Snow's 1936 photograph of the young Mao in an army uniform, to give him a kinder look.[10] The transformed photograph appeared as posters, badges, and ceramics and in the 1990s as a laminated print in vehicles as a talisman. A one-off poster and stamp (ca. 1967) (figure 7.1 [[N4]) is important in regard to the promotion of the cult of Mao's personality and the deployment of Cultural Revolution symbols. The poster shows Mao and Lin Biao in PLA uniforms with the caption "Our great and most beloved leader Chairman Mao with his closest comrade-in-arms, Comrade Lin Biao" ("Women zui aide weida lingxiu Mao zhuxi he tade qinmi zhanyou Lin Biao tongzhi zai yiqi"). Lin Biao was appointed minister of defense in 1959 and was designated Mao's successor after the summer of 1966. The post was not formally confirmed until 1969, and Lin fell out of favor by 1971. During the period

Fig. 7.1 [N4]. *Our great and most loved leader Chairman Mao with his closest com-rade-in-arms, Comrade Lin Biao (Women zui aide weida lingxiu Mao zhuxi he tade qinmi zhanyou Lin Biao tongzhi zai yiqi).* N.p., n.d (ca. 1967).

of Lin's ascendancy the PLA was chief promoter of the personality cult. Whether Lin undertook this commission on his own behalf or with the compliance of the Cultural Revolution group or under instruction from Chairman Mao has yet to be historically resolved. *Quotations of Chairman Mao* was published in 1964 primarily for use within the PLA, and the military was an important manufacturer of Mao badges. Posters and photographs presented PLA personnel waving the *Quotations* and wearing badges, often more than one. With Lin' s demise *Quotations of Chairman Mao* tends to disappear from posters (plate 29 [N8]), although attempts to curtail the badges were less effective.

The siting, hanging, and carrying of Mao's portraits served to reinforce distance and omnipresence. Face-on portraits occupied positions of honor in all workplaces and homes and featured in Cultural Revolution processions and demonstrations. His portrait dominates Tian'anmen today; when it was defaced during the protests of 1989, it was quickly repaired. It should be remembered with respect to this particular form of representation that, for different reasons, democracies—both people's democracies and liberal democracies—need icons of personality, while affecting to disdain them. The icons will differ, however, according to inspiration and intensity, range and resonance, source and scale.[11]

The posters in which Mao shares space, mainly with crowds, seek to humanize, secularize, and narrow (but not close) the distance between him and the viewer. At the same time, the cult of his personality is projected and he adds authority to the message. The crowd too is important as a signifier, and, as Gittings observes in this volume, posters provoked discussion.

Many Cultural Revolution posters, particularly those of the Red Guard years, display violence. A 1967 poster (E10, *Quotations of Chairman Mao [Mao zhuxi yulu]*) shows an air force man, peasant, soldier, and worker crushing tiny imperialist/capitalist figures with fists. Such posters attract the attention of the analyst as evidence of social upheaval and disorder. Posters presenting Mao in a crowd scene, however, tend towards peaceful expressions of social solidarity and celebration, created by the presence of the chairman.[12] Even where there is latent violence, as in posters showing Mao greeting the Red Guards, celebration and reverence predominate. Whatever the explicit message, Mao appears as the symbol of stability and order amid the chaos and upheaval for which he bears responsibility.

The poster of Mao addressing a Red Guard rally from the bridge outside Tian'anmen appeared in several versions. A 1967 painting, widely reproduced, shows Chairman Mao on the bridge with Zhou Enlai, Lin Biao, and the leaders of the Cultural Revolution Group, Chen Boda, Jiang Qing, and Kang Sheng. They wear Mao badges and hold the *Quotations of Chairman Mao*. Mao's right hand is stretched out as if to shake hands with the adoring crowd wearing Red Guard armbands and badges and carrying "little red books." The scene is one of Mao investing the crowd with a mission. The captions read, "The hearts of Chairman Mao and the revolutionary masses beat in union" and "Chairman Mao, to see you marks the realization of our most cherished dreams. We will never forget these happy times. Guided by your brilliant thoughts we will bring the revolution to a conclusion."[13]

A 1973 version, based on a painting by seven artists, is less militant but also less celebratory and more authoritarian. Mao is depicted in a Lenin-like pose with his left arm raised and outstretched towards the admiring crowd. Even though workers, peasants, and soldiers have replaced the Cultural Revolution Group, including Zhou Enlai and the disgraced and now dead Lin Biao, and the "little red book" has vanished, the physical and emotional distance between Mao and the crowd has increased. An inscription on the left reads, "Long Live the Communist Party of China" and, on the right, "Follow Chairman Mao's Long March." The caption reads, "March forward to achieve the Great Proletarian Cultural Revolution." The 1976 version in plate 29 [N8] is identical to that of 1973 with the exception of the caption, which now reads, "For consolidating the dictatorship of the proletariat, guarding against capitalist restoration, and establishing socialism, the Great Proletarian Cultural Revolution could not be more necessary or timely."

Crowd mobilization as a Cultural Revolution theme and Mao as the chief mobilizer are well expressed in other examples of poster art. In the poster shown in figure 7.2 [N59] and in N52 Mao appears as a larger-than-life figure dressed in the tunic originally styled by Sun Yatsen, widely worn in the People's Republic and achieving icon status as a "Mao jacket." In figure 7.2, *Closely follow our great leader Chairman Mao and go forward courageously!* Mao towers above the crowd as their leader, as the caption makes clear. Insofar as there is a relationship between Mao and the crowd, the crowd is serving the leader. In N52 Mao stands with the crowd but slightly ahead, in the center and as the largest figure, as appropriate for a great leader. The caption reads, "Unite to achieve great victories." Among those sporting smiles, wearing badges and carrying the *Quotations* are a peasant, a worker, a soldier, and a cadre in a Mao jacket. The crowd is also on the march but celebrating his leadership.

The posters discussed thus far position Mao before, above, or at the head of the crowd. They are as much about about projecting his image as promoting identification

紧跟伟大领袖毛主席奋勇前进!

Fig. 7.2 [N59]. *Closely follow our great leader Chairman Mao and go forward courageously (Jin gen weida lingxiu Mao zhuxi fenyong qianjin)*. Shanghai 1969.

with the viewer. Many posters, however, narrow the distance between Mao and the crowd and are thereby more accessible to the viewer, inviting identification. The settings tend to be rural, the themes less threatening, ranging from the serious to the celebratory, the crowds are drawn from the peasantry, there are allusions to historic Party struggles, and they are drawn in the spirit of the Yan'an talks, that is, learning from and serving the people.

The posters in plates 30 [N11] and 31 [N51] show Mao on inspection tours, a reference to his Report on the Investigation of the Peasant Movement in Hunan (1927) on the revolutionary potential of the peasantry. In the poster *Chairman Mao's rural investigations in the Jinggang mountains* (1971) (plate 30) Mao appears as a young revolutionary in uniform. Even though the crowd is made up of armed peasants who were supporting the early Red Army base, they do not appear aggressive or threatening. It is a meeting among equals. Mao and a crowd of peasants, some wearing badges, are pictured striding across the countryside in the poster *Chairman Mao visits the Guangdong countryside* (plate 31). Mao, accompanied by the team or brigade leader, is slightly in the lead. He cuts a striking figure, but not disproportionately so, as in the earlier posters. Yet his white shirt, open at the neck, and gray trousers are markedly different from the working clothes of the peasants. The hat in his right hand, however, as well as being functional, serves as a badge of identification as signified by two similar hats in the crowd. It is a happy scene; the crowd is pleased to show Chairman Mao their achievements and take pleasure in his presence.

A late poster (1977), *A heart-to-heart talk (Zhixin hua)* (figure 7.3 [N39]), reproduces a favorite theme. Mao is dressed so as to identify him with rural China, yet his

Fig. 7.3 [N39]. *A heart-to-heart talk (Zhixin hua).* Beijing 1977.

outfit contrasts with the peasants' clothing, which clearly identifies them with the Yan'an region. He sits chatting, smoking, drinking tea with, and listening to, the small crowd. Also set in Yan'an is another popular poster (plate 32 [N13]), which depicts Mao in a celebratory crowd. Here, in *New spring in Yan'an (Yan'an xin chun),* Mao as expected is center stage, wearing a dress tunic, smoking, and not portrayed markedly out of proportion with the crowd. What is most unusual, however, is that it is one of the few posters in which he is shown making human contact , in this instance with a child.[14] Even when he is sited as part of the crowd, narrowing the distance from the viewer, a degree of distance is usually maintained by the absence of physical contact. The crowd in *New spring* is also interesting for its representation of different groups in the area. The *Quotations* and Mao badges are absent from this 1972 poster, but note the slogans displayed by the children: "Be self-sufficient. Use your own resources."

There is no shortage of posters representing Mao indirectly through icons of activism. These icons were also used in posters in which Mao was directly represented (plate 31 [N51]) and N52 *(Unite, and achieve even greater victories)* frequently enough to make their absence, as in plate 29 (N8) noteworthy. The poster shown in figure 7.4 (E5) repeats the popular slogan, "Chairman Mao is the red sun in our hearts." Although the poster is dated 1966, in place of the Red Guards and the *Quotations of Chairman Mao,* it features the cultural-revolutionarily-correct triumvirate of worker, peasant (often female), and soldier, with minority nationalities in the background holding *The Selected Works of Mao Zedong.* While the worker in the foreground holds his copy aloft, the others hold their copies against their hearts.

Fig. 7.4 [E5]. *Chairman Mao is the red sun in our hearts (Mao zhuxi shi women xin zhong de hong taiyang)*. Shanghai 1966.

## The Red Badge of Power

The badge identified the wearer with Chairman Mao and, through him, with China and the party-state, workplace, and residence. It signified individualized power and demonstrated a peculiar mix of authority and rebellion. Not to wear a badge could be taken as a sign of disgrace, disloyalty, or bourgeois individualism, especially since those said to have a bad family background were forbidden to wear them.

Badges also served other purposes. They were issued to commemorate anniversaries such as the founding of the Party or the PLA; they had ceremonial functions commemorating visits or inspections by party-state leaders; and they were presented as rewards for achievements or attendance at meetings. What was special, however, was that in an environment that discouraged gifts and favors, badges acquired an exchange value and preserved the notion of reciprocity. For example, a badge *Chair-*

*man Mao goes to Anyuan* (discussed below) is inscribed on the reverse "Long Live Chairman Mao" but in addition has a personal inscription for presentation or exchange, "Keep in step with Chairman Mao and forge ahead courageously."[15] The more elaborate the badge and valuable the material, the greater the esteem. The badges' distinguishing feature was the omnipresent image of Mao Zedong.

Mao is shown facing left on over 85 percent of the badges, signifying the desired direction of change. As in the posters, he appears in different guises and poses: student, revolutionary, soldier, peasant, and, above all, Chairman Mao. Better use was made of less space than in the posters. The name and place of the issuing organization—factory, commune, PLA unit, revolutionary committee—was normally inscribed on the reverse side of the badge, and slogans and quotations may appear on both sides. One favorite reads, "Follow the Leadership of the Proletariat. Long Live Chairman Mao/Commission of People's Liberation Army in the Ministry of Construction/ Power in the fields of education, literature and the arts and the influence of the government has been controlled by the army during the Cultural Revolution."[16]

Many of the badges were loaded with symbolism. One of the most common replicated the slogan on the poster in figure 7.4; red rays surround Mao's image, portraying him as the red sun in the hearts of the Chinese people. Symbols of national unity include cogs of industry, sheaves of grain, and red flags. Sets of badges were issued adorned with the sacred sites and monuments of the revolution or with the important landmarks along the route of the Long March. Unlike posters, badges used traditional symbols: the pine tree connotes toughness; the palace lantern was an expression of love and respect for Mao; and sunflowers, since they always turn towards the sun, were likened to the people's devotion to Mao. Even so, the badge contributed, and was intended to contribute, to replacing the old ideas, beliefs, and traditions with the new ones identified with the chairman.

It comes as no surprise that the number of posters and "little red books" printed and distributed is paltry compared with the production of the ubiquitous badge, of which an estimated 2.5 *billion* to 5 *billion* were produced. More than twenty thousand different badges have been produced. Plated aluminum badges, red in color, were the most common, but twenty-seven different materials have been noted, ranging from expensively produced ceramic to the fragile bamboo. As the number manufactured and worn increased, so did the size of the badges, suggesting not only competition for favor but also a change of use, that is, the badge could serve as a plaque, a wall decoration, or a talisman.

This adds up to individualizing power and personalizing ideology and culture, sanctifying the badge through the wearer's identification with Chairman Mao. The badge is serving the leader not the people. Moreover, there was conflict and competition to determine the true wearer or believer as distinct from the ritual wearer. In this sense, the badge had become an icon of a process of indoctrination and an instrument to settle old scores.

By the autumn of 1968 the Cultural Revolution was out of control, and Mao directed the PLA to restore order. In June 1969, orders were issued seeking to limit the manufacture of the badges. It was during this period that the promotion of the cult of Mao's personality reached its peak. An examination of two badges illustrates the institutionalization of the cult and its relation to power.

The first badge is one of more than seventy different images of Mao in 1921 on his way to organize a miners' strike. They differ from the portrayal of Chairman Mao facing left, which adorned most badges, by showing the young Mao striding out in a scholar's gown. The images are based on an oil painting, credited mainly to Liu Chunhua, entitled *Chairman Mao goes to Anyuan*. Both Clunas and Gittings refer to the painting as a Cultural Revolution icon in its own right, while Laing argues that the "work politically is perhaps the single most important painting of the Cultural Revolution period."[17]

The painting was important in a number of ways. First, it fed into the power struggle between Mao and Liu Shaoqi, who by then was being referred to as China's Khrushchev and who died in disgrace in prison in 1969. The Anyuan miners' union was the first important union led exclusively by the Chinese Communist Party and was one of the strongest sources of support for the Party prior to 1949. A 1961 painting by Hou Yimin entitled *Liu Shaoqi and the Anyuan coal miners,* of which 172,077 copies were printed, shows the young Liu leading the strike.[18] Six years later, in 1967, the painting was denounced as an attempt to rewrite history and was labeled a "poisonous weed."[19] Instead, an exhibition was organized in the Museum of Revolutionary History in Tian'anmen Square to promote Chairman Mao's visits, in which the new painting of Chairman Mao on his way to organize the miners prominently featured.[20] Second, this painting signaled the shift away from the students/Red Guards to the workers/peasants/soldiers as the instruments of the Cultural Revolution, as signified by the mango in the second badge discussed below. Third, the painting represents the high point of the politicization of culture and the iconographic representation of Mao Zedong.

The artist claimed that nine hundred million copies of the painting were printed and distributed throughout China (plate 6 [N35]). Copies were also painted by established artists like Li Huasheng and Yu Jiwu.[21] The prints usually had a version of the following caption: "In autumn 1921 our great leader Chairman Mao went to Anyuan and personally kindled the flame of revolution there." It was ever present at meetings and demonstrations, along with other icons of the Great Helmsman. Red Guards even walked to Inner Mongolia holding aloft a reproduction of the painting. Jiang Qing, Mao's wife and arbiter of culture, declared it a model painting equal in stature to the eight model operas and ballets that she promoted. According to one Chinese analysis:

> Mao's eyes are gazing ahead over the road of revolutionary advance. His clenched fist shows his determination to smash the old world to smithereens. The old umbrella symbolizes his working style of shirking no hardships for the revolution.[22]

The artist's own description begins, "We placed the Chairman in the forefront of the painting, tranquil, farsighted and advancing towards us like a rising sun bringing hope to the people," thereby establishing an identification with the viewer. So while the painting identified Mao with the revolution and the Chinese people, the badge in its numerous versions identified the wearer with Mao and the revolution. A symbiotic relationship was established.

We are, however, still left with the romantic image of an effete young man in a scholar's gown who somehow is supposed to organize and lead those tough, exploited miners, as portrayed in the earlier painting of Liu Shaoqi, leading the strike. A later painting shows Mao in more convincing dress with the miners.[23]

Where the badges and posters of *Chairman Mao goes to Anyuan* illustrate how extensive and total the cult of Mao's personality and power was, the second badge signifies how intensive it had become. The different versions of the event that also led to more than seventy badges being produced can be reconstructed as follows. In August 1968 the foreign minister of Pakistan called upon Mao Zedong and presented him with a basket of mangoes. This was an appropriate gift since it represented agricultural produce of Pakistan. Even more, the red and golden colors of the mango traditionally symbolize happiness and prosperity for the Chinese; here they represent the red flag and yellow stars of the People's Republic, as well as the so-called red sun, that is, Mao, in the hearts of the Chinese people. There was one problem: Mao did not like mangoes.

After graciously accepting the basket of mangoes, he sent them to the worker–peasant–Mao Zedong–thought propaganda team that had been dispatched to Qinghua University to take over from the Red Guards and restore order after two months of campus warfare in which ten were reported dead and hundreds were injured. As with the portrait *Chairman Mao goes to Anyuan,* this was also a signal: Mangoes were in, the Red Guards were out. The *People's Daily* reported the receipt of the mangoes as follows:

> When this joyous news spread on the Tsinghua campus, every one of us was overjoyed. We sang one song after another. We held in our hands the precious gift from Chairman Mao and looked at his portrait. Our hearts swelled and tears ran down our cheeks. We waved our red-covered book *Quotations from Chairman Mao Zedong,* and all our feelings were concentrated in our cheers "Long live our great leader Chairman Mao! A long, long life to Chairman Mao!"[24]

The mangoes were placed on a red table in the middle of the campus, and people came and pledged themselves to Mao and the proletarian revolution. In order to preserve the mangoes for future generations, some of them were placed in glass containers filled with formaldehyde. As the happy news spread, celebrations were held throughout China and pilgrimages were organized to view the mangoes. Some of the mangoes, or replicas, were sent to other cities, placed in glass cases, and given an honor guard.

What is interesting about this episode is the coincidence of the present of mangoes and the leashing in of the Red Guards. On 27 July 1968 the worker-peasant work team was sent into Qinghua University with a directive that they should cooperate with the PLA in taking over the revolution in education. On 5 August, the very day that Mao received the mangoes, he forwarded them to the work team. Was this a ruler's inspiration, and, if so, how was the response orchestrated? It also raises the more general question of what constitutes people's art and how it is determined.[25] The painting of *Chairman Mao goes to Anyuan* had a clear purpose, and it was promoted by Mao's wife, Jiang Qing. But we are left to speculate how the mangoes became an icon of power and devotion, decorating badges portraying the benevolent, mature Mao and identifying the wearer with the shift in policy. An attempt to paint the celebration of the mangoes ranks as an inferior work of propaganda art.[26]

Although the Cultural Revolution decade lasted until Mao's death in 1976, the production of badges began to wind down in 1969. The generally accepted explanation stems from an incident in which, in response to a presentation of badges, Mao is alleged to have said, "Take them away and bring me airplanes." This is a reference to the use of aluminum as the material for the vast majority of badges. A more likely explanation is that the decline was part of the repudiation of Lin Biao, following his alleged attempted coup and flight from China in 1971.

## Mao Meets the Market

The policies of the post-Mao reformers are rooted in the determination to prevent a recurrence of the upheavals of the Cultural Revolution and to legitimate and secure their own power. Mao's mandate on earth had proved as unstable as the Emperor's mandate of heaven was remote. The main instrument of reform has been the market-orientated economy. The 1950s Maoist slogan, "Anything can be achieved through will" has been superseded by the entrepreneurial motto, "Everything possible, nothing too weird."[27] One expression of this is the commodification of Cultural Revolution relics in general and the Mao image in particular. This can be seen as signifying a further stage in the evolution of China's ideology and cultural values. Yet it does not explain the revival of the cult of Mao's personality, which may suggest the opposite, that is, a cultural and ideological vacuum—what Gordon White has described as the decline of ideocracy.[28]

The revival that began in the late 1980s manifested itself in a number of ways. Photographs of Mao appeared in taxis, minibuses, and official cars, and along with them came apocryphal tales of accidents avoided and lives saved. A transformation of Mao from revolutionary icon to pop icon was achieved in 1991 when the Cultural Revolution ode to Mao Zedong, "The Red Sun," topped the charts for a single videotape with a sale of 5.8 million, rising to 14 million in 1993.[29] The centenary of Mao's birth in 1993 produced a heady mix of commemoration, commodification, and caricature. The market was flooded with brand-new lines of Mao kitsch, including watches, alarm clocks with Red Guards waving copies of the "little red book," medallions, commemorative plates and plaques, and cigarette lighters that, when they worked, played the Cultural Revolution anthem, "The East Is Red." The advent of the karaoke bar opened opportunities for more Maoist golden oldies to make a comeback; the Central Propaganda Department got into the act by issuing an anthology of Maoist songs. But most of all, the revival has centered on recycled and reproduced Mao badges and the commercialization of Cultural Revolution art.

Throughout the 1980s the party-state issued directives calling in Mao badges, and by 1988 an estimated 90 percent had been recovered.[30] This would still have left 50 million badges unaccounted for, so it is not surprising that the official *Beijing Review* headlined an article in 1993, "Mao Badge Craze Returns to China." Collectors and collections appeared or reappeared. Moreover, in Shaoshan, Hunan Province, Mao's birthplace, and at the Mao Zedong Memorial Hall, the sale of badges had never been stopped. Research societies were formed, exhibitions held, and catalogues published assigning commercial value to the badges.

These badges are for sale, trade, or display rather than for identifying a wearer with Chairman Mao. When a badge is worn, it is as a fashion accessory to adorn denim or, more spectacularly, as an outfit displayed at the International China Young Fashion Designers' Contest in Beijing in April 1998. The number of badges that decorated the model's clothes exceeded the number worn by even the most fanatical PLA soldier in the 1960s.

Cultural Revolution posters can be bought, at a price, in flea markets or viewed, like the one shown in figure 7.2 (N59), in the Mao Zedong theme restaurants, of which more than forty exist in Beijing alone, serving what are purported to be Mao's favorite dishes, with Cultural Revolution Muzak in the background. A shrine with offerings to the chairman may dominate the entrance. and reproductions of Mao badges are distributed as souvenirs by table attendants dressed in regional costume. Paintings featuring Chairman Mao, some of which were reproduced as posters, command high prices at auction.[31] To the best of my knowledge, no badges with new images have been created. The deconstruction of the sacred Mao image has been left to Chinese artists at home and abroad.[32] The juxtaposition of Mao and other Cultural Revolution images with advertisements can be interpreted as satirizing the Yan'an talks on serving the people.

It is apparent that this commodification and revival of the cult of Mao's personality is tolerated by the party-state. The Mao image, whether viewed for profit or for nostalgia, is no longer an icon of power but remains useful in contributing to the legitimation of the party-state and for promoting the market economy. It is my contention, however, that Mao, born again, is symptomatic of the exigencies of the transfer to a market-oriented economy and of the transformation of the totalizing-individualizing power relationships of the Cultural Revolution and the terror it inspired to the faceless power of the post-Maoist regimes. These are related phenomena but will be taken in turn in order to distinguish, at least analytically, between commodification and the personality cult.

First of all there are the opportunities that the market has opened up and the improvement in living standards for a significant proportion of the population. Against this are rising expectations, massive unemployment, and the risks, insecurities, and inequalities that are market induced. Faceless power can also exercise terror, as in the Tian'anmen crackdown of 1989 and the subsequent attempts to stifle dissent. Moreover, widespread corruption and the limited means for expressions of discontent stretch the credibility of the party-state. The commodification of the Mao badge and related political icons signifies in the context of the market an independence from the party-state, while the Mao cult is representative of a failure to institutionalize political power. This disjuncture between economic and political change has also contributed to an ideological and cultural vacuum. The reformers, aware of the dilemma, have revised the official ideology from Marxism–Leninism–Mao Zedong thought to Marxism–Leninism–Mao Zedong thought and Deng Xiaoping's theory of Building Socialism with Chinese Characteristics. Many will argue that all power is faceless and that democratic politics also require icons, however much that need is denied. The differences between people's democracies and liberal democracies are more than matters of degree, however, and there is a responsibility to clarify the differences.[33]

## Postscript

In March 1998 Liu Chunhua's painting *Chairman Mao goes to Anyuan* was declared a cultural relic. Moreover, a spokesperson for the Cultural Relics Bureau declared that posters, badges, and so on have been recognized as part of China's past and "are of educational significance and should not be lost to history." The painting, which had been purchased at a record price by the Construction Bank of China for US$660,000, was reported as the first painting since 1949 to be officially recognized as a cultural relic.[34]

Just as the rehabilitation of Liu Chunhua's painting may serve as a reminder of the totalizing-individualizing power relationships of the Cultural Revolution, a 1995 painting suggests faceless power. Here is the artist Wang Xingwei in his painting *Road to Anyuan*. Like Mao he carries the old umbrella and his other fist is clenched. Immediately, his Armani suit and Gucci shoes seem as unconvincing as Mao's scholar's gown and cloth shoes. But there is a bigger difference. His back is to the viewer as he sets off in the other direction. This may have been prescient, for as the Anyuan coal mine prepared for its hundredth anniversary in 1998, it was reported that because of the mine's poor performance, most of the fifty thousand workers receive a low wage and some retired workers receive no living expenses.[35]

## Notes

Many people have contributed to this project. I wish to thank Sarah Cook, Laura Rifkin, Xiaoyuan Shang, Paul Wingrove, and our editors, Stephanie Donald and Harriet Evans, but none more than my beloved wife, colleague, and friend, Anne Benewick, who died on 8 December 1998.

1. *China Pictorial,* February 1968, 10.
2. Stefan R. Landsberger, "Mao as Kitchen God: Religious Aspects of the Mao Cult during the Cultural Revolution," *China Information* 11, nos. 2/3 (Autumn/Winter 1996): 202–4.
3. These categories are drawn from the University of Westminster collection.
4. While I was traveling by train in China in 1975, the "whole country" was full of graffiti, "Learn from Dazhai," a reference to the model production brigade. For a critique of explanations of the Cultural Revolution, see Lynn T. White III, *Policies of Chaos* (Princeton, N.J.: Princeton University Press, 1989), 3–49.
5. Yan Jiaqi and Gao Gao, *Turbulent Decade,* ed. and trans. D. W. Y. Kwok (Honolulu: University of Hawaii Press, 1996), 89–90.
6. Michel Foucault, "The Subject and Power," in *Michel Foucault: Beyond Structuralism and Hermeneutics*, ed. H. Dreyfus and P. Rabinew, 2d ed. (Chicago: University of Chicago Press, 1983), quoted in Mayfair Mei-hui Yang, *Gifts, Favors, and Banquets* (Ithaca, N.Y.: Cornell University Press, 1994), 245.
7. Geremie R. Barmé, *Shades of Mao* (Armonk, N.Y.: M. E. Sharpe, 1996), 8.
8. There were also separate posters of the "immortals," and their portraits were displayed on billboards in Tian'anmen Square for national celebrations.
9. Jerome Silbergeld with Gong Jisiu, *Contradictions: Artistic Life, the Socialist State, and the Chinese Painter Li Huasheng* (Seattle: University of Washington Press, 1993), 43.
10. Rone Tempest, "The Woman Who Touched Up Mao's Great Revolution," *Guardian*, 4 February 1997, 8.
11. Robert Benewick and Stephanie Donald, "Badgering the People: Mao Badges, a Retrospective, 1949–1995," in *Belief in China*, ed. Robert Benewick and Stephanie Donald (Brighton, England: Royal Pavilion/Green Foundation, 1996), 31.
12. For the peaceful crowd, see Robert Benewick and Robert Holton, "The Peaceful Crowd: Crowd Solidarity and the Pope's Visit to Britain," in *The Crowd in Contemporary Britain*, ed. George Gaskell and Robert Benewick (London: Sage Publications, 1987), 200–211.
13. *La Chine en construction* 6, no. 2 (February 1968): 22–23.
14. See also Ellen Johnston Laing, *The Winking Owl: Art in the People's Republic of China* (Berkeley and Los Angeles: University of California Press, 1988), figs. 65–67.
15. Circa 1967, author's collection.
16. Benewick and Donald, "Badgering the People," 36.
17. Laing, *Winking Owl,* 67. For other detailed analyses, see Julia F. Andrews, *Painters and Politics in the People's Republic of China, 1949–1979* (Berkeley and Los Angeles: University of California Press, 1994); Landsberger, "Mao as Kitchen God."
18. Andrews, *Painters and Politics*, 328.
19. The painting is reported to be destroyed. Andrews, *Painters and Politics*, 245.
20. According to the Party's official biography of Mao, although Mao visited Anyuan seven

times, Li Lisan was "overall strike commander" and Liu Shaoqi "workers' representative" of the strike that took place in 1922. Unpublished English manuscript of the Department of Research of Party Literature, Central Committee of the Communist Party of China, "Mao Zedong: A Biography (1893–1949)," 62. Originally published in Chinese in Bejing by the Central Party Literature Press, 1996.

21. Silbergeld and Gong, *Contradictions,* 44.

22. *China Pictorial,* September 1968, 13.

23. *China Reconstructs,* August 1969, 9.

24. Quoted in Edward E. Rice, *Mao's Way* (Berkeley and Los Angeles: University of California Press, 1972), 455–56.

25. Michael Schoenhals, ed., *China's Cultural Revolution, 1966–1969* (Armonk, N.Y.: M. E. Sharpe, 1996), 185.

26. See *Chinese Literature,* November 1968, 12 ff.

27. Matt Forney, ''Record Maker,'' *Far Eastern Economic Review,* 3 October 1996.

28. Gordon White, "The Decline of Ideocracy," in *China in the 1990s,* ed. Robert Benewick and Paul Wingrove (London: Macmillan, 1995), 21–33.

29. Jing Wang, *High Culture Fever* (Berkeley and Los Angeles: University of California Press, 1996), 266.

30. Bill Bishop, "Badges of Chairman Mao Zedong," <http://www.cind.org/CR/Maobadge/index.html>, 11 [accessed in 1995 but no longer available].

31. China Guardian Auctions, *Important Art of New China, 1949–1979,* catalogue of auction, 19 October 1996 (Beijing: China Guardian Auction, 1996), items 405, 431, 443, 446, 450, 451, 457, 458, 460, 495, 497, 502, 511.

32. See, e.g., Erró, "Young Mao at San Marco, 1974," in *Von Mao bis Madonna* (Palais Lichtenstein, Vienna: Museum Moderner Kunst Stiftung Ludwig, 1996), 117. Exhibition catalogue.

33. See Michael Walzer, *The Company of Critics* (London: Peter Halban, 1989).

34. Wang Xingwei, "Road to Anyuan," in *Reckoning with the Past* (Edinburgh: Fruitmarket Gallery, 1996), 45. Exhibition catalogue.

35. Summary of World Broadcasts, FE/3244/G6, 4 June 1998.

# 8

# Afterword

*Stephanie Donald and Harriet Evans*

*Picturing Power,* a title we borrowed from Jeffrey Wasserstrom's description of historical *visual* analysis, has been an enlightening project.[1] As editors and as contributors to this volume, we have appreciated the presence of a multiplicity of images and of many and diverse invitations to description and interrogation. We have brought disciplinary structures of academic thinking, as well as our personal memories and impressions, to the job of re-presenting the body of posters to the reader. At the same time, these posters have addressed *us* as a small body of spectators, caught up in our own times and our own perspectives.

Through these different approaches, and our own reflections and discussions as we have tried to think our way through them, two linked points emerge. The first is that visual analysis, in this case of a specific visual discourse of the Cultural Revolution, introduces a range of possible readings into the interpretation of history, which may be neglected by other modes of study. Together, our arguments challenge dominant narratives of the Cultural Revolution as the totalitarian obliteration of all difference. They reintroduce into public view the possibility of retrieving a memory and knowledge of China's recent past that has been denied by the political exigencies of the past two decades. The chapters also remind us of quite obvious categories of difference, those marked by generation, gender, and ethnicity. Questions of class and the separations of rural and urban, Han and non-Han experience are still to be fully explored. The second point is to reiterate the truism that the act of making meaning of any text, whether image or written word, is always a two-way street, even though one in which the "ways" may not be evenly tabulated. Whether the posters are seen as reminders of horror and brutality or of youthful excitement and passion, the readings made of them depend on the knowledge, fears, expectations, cultural specificities, and emotional or psychic needs of their spectators, moving between different moments of experience, memory, and place. We want to use the concluding pages of this book to explore further some of the implications of these two points.

We have viewed these posters as a collection, a bundled fragment of the recent past. In the introduction, we demonstrated how this past is now predominantly reconstructed as a universal tragedy, the responsibility for which lay with the totalitarian designs of a misguided autocrat, blinded by his own version of revolutionary truth. As part of this dominant narrative, the posters that we have looked at here were produced by the Communist Party apparatus as a means of imposing a uniform and obligatory vision of the future. This rendering of the Cultural Revolution suggests that both its producers (here of posters) and its publics were uniformly fixed in set patterns of intention and response. It is, moreover, a narrative that is prevalent in contemporary accounts—autobiographical, popular, and political—of the Cultural Revolution, both within and outside China. However, scholars are beginning to unpack this version of the story, mainly through attention to the details of language, political thought and structure, and individual memories. The Westminster collection affords a matchless opportunity to further this work. A mere glance at the posters reproduced in this book shows that they contain a diversity of aesthetic qualities and symbolic references, indicative of a range of cultural and social relationships, that makes nonsense of the single narrative. They contain visual clues and compositional arrangements that contradict the egalitarianism of Party rhetoric. They indicate that Mao, as image, was by no means omnipresent in the conduct of the Cultural Revolution. As a dominant visual discourse, they constructed not a single message—they were not simply "propaganda"—but alternative possibilities. Even though the outer parameters of these possibilities were clear, they contained within them inconsistencies and tensions often obscured by current dominant accounts.

This book has also shown that the ways in which these posters are viewed goes much further than analysis of the visual items that they materially contain. Exponents of "propaganda" see the posters' spectators as a uniform public; yet as spectators, we are necessarily caught up in a grid of shifting, even conflicting, responses. In writing this book, we have engaged in editorial discussion on matters ranging from the precise relationship between toys and playthings to the point at which art memory becomes art history. It would be inaccurate to dismiss such discussions as intrinsically academic. They have been couched in academic formulae, but the bones of contention are lodged at peculiarly subjective points of conflict and debate. Such discussions exemplify the differences among spectators, now outside China. More interestingly, the posters' own delineation of representational groups—women, men, children; cadres, workers, students, schoolchildren; political leaders, people's martyrs, revolutionary heroes—already marks out a range of different publics. All of these familiar categories will be subdivided by experience, and now by the distance of time, into a far more complex set of spectator groups. These groupings can be seen as components of an overarching narrative of revolutionary practice. Our emphasis here is that they may also be understood as separate groupings with discrete narratives. As such they deserve detailed attention on their own account from students and scholars and in the realms of public history. We cannot comment in any decisive way on the intricacies of belief, irony, terror, pleasure, and cynicism that must have been elicited by certain images at certain times. What we do suggest is that *the very recognition* of the differences, as well as the continuities, within the structures of address in poster art should remind us to look for a multiplicity of meanings in the day-to-day unfolding of history.

We have noted the importance to historical thinking of at least considering the great range of response to any historical document or object-as-document. Neither should we forget the contingencies of production. These posters were produced at different moments. Their images and texts constructed, and were constructed by, in conjunction with the fluctuations of policy and politicking, a continuum of spectatorship across several extraordinary years. Beijing's recent decision to translate *xuanchuan* as *publicity* rather than *propaganda* is thus a timely prompt for our own impulses in looking at these quintessential organs of xuanchuan.[2] They offer both propaganda and publicness, which is rather different from the bland connotations of "publicity." The spectatorships of posters-as-xuanchuan have formed many publics in the last three decades. Those publics, mainly although not exclusively consisting of the citizens of the People's Republic of China, have brought a wide diversity of experience and knowledge to bear on their reception of political posters. Whatever current thinking may be, say, on the absence of civil society in modern China, that should not allow us to assume that there is no publicness. These posters took up space. Much of that inhabitation could be accounted for as the unilateral encroachment of party-state interests in the civil and domestic byways of everyday life. Yet, if we recollect that primary tenet of spectatorship, the two-way street, or if we simply give credit to people's active intelligence, we cannot but look again at so-called ephemera of past times. To do so in a context such as that presented by this book offers the possibility of unburdening or unraveling the past in ways that continuing political constraints have denied. For each insight afforded by the posters there is also the gathering dusk of memory—the memory of the original publics and the knowledge that art is only "memory organised."[3] The posters were not so much memory organized, as politics and aesthetics and cultural expectations organized to address a particular moment in contemporary Chinese history. Now, however, if these posters are drifting to the interest of the connoisseur, as Clunas suggests, then there is a reorganization of culture, memory, and history into art. The movement makes our task more timely. It also requires that both the reader and we should be eventually cautious in our conclusions.

The obvious comment to make on our project is that it is primarily an outsiders' view of a Chinese cultural and political product. With the crucial exception of Xiaomei Chen's piece on memory and continuity in popular art, we are third and fourth party to posters of the Cultural Revolution. That said, we are also very much aware of the very slippery politics of cultural production, spectatorship, and exchange in global markets of the intellectual and the artistic. The decision to *collect* these posters was made, by a non-Chinese scholar, in China at the time of their distribution. They were collected not for investment purposes but for their value as records of a time and place and of how communications happened then and there. Even so, the decision to purchase was strongly influenced by the appeal of the images, if not of the politics that underlay them—although sometimes both were attractive to the purchaser. This raises the question that arises every time we read the literature of Jorge Luis Borges or the poetry of Ezra Pound or listen to the music of Richard Wagner. How is it possible to deny and enjoy, to simultaneously challenge, reject, and take pleasure? One answer may be simply that it is not possible, that aesthetic and phenomenal pleasures can only be read off the intellectual and historical template of experience. This argument was upheld during the Cultural Revolution under the "class-line" theory: the spirit of the true revolutionary is apparent in her or his writing and art. Conversely, counter-revolutionary art can be read from the political credentials of the artist. Beethoven's works were logically banned in China until the late 1970s. The same view continues to be upheld, in different form, by the current Beijing regime in its insistence on the correspondence between the architects and artifacts (effects) of the Cultural Revolution. However, this argument falters when we recall how it legitimized the absolute tessellation of the body, the eye, and the mind by Jiang Qing's cultural authoritarianism during the late 1960s and early 1970s. Perhaps a more tolerant answer might be to accept pleasure but to constantly resituate the product in the period of its manufacture. In our experience, this approach contains and fractures the image in ways that allow for inconsistent and uncomfortable knowledge to enter into the shifting lines of spectatorship.

Analyzing posters has thus enabled us to take a new look at the Cultural Revolution as well as reflect upon the publics it constituted and upon ourselves as components of those publics. John Gittings challenges the monolith of official history by insisting on the publicness of the posters and on their value in terms both of art and of address to the people who lived with them. The posters pictured social relations and problems as well as the political directives that framed each issue. Gittings also reminds us that the posters are a valuable resource for the study and record of revolutionary art in an extraordinary section of world history. That reminder seems all the more urgent at the end of the twentieth century, when so much that seemed monolithic now looks frail or has already disintegrated.

Craig Clunas's emphasis on the singularity of memory within spectatorship in general, and academic spectatorship in particular, also poses a threat to monolithic accounts of cultural formations. He remembers the Maoist propaganda team that set up shop in Aberdeen, Scotland, for one morning in the 1960s and recalls the omnipresence and—for him but not for Gittings—distinct unsexiness of the posters of the Cultural Revolution. He admits his connection to these posters as part of a shared history, and he notes their current value to Chinese and international collectors. Clunas also remarks on the importance of feminist scholarship to his own place in the academy and notes the misogyny that characterizes much Chinese writing on art, and Cultural Revolution art in particular. It seems that the tension between misogyny and feminism operates transculturally in this area of study. Harriet Evans's work is focused on and within such a dialectic of misunderstanding. She revisits both the assumptions of female equality as pictured in the posters and the skepticism of Western feminisms towards *any* image of woman in a man's world. Evans suggests that, while the equality is clearly undermined by the semiotic structure of the posters, the possibilities for new practice associated with the Cultural Revolution's rhetoric featured positively in the experience of many women. The mobile woman is always an ambiguous figure in wars and revolutionary upheavals—from the French Revolution in 1789, to World Wars I and II in Europe, to the militant women of the early communist movements in China and Vietnam, to the guerrilla fighters of the Sandinistas. The mobile woman's presence in and alongside these posters upsets any easy summation of the direction and meaning of change in social relations of gender.

A similar fissure is opened up in Stephanie Donald's chapter on children. She sees the figuration of children in posters of the 1970s in a continuum beginning with early revolutionary images, many of which provide nostalgic entertainment to contemporary Chinese mainlanders. Furthermore, the emergence of a strong culture of advertisement in the 1980s draws strength from received "revolutionary" practices of representation and organization. The question inevitably arises, where does the culture of the Cultural Revolution begin and end? This point is taken up with personal hindsight, coupled with academic experience in both China and America, by Xiaomei Chen. She describes memories of her own childhood, bound up with small picture books and pinups of favorite heroines from revolutionary operas. She wonders at the harshness of remembering traumatic times, as though China is but the sum of trauma and not a larger, longer history in which cultural artifacts have played a complex role across the years. Her work reminds at least one of the editors of this book of a slight envy of Chinese girlfriends who can still hum along to all the operas now on disk and who claim to have played the leads in small productions in the 1970s. It all seems rather special compared to playing Mary (or an unnamed shepherd) in the Christmas pageant.

Finally, Robert Benewick returns to where we started at the beginning of the introduction to the book. How important is Mao to the history of the Cultural Revolution? In many accounts, both popular and scholarly, he is at the center of the story, with his wife Jiang Qing hovering like an evil genius in his shadow. Benewick's chapter assesses his importance as an icon, a political trump card that operates almost independently of the man himself. Benewick's most exciting insight is perhaps the isolation of Mao as a symbol of national security and social stability, within which extreme political destabilization and disorder could be played out, and played with, for factional advantage.

If we have achieved nothing else, we hope that we have persuaded readers to value the momentary experience in history and that we have shown that revisiting history by examining specific discourses produced at specific times can shed considerable light on a range of related but not obvious issues. This book has shown that the posters of the Cultural Revolution invite interpretations and reflections that go far beyond the limited frame of the posters themselves. In some cases, our interpretations contradict the overt message of the poster. In others, we acknowledge our own subjective function in the "writing" of our own and others' histories. In all these senses, picturing power is an exercise with ambiguous and uncertain results but, we think, one that will help us come a little closer to breaking the mold of received wisdom.

## Notes

1. The title of an Association of Asian Studies panel in the March 1998 meeting in Washington, D.C. Panelists were Jeffrey Wasserstrom, Marilyn Young, Harriet Evans, Carma Hinton, Paola Voci, and Stephanie Donald.

2. See chap. 1, note 57.

3. A quote attributed to Goethe in Jay Parini, *Benjamin's Crossing* (New York: Henry Holt, 1998), 268.

# Poster References

Posters are listed according to the categories and alphanumerical references of the University of Westminster poster catalogue.

## A: Agriculture

A2      *Criticize hard, work hard, and greatly improve the Dahzai standard (Zai da pi, zai da gan, jianshe gao biaozhun de Dazhai xian).* Tianjin 1977.

A4      *We can certainly triumph over nature (Ren ding sheng tian).* N.p., n.d.

A5      *Go full steam ahead and speed up the building of Dazhai counties (Shuai kai bangzi gan, jiasu jianshe Dazhai xian).* Xinjiang 1977.

A11      *The brigade's ducks (Dadui ya qun).* Shanghai 1974.

A34      *The people rejoice as the fish jump (Ren huan yu yue).* Shanghai 1978.

A36      *Hold high the red banner of Dazhai and reap a rich harvest (Gao ju Dazhai hongqi duoqu nongye fengshou).* Prob. Shanghai 1976.

A41      *The new song of the Huai River (Huaihe xin ge).* N.p., n.d.

A42      *Move mountains and make new land (Yi shan zao tian).* Shanghai 1977.

## B: Four Modernizations

B5      *Science is a productive force (Kexue shi shengchan li).* Tianjin 1979.

## C: Industry and Commerce

C4      *Learn from the spirit of Daqing (Xue Daqing jingshen).* Shanghai 1965.

C10      *Develop the economy and guarantee supplies (Fazhan jingji, baozhang gongji).* Beijing 1971.

## D: International Relations

D6      *The Chinese people are not easily humiliated (Zhongguo renmin bu shi hao nuode).* Beijing 1966–1967(?).

D7        *Down with Soviet revisionism (Dadao Su xiu).* Shanghai 1967.

D11       *Our victory is certain, so is the defeat of the Hong Kong English (Women bi sheng, Gang Ying bi bai).* Guangdong 1967(?).

## E: Politics

E2        *The proletarian revolutionaries hold power (Wuchanjieji geming pai lao wo da quan).* Hebei, ca. 1966–1967.

E9        *Oppose economism (Fandui jingjizhuyi).* Shanghai 1967.

E10       *The Quotations of Chairman Mao (Mao zhuxi yulu).* Tianjin 1967.

E19       *Study and use Chairman Mao's glorious philosophical thought on a large scale (Da xue da yong Mao zhuxi guanghui zhexue sixiang).* Shanghai 1971.

E24       *Spread revolutionary criticism in a deep-going way (Shenru kaizhan geming da pipan).* Beijing 1971.

E31       *People's communes are good (Renmin gongshe hao).* N.p., n.d.

E39       *Smash the old world and build a new one (Dasui jiu shijie, chuangli xin shijie).* Beijing 1967.

E43       *Thoroughly expose the monstrous crimes committed while attempting to take over Party power by the anti-Party clique Wang Hongwen, Zhang Chunqiao, Jiang Qing, and Yao Wenyuan (Chedi qingsuan Wang Hongwen, Zhang Chunqiao, Jiang Qing, Yao Wenyuan fandang jituan zuan dang duo quan de taotian zuixing).* Beijing 1976.

## F: Revolutionary History

F3        *Gutian conference (Gutian huiyi).* N.p., n.d.

## H: Health, Education, and Society

H1        *Chart for preventive exercises for the eyes (Yan baojian caotu jie).* Shanghai 1979.

H17       *One child is enough (Du sheng zinü yi zhi hua).* Jiangsu 1980.

## J: Military and Sport

J22       *Furiously criticize [Confucius's doctrine of] "restrain the self and return to the rites" and grasp your gun firmly (Hen pi ke ji fu li, jianwo shouzhong qianggan).* Huxian(?) 1974(?).

J30       *The new soldiers of Nanniwa (Nanniwa de xin zhanshi).* Beijing 1974.

**K: National Festivals and Patriotism**

K13      *Our great homeland is full of life and vigor (Weida zuguo xinxin xiang-rong)*. Shanghai 1974.

**L: Art**

L5      *Our literature and art is all for the masses, and in the first place for the workers, peasants, and soldiers; it has been created for them and is for their use (Women de wenxue yishu dou shi wei renmin dazhong, shouxian shi wei gong nong bing de, wei gong nong bing er chuangzuo, wei gong nong bing suo liyong de)*. Beijing 1967.

L16      *Our literature and art must become a component part of the whole revolutionary machine (Yao shi wenyi hen haode chengwei zhengge geming jiqi de yige zuchengbufen)*. Beijing 1967.

L40      *Spring colors fill the gardens (Chun se man yuan)*. Jiangsu 1980.

**M: Children**

M8      *Isn't our life wonderful! (Women shenghuo duomo meihao)*. Jiangsu 1980.

M9      *Health, long life, and happiness are on their way (Jiankang, chang shou, xingfu lai)*. Liaoning 1981.

M17      *The flower of friendship blossoms (Youyi hua kai)*. Shanghai 1980.

M28      *A happy generation (Xingfu de yi dai)*. Tianjin 1978.

M33      *We love science (Women ai kexue)*. Jiangsu 1978.

M42      *A new classroom (Xin ketang)*. Shanghai 1975.

**N: Leaders**

N1      *Chairman Mao is the reddest red sun in our hearts (Mao zhuxi shi women xinzhong zui hong zui hongde hong taiyang)*. Jilin 1967(?).

N27      *Premier Zhou shares our hardship and happiness (Zhou zongli he women tong gan ku)*. Shanghai 1978.

N28      *Let new socialist culture occupy every stage (Rang shehuizhuyi xin wenyi zhanling yiqie wutai)*. Beijing 1967.

N30      *Long live Chairman Mao; we wish him a long life without end (Mao zhuxi wansui, jingzhi Mao zhuxi wansui wujiang)*. Beijing 1967.

N41      *Asking who is in charge of the universe (Wen cangmang dadi shei zhu chenfu)*. Shanghai 1978.

N42         *Comrades-in-arms (Zhanyou).* Beijing 1977.

N43         *China ought to contribute greatly to humanity (Zhongguo yingdang duiyu renlei you jiaoda de gongxian).* Shanghai 1978.

N52         *Unite, and achieve even greater victories (Tuanjieqilai, zhengqu geng da de shengli).* N.p., n.d.

## Q: Women

Q5          *Women shock troops (Nüzi tuji dui).* Beijing 1975.

Q6          *Graduation report (Biye huibao).* N.p., mid-1970s.

Q15         *I accompany Grannie on her way to night school (Wo song nainai shang yexiao).* Tianjin 1973.

Q19         *Vigorous and spirited; thriving and dynamic (Shengqi bobo).* Jiangsu 1975.

Q22         *Embroidering goldfish which make the waves red (Xuichu jinyu yang po hong).* Shanghai 1979.

## Z: Nianhua (New Year Prints)

Z17–18      *An auspicious official,* recent copy of old blocks, Gugong Museum, Beijing.

Z25         *Welcoming the spring (Ying chun).* Tianjin 1979.

Z28         *The spring wind brings warmth (Chun feng song nuan).* Shanghai 1975–76.

Z30         *This year there will be much rejoicing (Jinnian xi shi duo).* Shanghai 1978.

Z32         *Child and cockerel.* Shanghai, early 1960s(?).

# Bibliography

Ahn, Byung-joon. *Chinese Politics and the Cultural Revolution*. Seattle: University of Washington Press, 1976.

Anagnost, Ann. "Socialist Ethics and the Legal System." In *Popular Protest and Political Culture in Modern China: Learning from 1989*, ed. Jeffrey N. Wasserstrom and Elizabeth J. Perry, 177–205. Boulder, Colo.: Westview Press, 1992.

———. "The Politicized Body." In *Body, Subject, and Power in China*, ed. Angela Zito and Tani Barlow, 131–56. Chicago: University of Chicago Press, 1994.

———. "Children and National Transcendence in China." In *Constructing China: The Interaction of Culture and Economics,* ed. Kenneth G. Lieberthal, Shuen-fu Lin, and Ernest P. Young, 195–221. Ann Arbor: Center for Chinese Studies, University of Michigan, 1997.

———. *National Past-Times: Narrative, Representation, and Power in Modern China*. Durham, N.C.: Duke University Press, 1997.

Andors, Phyllis. *The Unfinished Liberation of Chinese Women, 1949–1980*. Bloomington: Indiana University Press, 1983.

Andrews, Julia F. *Painters and Politics in the People's Republic of China, 1949–1979*. Berkeley and Los Angeles: University of California Press, 1994.

Apter, David, and Tony Saich. *Revolutionary Discourse in Mao's Republic*. Cambridge: Harvard University Press, 1994.

Ariès, Philippe. *Centuries of Childhood: A Social History of Family Life*. Harmondsworth, England: Penguin Books, 1973. Originally published in French as *L'enfant et la vie familiale sous l'ancien régime* (Paris: Libraire Plon, 1960).

Barmé, Geremie. "The Chinese Velvet Prison: Culture in the 'New Age,' 1976–89." *Issues and Studies* 25, no. 8 (August 1989): 54–79.

———. *Shades of Mao: The Posthumous Cult of the Great Leader*. Armonk, N.Y.: M. E. Sharpe, 1996.

Benewick, Robert, and Stephanie Donald. "Badgering the People: Mao Badges, a Retrospective 1949-1995." In *Belief in China: Art and Politics, Deities and Mortality*, ed. Robert Benewick and Stephanie Donald, 28–39. Brighton, England: Royal Pavilion/Green Foundation, 1996.

Benewick, Robert, and Robert Holton. "The Peaceful Crowd: Crowd Solidarity and the Pope's Visit to Britain." In *The Crowd in Contemporary Britain,* ed. George Gaskell and Robert Benewick, 200–211. London: Sage, 1987.

Benewick, Robert, and Stephanie Donald, eds. *Belief in China: Art and Politics, Deities and Mortality*. Brighton, England: Royal Pavilion/Green Foundation, 1996.

Benewick, Robert, and Paul Wingrove, eds. *China in the 1990s*. London: Macmillan, 1995.

Benjamin, Walter. "The Work of Art in the Age of Mechanical Reproduction." In *Illuminations*. 1955. Reprint in translation, London: Fontana, 1992, 211–44.

Bettleheim, Charles. *Cultural Revolution and Industrial Organization in China*. New York: Monthly Review Press, 1974.

Bhabha, Homi K. "The Commitment to Theory." *New Formations* 5 (1988): 5–23.

———. *The Location of Culture*. London: Routledge, 1994.

Bishop, Bill. "Badges of Chairman Mao Zedong." <http://www.cind.org/CR/Maobadge/index.html>. Accessed in 1995; no longer available.

Blumenthal, Eileen P. *Models in Chinese Moral Education: Perspectives from Children's Books.* Ann Arbor: University of Michigan Press, 1979.

Bolton, Andrew. "Chinese Papercuts from the Cultural Revolution at the Victoria and Albert Museum." *Arts of Asia,* November–December 1997, 79–86.

Bonnell, Victoria E. *Iconography of Power: Soviet Political Posters under Lenin and Stalin.* Berkeley and Los Angeles: University of California Press, 1997.

Bourdieu, Pierre. *In Other Words.* Cambridge, England: Polity Press, 1990.

Bourdieu, Pierre, and Jean-Claud Passeron. *Reproduction in Education, Society, and Culture,* trans. Richard Nice. London: Sage, 1977.

Bronfenbrenner, Urie. *Two Worlds of Childhood: USA and USSR.* 2d ed. London: Penguin Education, 1974.

Burch, Betty B. "Models as Agents of Change in China." In *Value Change in Chinese Society,* ed. Richard W. Wilson, Amy Auerbacher Wilson, and Sidney L. Greenblatt, 122–37. (New York: Praeger, 1979).

Cai Tilian. "Xinchao qifu yi quanquan" (Surging thoughts and emotions with a sincere heart). *Qingyi* (Journal of China Youth Art Theater) 58, no. 2 (December 1994): 31–36.

Calhoun, Craig, and Jeffrey N. Wasserstrom. "Wenhua da geming yu 1989 nian minzhu yundong zhijian de lishi guanxi" (Historical connection between the Cultural Revolution and the Democracy Movement of 1989). *Xianggang shehui kexue xuebao* (Hong Kong Journal of Social Sciences), no. 11 (Spring 1998): 129–49. Also to be published as "Legacies of Radicalism: China's Cultural Revolution and the Democracy Movement of 1989," *Thesis* 11, (forthcoming).

Cao Yiqiang and Fan Jingzhong, eds. *Ershi shiji Zhongguo hua: "Chuantong de yanxu yu yanjin"* (Chinese painting in the twentieth century: "Creativity in the aftermath of tradition"). Hangzhou: Zhejiang renmin meishu chubanshe, 1997.

Cavallero, Dani. *The Body for Beginners.* London: Writers & Readers, 1998.

Caygill, Howard. *Walter Benjamin: The Colour of Experience.* London: Routledge, 1998.

*CCP Documents of the Great Proletarian Cultural Revolution, 1966–1967.* Hong Kong: Union Research Institute, 1968.

Chan, Anita. *Children of Mao: Personality Development and Political Activism in the Red Guard Generation.* Seattle: University of Washington Press; London: Macmillan, 1985.

Chan, Anita, Richard Madsen, and Jonathan Unger. *Chen Village: The Recent History of a Peasant Community in Mao's China.* Berkeley and Los Angeles: University of California Press, 1984.

Chan, Anita, and Jonathan Unger. "Voices from the Protest Movement, Chongqing, Sichuan." *Australian Journal of Chinese Affairs* 24 (1990): 259–79.

Chang Jung. *Wild Swans: Three Daughters of China.* London: HarperCollins, 1991; New York: Doubleday, 1992.

Chang, Parris H. "Children's Literature and Political Socialization." In *Moving a Mountain,* ed. Godwin C. Chu and Francis L. K. Hsu, 237–56. Honolulu: University Press of Hawaii, 1979.

Chen, Xiaomei. *Occidentalism: A Theory of Counter-Discourse in Post-Mao China.* New York: Oxford University Press, 1995.

———. "Global Transactions of Chinese Country and City in the Formation of Transnational Cultural Capital in Chinese American Best-Sellers." Paper presented at the American Association of Anthropology meeting, Philadelphia, 2 December 1998. A different version can be found in "Time, Money, and Work," *Journal of American Studies* (Seoul, Korea) 29, no. 2 (Winter 1997): 414–21.

———. "Picture Stories of the People's Republic of China: Images from Popular Culture." In *Literature in Line: Lianhuanhua Picture Stories from China,* ed. Julia F. Andrews and Kuiyi Shen. Exhibition catalogue. Columbus: Ohio State University Cartoon Research Library, forthcoming.

―――. "From the 'Lighthouse': 'Mingdeng' and the Discourse of Fame and Subaltern in Maoist China: A Personal Account." In *Some of Us: Chinese Women Growing up in the Mao Era*, ed. Zhong Xueping, Wang Zheng, and Bai Di. New Brunswick, N.J.: Rutgers University Press, forthcoming.

Chen Xiaoming. "The Mysterious Other: Postpolitics in Chinese Film." *boundary 2* 24, no. 3 (Fall 1997): 123–41.

Chen Yingzheng. "Wo zai Taiwan suo tiyan de wenge" (My experience of the Cultural Revolution in Taiwan). *Yazhou zhoukai*, 26 May 1996. Reprinted in *Huaxia wenzhai* (*zengkan*) (supplement to *China News Digest*), *Wenge bowuguan zhuanji* (special issue on the Cultural Revolution Museum), 13 March 1997, 14–16.

Cheng Nien. *Life and Death in Shanghai*. London: Grafton Books, 1986.

Chi P'ing. "Attach Importance to the Role of Teachers by Negative Example." *Peking Review*, 31 March 1972, 5–8.

Chiang Chen-ch'ang. "The New Lei Feng's of the 1980s." *Issues and Studies* 20, no. 5 (May 1984): 22–42.

China Guardian Auctions. *Important Art of New China, 1949–1979*. Catalogue of auction, 19 October 1996. Beijing: China Guardian Auction Co., 1996.

China Revolutionary Museum. *Kangri zhanzheng shiqi xuanchuanhua* (Propaganda pictures of the anti–Japanese war period). Beijing: Cultural Press, 1979.

*La Chine en construction* 6, no. 2 (February 1968).

Chow, Rey. "Male Narcissism and National Culture: Subjectivity in Chen Kaige's *King of the Children*." *Camera Obscura* (1991): 9–41.

―――. *Primitive Passions: Visuality, Sexuality, Ethnography, and Contemporary Chinese Cinema*. New York: Columbia University Press, 1995.

Chu, Godwin C., and Francis L. K. Hsu, eds. *Moving a Mountain: Cultural Change in China*. Honolulu: University Press of Hawaii, 1979.

Clark, John, ed. *Modernity in Asian Art*. University of Sydney East Asian Studies, no. 7. Broadway: University of Sydney, 1993.

Clark, Paul. *Chinese Cinema: Culture and Politics since 1949*. Cambridge: Cambridge University Press, 1987.

Clark, Toby. *Art and Propaganda in the Twentieth Century*. New York: Harry N. Abrams, 1997.

Clifford, James, and George E. Marcus, eds. *Writing Culture: The Poetics and Politics of Ethnography*. Berkeley and Los Angeles: University of California Press, 1986.

Clunas, Craig. *Fruitful Sites: Garden Culture in Ming Dynasty China*. London: Reaktion Books, 1996.

―――. *Art in China*. Oxford History of Chinese Art. Oxford: Oxford University Press, 1997.

Cohen, Joan Lebold. *The New Chinese Painting, 1949–1986*. New York: Harry N. Abrams, 1987.

Croizier, Ralph. "Chinese Art in the Chiang Ch'ing Era." *Journal of Asian Studies* 38 (February 1979): 303–11.

―――. "The Thorny Flowers of 1979: Political Cartoons and Liberalization in China." In *China from Mao to Deng: The Politics and Economics of Socialist Development*, ed. Bulletin of Concerned Asian Scholars, 29–38. Armonk, N.Y.: M. E. Sharpe; London: Zed Press, 1983.

Croll, Elisabeth. *Feminism and Socialism in China*. London: Routledge, 1978.

Dai Qing and Luo Ke. "Nü zhengzhi fan" (Woman political prisoners). In *Weibei weiguan wang youguo* (A humble position does not allow one to forget one's duties to the country), ed. Yu Xiguang, 52–74. Changsha: Hunan renmin chubanshe, 1989.

Davis, Deborah. "My Mother's House." In *Unofficial China: Popular Culture and Thought in the People's Republic*, ed. Perry Link, Richard Madsen, and Paul Pickowicz, 88–102. Boulder, Colo.: Westview Press, 1989.

Davis, Deborah, and Ezra J. Vogel, eds. *Chinese Society on the Eve of Tiananmen: The Impact of Reform*. Cambridge: Harvard University Press, 1990.

Deaubier, Jean. *A History of the Chinese Cultural Revolution*. New York: Vintage, 1974.

Deng Liqun, et al., eds. *Dangdai Zhongguo meishu* (Fine arts of contemporary China). Beijing: Contemporary China Press, 1996.

Deng Xian. *Zhongguo zhiqing meng* (The dreams of the Chinese educated youth). Beijing: Renmin wenxue chubanshe, 1993.

*Diguo zhuyi he yiqie fandongpai doushi zhilaohu* (Imperialism and all reactionaries are nothing but paper tigers). Beijing: Renmin chubanshe, 1958.

Dittmer, Lowell. *Liu Shao-ch'i and the Chinese Cultural Revolution: The Politics of Mass Criticism*. Berkeley and Los Angeles: University of California Press, 1974.

———. "The Chinese Cultural Revolution Revisited." *Journal of Contemporary China* 5, no. 13 (November 1996): 255–68.

Dittmer, Lowell, and Chen Ruoxi. *Ethics and Rhetoric of the Chinese Cultural Revolution*. Berkeley: Center for Chinese Studies, University of California, Berkeley, 1981.

Donald, Stephanie. "Chinese Cinema and Civil Society in the Post-Maoist Era." Ph.D. diss., University of Sussex, 1996.

———. "Landscape and Agency: Yellow Earth and the Demon Lover." *Theory, Culture, and Society* 14, no. 1 (February 1997): 97–112.

Erró. *Von Mao bis Madonna*. Palais Lichtenstein, Vienna: Museum Moderner Kunst Stiftung Ludwig, 1996.

Evans, Harriet. *Women and Sexuality in China: Dominant Discourses of Female Sexuality and Gender since 1949*. Cambridge, England: Polity Press, 1997.

Farquhar, Mary Ann. "Revolutionary Children's Literature." *Australian Journal of Chinese Affairs*, no. 4 (1980): 61–84.

———. "Children's Literature in China." Ph.D. diss., Griffith University, 1983.

———. "*Sanmao*: Classic Cartoons and Chinese Popular Culture." In *Asian Popular Culture*, ed. John Lent, 139–58. Boulder, Colo.: Westview Press, 1995.

Feng Jicai. "Zhongjie wenge" (On the conclusion of the Cultural Revolution). *Huaxia wenzhai* (*zengkan*) (supplement to *China News Digest*), *Wenge bowuguan zhuanji* (special issues on the Cultural Revolution Museum), 13 March 1997, 6–9.

———. *Ten Years of Madness: Oral History of China's Cultural Revolution*. San Francisco: China Books & Periodicals, 1996.

*Folk Arts of New China*. Beijing: Foreign Languages Press, 1954.

Forman, Harrison. *Report from Red China*. London: Pilot Press, 1945.

Forney, Matt. "Record maker." *Far Eastern Economic Review*, 3 October 1996.

Foucault, Michel. "The Subject and Power." In *Michel Foucault: Beyond Structuralism and Hermeneutics*, ed. H. Dreyfus and P. Rabinew. 2d ed. Chicago: University of Chicago Press, 1983.

———. *The Order of Things: An Archaeology of the Human Sciences*. London: Tavistock/Routledge, 1989.

Fraser, Stewart E., ed. *One Hundred Great Chinese Posters*. New York: Images Graphiques, 1977.

Freedman, Maurice, ed. *Family and Kinship in Chinese Society*. Stanford, Calif.: Stanford Univerity Press, 1970.

Freeman, Derek. *Margaret Mead and the Heretic: The Making and Unmaking of an Anthropological Myth*. Harmondsworth, England: Penguin Books, 1996.

Gallinowski, Maria. *Art and Politics in China, 1949–1984*. Hong Kong: Chinese University Press, 1998.

Gallop, Jane. *Feminism and Psychoanalysis: The Daughter's Seduction*. London: Macmillan, 1982.

Gao, Mobo C. F. "Maoist Discourse and a Critique of the Present Assessment of the Cultural Revolution." *Bulletin of Concerned Asian Scholars* 26, no. 3 (July–September 1994): 13–31.

———. "Memoirs and Interpretations of the Cultural Revolution." *Bulletin of Concerned Asian Scholars* 27, no. 1 (January-March 1995): 49–57.

Gao Yuan. *Born Red: A Chronicle of the Cultural Revolution*. Stanford, Calif.: Stanford University Press, 1987.

Garber, Margorie. *Vested Interests*. New York: Routledge, 1992.

Gittings, John. *A Chinese View of China*. New York: Pantheon, 1973.
———. *China Changes Face*. Oxford: Oxford University Press, 1989.
———. *Real China: From Cannibalism to Karaoke*. London: Simon & Schuster, 1996.
Golomstock, Igor. *Totalitarian Art in the Soviet Union, the Third Reich, Fascist Italy, and the People's Republic of China*. London: Collins Harvell, 1990.
Guha, Ranajit, and Gayatri Chakravorty Spivak, eds. *Selected Subaltern Studies*. New York: Oxford University Press, 1988.
Hall, David L., and Roger T. Ames. *Thinking through Confucius*. Albany: State University of New York Press, 1987.
Han Minzhu, ed. *Cries for Democracy*. Princeton, N.J.: Princeton University Press, 1990.
Hershatter, Gail. "The Subaltern Talks Back: Reflections on Subaltern Theory and Chinese History." *Positions* 1, no. 1 (1993): 103–30.
Hinton, William. *Hundred Day War: The Cultural Revolution at Tsinghua University*. New York: Monthly Review Press, 1972.
Honig, Emily. "Maoist Mappings of Gender: Reassessing the Red Guards." In *Chinese Femininities/Chinese Masculinities,* ed. Jeffrey N. Wasserstrom and Susan Brownell. Berkeley and Los Angeles: University of California Press, forthcoming.
Honig, Emily, and Gail Hershatter. *Personal Voices: Chinese Women in the 1980s*. Stanford, Calif.: Stanford University Press, 1988.
Hong Chanying. "Xiongwei zhuangmei, guangcai zhaoren" (The magnificent and brilliant ballet performance). *Jiefang ribao* (Liberation daily), 15 July 1970. Reprinted in *Zan Hongse niangzijun* (Praising *The Red Detachment of Women*), 29–37. Guangzhou: Guangdong renmin chubanshe, 1970.
Huang Shaorong. *To Rebel Is Justified*. Lanham, Md.: University Press of America, 1996.
*Huang Xinbo banhua xuan* (Selection of woodcuts by Huang Xinbo). Beijing: People's Arts Press, 1961.
Hunter, Neale. *Shanghai Journal: An Eyewitness Account of the Cultural Revolution*. 2d ed. Hong Kong: Oxford University Press, 1988. (Originally published in 1969.)
*Huxian nongminhua xuanji* (Selection of Huxian peasants' paintings). Xi'an: Shaanxi renmin meishu chubanshe, 1974.
Jin Chunming. *Wenhua da geming de shigao* (Outline history of the great Cultural Revolution). Chengdu: Sichuan renmin chubanshe, 1995.
*Joris Ivens and China*. Beijing: New World Press, 1983.
Joseph, William, Christine Wong, and David Zweig, eds. *New Perspectives on the Cultural Revolution*. Harvard Contemporary China Series, no. 8. Cambridge: Harvard University Press, 1991.
Joyce, James. *Dubliners*. London: Penguin Books, 1975.
Karnow, Stanley. *Mao and China: Inside China's Cultural Revolution*. Harmondsworth, England: Penguin Books, 1972.
Kessen, William, ed. *Childhood in China*. New Haven: Yale University Press, 1975
Kinney, Anne Behnke. *Chinese Views of Childhood*. Honolulu: University of Hawaii Press, 1995.
Krips, Valerie. "Imaginary Childhoods: Memory and Children's Literature." *Critical Quarterly* 39, no. 3 (1997): 42–50.
Laing, Ellen Johnston. *The Winking Owl: Art in the People's Republic of China*. Berkeley and Los Angeles: University of California Press, 1988.
———. "Chinese Peasant Painting, 1958–1976: Amateur and Professional." *Art International* 27, no.1 (January–March 1984): 2–12.
———. "Auspicious Images of Children in China: Ninth to Thirteenth Century." *Orientations* 27, no. 1 (January 1996): 47–52.
Landsberger, Stefan R. *Chinese Propaganda Posters*. Amsterdam: Pepin Press, 1995.
———. "Mao as Kitchen God: Religious Aspects of the Mao Cult during the Cultural Revolution." *China Information* 11, nos. 2/3 (Autumn/Winter 1996): 202–4.
———. *Paint It Red: Fifty Years of Propaganda Posters*. Gröningen: Gröninger Museum, 1998.

Larson, Wendy. "Women and the Discourse of Desire in Postrevolutionary China: The Awkward Postmodernism of Chen Ran." *boundary 2* 24, no. 3 (Fall 1997): 201–23.

Lee, Hong Yung. *The Politics of the Chinese Cultural Revolution*. Berkeley and Los Angeles: University of California Press, 1978.

Liang Heng and Judith Shapiro. *Son of the Revolution*. New York: Knopf, 1983.

Li Shibin et al., *Qixi Baihutuan*. Beijing: Zhongguo xiju chubanshe, 1964.

Lin Piao. *Long Live the Victory of People's War!* (Renmin zhanzheng shengli wansui). Beijing: Foreign Languages Press, 1965.

Link, Perry, Richard Madsen, and Paul G. Pickowicz, eds. *Unofficial China: Popular Culture and Thought in the People's Republic*. Boulder, Colo.: Westview Press, 1989.

Liu, Guokai. *A Brief Analysis of the Cultural Revolution*, ed. Anita Chan. Armonk, N.Y.: M. E. Sharpe, 1984.

Liu Zengrong. "Ganwen qianlu zai he chu" (Dare to ask where the road leads). *Beijing qingnian bao* (Beijing Youth Newspaper), 23 October 1996, 3.

Lupher, Mark. "Revolutionary Little Red Devils: The Social Psychology of Rebel Youth, 1966–1967." In *Chinese Views of Childhood*, ed. Anne Behnke Kinney, 321–44. Honolulu: University of Hawaii Press, 1995.

MacFarquhar, Roderick, and John K. Fairbank, eds. *The Cambridge History of China*, Vol. 15, *The People's Republic, Part 2: Revolutions within the Chinese Revolution, 1966–1982*, 880–911. Cambridge: Cambridge University Press, 1991.

Magginis, Hayden B. "The Role of Perceptual Learning in Connoisseurship: Morelli, Berenson, and Beyond." *Art History* 13, no. 1 (1990): 104–17.

*Manhua xuanji: quanguo meishu zuopin zhanlan* (Collection of cartoons: national fine arts exhibition). Beijing: People's Arts Press, 1977.

Mao Zedong. "Take the Characteristics of Youth into Consideration" (1953). In *Selected Works*. Vol. 5. Beijing: Foreign Languages Press, 1977.

*Mao Zedong sixiang xuanchuan lan: baotou ziliao* (Mao Zedong Thought propaganda column: masthead selection). Shanghai: People's Press, 1970.

*Mao zhuxi de hao zhanshi Li Feng* (Chairman Mao's good soldier Lei Feng). Hong Kong: Chaoyang chubanshe, 1971.

Mead, Margaret. "*Monkey*: A Chinese Children's Classic." In *Childhood in Contemporary Cultures*, ed. Margaret Mead and M. Wolfenstein, 246–52. Chicago: University of Chicago Press, 1955.

*Meishu cankao ziliao 2: baotou xuanji* (Art reference material 2: masthead selection). Beijing: People's Arts Press, 1972.

Meisner, Maurice. *Mao's China and After: A History of the People's Republic*. New York: Free Press, 1977.

Min, Anchee. *Red Azalea*. London: Victor Gollancz, 1993; New York: Pantheon, 1994.

Moore, Henrietta. *A Passion for Difference: Essays in Anthropology and Gender*. Cambridge, England: Polity Press, 1994.

National Palace Museum, Taiwan. *Paintings of Children at Play*. Taiwan: National Palace Museum, 1997.

Pack, Susan. *Film Posters of the Russian Avant-Garde*. Germany: Benedikt Taschen Verlag, 1995.

Pan Jia-ching. "Mass Political and Ideological Dissent: Big-Character Posters and Underground Publications in Mainland China." *Issues and Studies* (August 1980): 42–62.

Parini, Jay. *Benjamin's Crossing*. New York: Henry Holt, 1998.

*Peasant Paintings from Hu County*. London: Arts Council, 1976.

Perry, Elizabeth J., and Li Xun. "Revolutionary Rudeness: The Language of Red Guards and Rebel Workers in China's Cultural Revolution." Indiana East Asian Working Paper Series on Language and Politics in Modern China, no. 2 . Bloomington: Indiana University East Asian Center, July 1993.

———. *Organized Disorder: Shanghai Workers in the Cultural Revolution*. Boulder, Colo.: Westview Press, 1997.

Pommier, Gérard. "The Psychoanalytic Concept of Childhood." *Critical Quarterly* 39, no. 3 (1997): 8–15.

Powell, Patricia, and Shitao Huo, eds. *Mao's Graphic Voice: Pictorial Posters from the Cultural Revolution.* Madison: University of Wisconsin Press, 1996.

Preziosi, Donald. *Rethinking Art History: Meditations on a Coy Science.* New Haven: Yale University Press, 1989.

Pye, Lucien W. *Mao Tse-tung: The Man in the Leader.* New York: Basic Books, 1976.

Rabinow, Paul. "Representations Are Social Facts: Modernity and Post-Modernity in Anthropology." In Writing Culture: The Poetics and Politics of Ethnography, ed. James Clifford and George E. Marcus. Berkeley and Los Angeles: University of California Press, 1986.

*Renwu hua cankao ziliao* (Figure painting reference material). Shanghai: People's Press, 1973.

Rice, Edward E. *Mao's Way.* Berkeley and Los Angeles: University of California Press, 1972.

*Reckoning with the Past.* Edinburgh: Fruitmarket Gallery, 1996.

Rose, Jacqueline. *The Case of Peter Pan: Or the Impossibility of Children's Fiction.* London: Macmillan, 1984.

Rosen, Stanley. *Red Guard Factionalism and the Cultural Revolution in Guangzhou (Canton).* Boulder, Colo.: Westview Press, 1982.

———. "Value Change amongst Post-Mao Youth: The Evidence from Survey Data." In *Unofficial China: Popular Culture and Thought in the People's Republic,* ed. Perry Link, Richard Madsen, and Paul Pickowicz, 193–216. Boulder, Colo.: Westview Press, 1989.

———. "The Impact of Reform Policies on Youth Attitudes." In *China on the Eve of Tiananmen,* ed. Deborah Davis and Ezra F. Vogel, 283–304. Cambridge: Harvard University Press, 1990.

Russo, Alessandro. "The Probable Defeat: Preliminary Notes on the Chinese Cultural Revolution." *Positions* 6, no. 1 (Spring 1998): 179–202.

Schein, Louisa. "Gender and Internal Orientalism in China." *Modern China* 23, no. 1 (January 1997): 69–98.

Schoenhals, Michael. "Unofficial and Official Histories of the Cultural Revolution: A Review Article." *Journal of Asian Studies* 48, no. 3 (August 1989): 563–72.

———. *Doing Things with Words in Chinese Politics: Five Studies.* China Research Monographs, no. 41. Berkeley and Los Angeles: University of California Press, 1992.

———. "Proscription and Prescription of Political Terminology by the Central Authorities, 1949–1989." In *Norms and the State in China,* ed. Chun-chieh Huang and Erik Zurcher, 337–59. Sinica Leidensia 28. Leiden: Brill, 1993.

———. "Talk about a Revolution: Red Guards, Government Cadres, and the Languages of Political Discourse." Indiana East Asian Working Paper Series on Language and Politics in Modern China, no. 1 (June 1993). Bloomington: Indiana University East Asian Studies Center, June 1993.

———. "Posters and Poster Art in China's Cultural Revolution: The Political and Social Contexts." Lecture given at the exhibit "Mao's Graphic Voice: Pictorial Posters from the Cultural Revolution," Elvehjem Museum of Art, University of Wisconsin, Madison, 1996.

———. ed. *China's Cultural Revolution, 1966–1969: Not a Dinner Party.* Armonk, N.Y.: M. E. Sharpe, 1996.

Schram, Stuart R., ed. *Authority, Participation, and Cultural Change in China.* Cambridge: Cambridge University Press, 1973.

*Shaan-gan-ning bianqu funü yundong wenxian ziliao xuanbian* (Selected materials on the women's movement in the Shaan-Gan-Ning border region). Xi'an: Shaanbei sheng funü lianhehui, 1982.

*Shanghai gongren meishu zuopin xuan* (Selection of workers' art from Shanghai). Shanghai: People's Press, 1975.

Shue, Vivienne. *The Reach of the State.* Stanford, Calif.: Stanford University Press, 1988.

Silbergeld, Jerome, with Gong Jisiu. *Contradictions: Artistic Life, the Socialist State, and the Chinese Painter, Li Huasheng.* Seattle: University of Washington Press, 1993.

Snow, Edgar. *Red Star over China.* London: Gollancz, 1937.

Solomon, Richard H. *Mao's Revolution and the Chinese Political Culture.* Berkeley and Los Angeles: University of California Press, 1971.

Song Jiami, ed. *Lao Yuefen Pai* (Old calendar pictures). Shanghai: Shanghai huabao chubanshe, 1997.

Song Liyi. Foreword to *Paintings of Children at Play.* Taipei: National Palace Museum, 1997.

Stewart, Susan. *On Longing: Narratives of the Miniature, the Gigantic, the Souvenir, the Collection.* Durham, N.C.: Duke University Press, 1993.

Sullivan, Michael. *Art and Artists of Twentieth Century China.* Berkeley and Los Angeles: University of California Press, 1996.

Tempest, Rone. "The Woman Who Touched Up Mao's Great Revolution." *Guardian,* 4 February 1997, 8.

Thompson, John D. *The Media and Modernity: A Social Theory of the Media.* Cambridge, England: Polity Press, 1995.

Tsai Jo-hung. "New Year Pictures: A People's Art." *People's China* 4, nos. 1–2 (February 1950): 12–18.

*Tu an ji: banbao changyong baotou* (Design collection: commonly used mastheads in blackboard newspapers). Beijing: China Illustrated Press, 1995.

Voci, Paola. "The Effect of Post–June 4 Re-education Campaigns on Chinese Students." *China Quarterly,* no. 134 (June 1993): 310–34.

―――. "The Aesthetic of Dissent in Chinese Cinema: Choosing Shots to Say What Words Do Not." Paper presented at American Asian Studies conference, Washington D.C., March 1998.

Wagner, Rudolph G. "Reading the Chairman Mao Memorial Hall in Peking: The Tribulations of the Implied Pilgrim." In *Pilgrims and Sacred Sites in China,* ed. Susan Naquin and Chünfang Yü, 378–423. Berkeley and Los Angeles: University of California Press, 1992.

Wagner, Vivian. "Die Lieder der Roten Garden" (Songs of the Red Guards). M.A. thesis, University of Munich, 1995.

Walder, Andrew. "Cultural Revolution Radicalism: Variations on a Stalinist Theme." In *New Perspectives on the Cultural Revolution,* ed. William Joseph, Christine S. Wong, and David Zweig, 41–61. Harvard Contemporary China Series, no. 8. Cambridge: Harvard University Press, 1991.

Walzer, Michael. *The Company of Critics.* London: Peter Halban, 1989.

Wang, Jing. *High Culture Fever.* Berkeley and Los Angeles: University of California Press, 1996.

Wang Nianyi. *Da dongluan de niandai* (Decade of great chaos). Zhengzhou: Henan renmin chubanshe, 1988.

Wang Xingwei. "Road to Anyuan." In *Reckoning with the Past.* Edinburgh: Fruitmarket Gallery, 1996.

Wasserstrom, Jeffrey N. "Presentations of Progress in PRC Primers and Pictorial Histories, or What do Modern Cities and Citizens Look Like?" Paper presented at the Association of Asian Studies conference, Washington D.C., March 1998.

Wasserstom, Jeffrey N., and Elizabeth J. Perry, eds. *Popular Protest and Political Culture in Modern China: Learning from 1989.* Boulder, Colo.: Westview Press, 1992.

Watson, James L. "The Renegotiation of Chinese Cultural Identity." In *Popular Protest and Political Culture in Modern China: Learning from 1989,* ed. Jeffrey N. Wasserstom and Elizabeth J. Perry, 67–84. Boulder, Colo.: Westview Press, 1992.

West, Shearer, ed. *The Bulfinch Guide to Art History.* Boston: Bulfinch, 1996.

White, Gordon. "The Decline of Ideocracy." In *China in the 1990s,* ed. Robert Benewick and Paul Wingrove, 21–33. London: Macmillan, 1995.

White, Lynn T., III. *Policies of Chaos.* Princeton, N.J.: Princeton University Press, 1989.

Wilson, Richard W., Amy Auerbacher Wilson, and Sidney L. Greenblatt, eds. *Value Change in Chinese Society.* New York: Praeger, 1979.

Wolf, Margery. "Child Training and the Chinese Family." In *Family and Kinship in Chinese Society,* ed. Maurice Freedman, 37–62. Stanford, Calif.: Stanford University Press, 1970.

―――. *Revolution Postponed: Women in Contemporary China.* London: Methuen, 1985.

Wu Hung. "Private Love and Public Duty: Images of Children in Early Chinese Art." In *Chinese Views of Childhood*, ed. Anne Behnke Kinney, 79–110. Honolulu: University of Hawaii Press, 1995.

Xiao Ruiyi. "Wode shangshu huiyi" (Recollections of submitting letters to Mao). In *Weibei weiguan wang youguo* (A humble position does not allow one to forget one's duties to the country), ed. Yu Xiguang. Changsha: Hunan renmin chubanshe, 1989.

*Xinnianhua xuan* (Selection of New Year paintings). Beijing: People's Arts Press, 1974.

*Xuexi Mao zhuxi lun 'zhilaohu'' wenxian* (Studying Chairman Mao's thoughts on paper tigers) (Hong Kong: Wenhui bao, 1958).

Yan Jiaqi and Gao Gao. *Turbulent Decade: A History of the Cultural Revolution*. Ed. and trans. D. W. Y. Kwok. Honolulu: University of Hawaii Press, 1996.

Yang, Mayfair Mei-hui. *Gifts, Favors, and Banquets*. Ithaca, N.Y.: Cornell University Press, 1994.

Yang, Rae. *Spider Eaters: A Memoir*. Berkeley and Los Angeles: University of California Press, 1997.

*Yangquan gongren meishu dazibao, bihua xuan* (Selection of art: big-character posters and wall paintings by Yangquan workers). Beijing: Peoples' Arts Press, 1976.

Yau, Esther C. M. "Filmic Discourses on Women in Chinese Cinema (1949–1965); Art, Ideology, and Social Relations." Ph.D. diss., University of California, 1990.

Yi Bin, ed. *Lao Shanghai guanggao* (Advertisements of old Shanghai). Shanghai: Shanghai huabao chubanshe, 1995.

*Youhua: Hongse niangzijun* (Oil paintings of *The Red Detachment of Women*). Shanghai: Shanghai renmin chubanshe, 1972.

Young, Marilyn. "Chicken Little in China: Some Reflections on Women." In *Marxism and the Chinese Experience: Issues in Contemporary Chinese Socialism,* ed. Arif Dirlik and Maurice Meisner, 253–68. Armonk, N.Y.: M. E. Sharpe, 1989.

Yue Daiyun and Carolyn Wakeman. *To the Storm: The Odyssey of a Revolutionary Chinese Woman*. Berkeley and Los Angeles: University of California Press, 1985.

*Zai guangkuo tiandi li: meishu zuopin xuan* (In the wide world: selection of artworks). Beijing: People's Arts Press, 1974.

Zhang, Xudong. *Chinese Modernism in the Era of Reforms: Cultural Fever, Avant-Garde Fiction, and the New Chinese Cinema*. Durham, N.C.: Duke University Press, 1997.

Zhang Zhizhong. "Lishi zhi mi he qingchun zhi wu" (The mystery of history and the mistake of youth). *Zhongguo yanjiu yuekan* (China Research Monthly), August 1996, 64–70.

Zhao Bin and Graham Murdock. "Young Pioneers: Children and the Making of Chinese Consumerism." *Cultural Studies* 10, no. 2 (1996): 201–17.

*Zhongguo dianying da cidian* (Dictionary of Chinese film). Shanghai: Shanghai Publishing House, 1994.

Zhongguo quanquo funü lianhehui funü yundong lishi yanjiu shi (Research Department of the All-China Women's Federation), ed. *Zhongguo funü yundong lishi ziliao* (Materials on the history of the Chinese women's movement). Vols. 1–4. Beijing: Renmin chubanshe, 1986.

# Index

Page numbers in boldface indicate illustrations. **P** refers to a color plate, **f** to a black-and-white figure.

# About the Contributors

ROBERT BENEWICK is research professor of politics at Sussex University. His recent publications include *The Routledge Dictionary of Twentieth-Century Political Thinkers,* edited with Philip Green (2d ed.,1998), and "China in the 1990s," edited with Paul Wingrove (rev. ed., 1999). With Stephanie Donald he has written an essay on Mao Zedong badges, which appears in their edited volume, *Belief in China: Art and Politics, Deities and Mortality* (1996). They also coauthored *The State of China Atlas* (forthcoming).

XIAOMEI CHEN is associate professor of Chinese and comparative literature at Ohio State University. She received her Ph.D. in comparative literature from Indiana University in 1989. Her publications include *Occidentalism* (1995) and numerous articles in journals such as *Critical Inquiry, New Literary History, Journal of Asian Studies, Comparative Literary Studies,* and *Chinese Literature: Essay, Article, and Review.* She has just completed two book manuscripts, "Acting the Right Part: Cultural Performance and Contemporary Chinese Drama" and "Reading the 'Right' Texts: An Anthology of Contemporary Chinese Plays with a Critical Introduction." She is currently working on a book on modern Chinese women playwrights (1928–1998).

CRAIG CLUNAS is professor of the history of art at the University of Sussex, having previously worked as a curator of Chinese collections at the Victoria and Albert Museum, London. He has published extensively on Chinese art, mostly of the Ming and Qing periods, and on cultural contacts between China and Europe. His books include *Superfluous Things: Material Culture and Social Status in Early Modern China* (1991), *Fruitful Sites: Garden Culture in Ming Dynasty China* (1996), *Art in China* (1997), and *Pictures and Visuality in Early Modern China* (1997).

STEPHANIE DONALD is lecturer in media studies at Murdoch University, Western Australia. She has also been a research fellow in Chinese at the University of Westminster. She has edited, with Robert Benewick, a collection of essays on Chinese art and iconography, *Belief in China: Art and Politics, Deities and Mortality* (1996). She has also published articles on Chinese film in *Screen; Theory, Culture, and Society; Continuum;* and *diatribe.* Her book about public space in Chinese cinema, *Public Secrets, Secret Spaces: Cinema and Civility in Post-Maoist China,* and *The State of China Atlas* are due out in 1999. She is also working with Harriet Evans on a special issue of the journal *New Formations* about "Cultural China," gender, and diaspora.

HARRIET EVANS is senior lecturer in Chinese studies at the Centre for the Study of Democracy, University of Westminster. She studied in Beijing between 1975 and 1977 and taught modern Chinese history in El Colegio de México, Mexico City (1979–1984). She has written extensively on gender and sexuality in China, with articles in *SIGNS, Intersections,* and other journals and collections. She published *La historia moderna de China, 1800–1949* in 1991, and her *Women and Sexuality in China: Dominant Discourses of Female Sexuality and Gender since 1949* was published in 1997.

JOHN GITTINGS graduated in oriental studies from the University of Oxford and worked in Hong Kong during the Cultural Revolution. He first visited mainland China in 1971. From 1976 to 1983, he taught Chinese politics at the Polytechnic of Central London, where he established the Chinese poster collection with the help of colleagues and students. He is now based in Hong Kong as the East Asia correspondent for the *Guardian.* His recent publications on China include *China Changes Face: The Road from Revolution* (1990), *Real China: From Cannibalism to Karaoke* (1996), and *China through the Sliding Door: Reporting Three Decades of Change* (1999).